3/91

Commission on Cults and Missionaries

Maynard Bernstein, Chair - 1981-1988
Rabbi Stephen Robbins, Chair - 1979-1986

Marsha Emmer Addis, Chair
Rabbi Shelton Donnell, Co-Chair
Rachel Andres, Director

Community Relations Committee

Marcia F. Volpert., Chair
Steven F. Windmueller, Ph.D., Executive Director

Jewish Federation Council of Greater Los Angeles

George Caplan, Esq., President
Wayne Feinstein, Executive Vice President

CULTS

&

CONSEQUENCES

The Definitive Handbook

Edited by

Rachel Andres
and **James R. Lane**

Published by

Commission on Cults & Missionaries

Community Relations Committee
Jewish Federation Council of Greater Los Angeles

ISBN 0-9621478-7-7

Third Printing, April 1990

Grateful Acknowledgement is made for permission to reprint:

Coming Out of the Cults by Margaret Thaler Singer
Reprinted from Psychology Today magazine copyright ©1979 (APA).

Intervarsity Press - Taken from *What is a Cult?* by Ronald Enroth.
©1982 by Inter-Varsity Christian Fellowship of the USA and used by
permission of InterVarsity Press, Downers Grove, Il. 60515, USA.

U. S. News and World Report - *One Moonie and How I Left*
Reprinted from U.S. News and World Report issue of July 5, 1982.
©1982, U.S. News and World Report, Inc.

West, L. J. and Singer, M. T. - *Cults, Quacks, and Non-Professional
Psychotherapies*
Reproduced with permission from West, L. J. and Singer, M.T. In
Comprehensive Testbook of Pschiatry/III, Edited by H. I. Kaplan, A. M.
Freedman, and B. J. Sadock, pp. 3245-3258.
Williams and Wilkins, Baltimore, 1980.

The Psychology of the Cult Experience by Glen Collins,
March 15, 1982. Copyright ©1982 by The New York Times Company.
Reprinted by permission.

Group Work with Former Cultists by Lorna Goldberg and William Goldberg.
Copyright ©1982, National Association of Social Workers, Inc. Reprinted
with permission, from *Social Work*, Vol. 27, No. 2 (March 1982), pp. 165-170.

Information Disease by Jim Siegelman and Flo Conway.
Reprinted by permission of The Sterling Lord Agency, Inc.
Copyright ©1982 by Jim Siegelman and Flo Conway.

Emphasis in the text does not necessarily reflect the writer, but rather that of the
editors.

ACKNOWLEDGEMENTS

Without the selfless contributions of many devoted, caring, and persistent individuals, we never could have navigated this long, sometimes treacherous and most rewarding road.

Rabbi Stephen Robbins for dreaming big and never doubting our potential; Jim Lane for transforming a blueprint into a dynamic foundation; Beth Hersh Goldsmith for believing in and beginning this wonderful project; Barbara Blake Levine for trusting me, and providing supervision, support and most of all friendship; Elizabeth Brenner Danziger for her organizing capabilities; Hal Berlfein for understanding the importance of this book and his financial assistance, Jean Berlfein for her patience and imparting her wisdom about self-publishing; Barbara Bruno Lancaster for her creativity, talent, and boundless ideas and energy; Steve Windmueller and Michael Hirschfeld for their persistent efforts to help us over the many hurdles; Jack Roberts from whose creative genius came our title: *Cults & Consequences*; the Cult Awareness Network for sharing their wealth of information; all of the contributing authors, for their boldness and tenacity in an especially difficult field and for giving me the courage to work on this issue.

The Jewish Community Foundation for supporting us in this endeavor; George Caplan and the law firm of Irell and Manella for their legal advice and assistance; LSW Insurance for their persistence; the Bureau of Jewish Education for their support. Most gratefully to Wayne Feinstein and the Jewish Federation Council of Greater Los Angeles for being ahead of their time in recognizing the urgency of the cult problem and the value of getting *Cults & Consequences* to the public. Many thanks to:

Marsha Emmer Addis	Dr. John Hochman	Rabbi Shelly Donnell
Shaari Freed	Mark Friedman	Eric Heilman
Aaron Fenton	Audrey Steinhaus	Patty Glickman
Terry Burns	Al Saunders	Ron Lancaster

My love and thanks to those who have kept me sane always: Mom & Dad, Bubbie, Jill, Mitch, Benjamin, Roger, Marc, Teri Horowitz, Michael Zucker, Susan Bakota, Carrie Ungerman, Arthur Pinchev, and Cindy Sweet.

Most of all, I thank Maynard. Without his insight, guidance, dedication, and humor this book would not have been published. His righteous and loving ways will forever bless my life.

Rachel Andres

CONTENTS

INTRODUCTION

Crisis Proportions!

- **Are you aware of the growth of destructive cultism?**

- **Do you realize that on almost every college campus in America there are cult recruiters seeking new members?**

- **With less than 3% of the American population identifying with Judaism, is it possible that as much as 12% of cult membership is Jewish?**

The Commission on Cults and Missionaries was formed in response to the community's need to monitor destructive cult groups. The Commission is charged "to act as a coordinating agency, building a coalition of Jewish Community organizations and/or agencies to respond to the problems of cult and missionary groups in the Jewish community."

Although initially established to respond to problems reported by Jewish families, the Commission has found the cult issue to be a crisis throughout American society. The Commission's emphasis is to educate the public on the dangers of destructive cultism.

This book is not intended to be merely a compendium, but rather **to present replies to the questions most often asked of us.** In order to give a thorough and complete coverage of this issue, we sought responses from a wide variety of persons experienced in the cult phenomenon and solicited information from them about the work they are doing. Additionally, we have included articles and excerpts to further cover and complete each section.

Most of this book does not specifically address questions of theology. Although as Jews we are concerned with religious questions, our disagreement with cults does not focus on the content of their beliefs. Rather, we are concerned with what is, in our opinion, deceptive proselytizing and unethical conduct (i.e., front organizations, mind control practices). We expect these groups to accept the same social and legal accountability as do mainstream religious organizations. We expect openness in accessibility of information, and an honest declaration of goals and principles to potential new members.

We are also concerned about the political activities of these organizations, many seeming to view the First Amendment guarantee of freedom of religion as granting license to function in any manner they choose. They expect their proclamation of religious belief sufficient to obviate any criticism or investigation. We believe that the First Amendment was not established to *protect* religious organizations, but rather, to *insure the freedom* of individuals to hold and express their own religious ideas, and to congregate so that those ideas can be furthered. The Constitutional guarantee of freedom of religion was not created to protect the business dealings of religious organizations (thereby granting tax-exempt status for non-church related business income), nor was it created to give them the right to enter, in any means they see fit, the lives of individuals in ways that violate freedom of religion and freedom of thought.

We cannot blindly protect destructive organizations at the expense of the rights of the individuals involved. We are concerned with the need to educate individuals *to protect themselves* from manipulative and coercive techniques by religious organizations and cults who claim to bring salvation without effort. This book can make it easier for individuals to properly consider any religious or quasi-religious approach made to them. We offer this information for persons on an emotional and spiritual quest, so that they may not fall prey to people who use fraudulent means to entrap them in a belief system that forbids free choice and personal autonomy. The empty promise of "authentic spirituality" is often a successful cult tool.

We must also educate the families of cult members, since they suffer too. A new cult member may just disappear, rejecting parents and siblings, friends and community, having only the cult for emotional support. Those left behind may suffer a tremendous sense of loss.

The study guide in each section may be used to stimulate further discussion on the many controversial aspects of the cult phenomena. As with most complex issues, there are many gray areas. Some study questions have no clear cut answers; these are the real issues the Commission faces in its work for the community. Additionally, we have included resources and references on international, national, and local levels.

The Commission does not have the solution to the problem of cults. We do have responses to the many issues that cults raise. Some may find personal answers here, although we realize that each individual's situation is unique.

> **Anyone having a close friend or relative involved in a destructive cult should not rely solely on this book. Seek professional advice. This handbook is not intended to be, nor should it be construed as, a substitute for counseling that focuses on individual problems.**

PART 1:

CULTS
&
SOCIETY

Part 1:   CONTENTS

PART 1: *CULTS & SOCIETY*

What is a Cult?

___

How Does it Differ From a Religion?

What is the Difference Between a Destructive and a Benign Cult?

There's always a pretty good number of self-appointed pied pipers, self-appointed messianic people, self-appointed gurus in any society who say to the confused masses: "Follow me! I have a simple solution for the complex problems of life." But if the social structure has not broken down, very few people will follow them.

Dr. Margaret Thaler Singer
Clinical Psychologist Professor,
The University of California Berkeley
and The University of San Francisco

It seems as modern social structures are breaking down, more and more people are drifting into organizations which use deceptive and manipulative practices that offer "simple" solutions to today's complex problems. These organizations usually cloak themselves under the mantle of "religion," and chastise their critics as the worst kind of anti-religious bigots. **But *not every* organization which calls itself "religious" *is* religious in the traditionally accepted sense of the word**, and if an organization damages the mental and/or physical health of its members, it may have to be opposed. The separation of Church and State in America (guaranteed by the First Amendment) appears to allow any organization declaring itself a religion, immunity from laws that govern other non-"religious" organizations. However, it is difficult to believe that the framers of the Constitution would have condoned the protection of groups which practice brutal brainwashing techniques and encourage members to renounce connections with their families and with society at large. Claiming the right to religious freedom, these organizations have also moved into other areas of the community, such as business and education, thus making their activities harder to counteract.

The longer a community waits to respond to these organizations the more complex the problem becomes.

Once the destructive cults have become entrenched in many areas of society, it becomes extremely difficult for a cult awareness group to reach a consensus on one effective form of action. We at the Commission on Cults believe that some action must be taken to counteract the growth of cults, particularly the cults who direct recruiting toward Jews. **We hope that the information in this handbook will help readers decide what, if any, action they will take.** If Dr. Singer's belief is correct (when social structures weaken, destructive cults prosper) what course of action should society take? Should we first bolster faltering institutions, act against the organizations which have coerced and manipulated our citizens, or do both? More importantly, will either alternative succeed in uprooting destructive cults?

Cults have existed since history began. Every society has encountered groups outside of the mainstream. Does this mean that cults will continue regardless of what is done? We think the answer is yes, **but our problem is not cults in general.** Our goal is counteracting *destructive* cults.

We do not want to "throw the baby out with the bath water" and undertake a program whose ultimate goal is to bring about the disappearance of all cults. Many cults are benign, legitimate alternatives to the mainstream. By narrowing our focus, we must answer the following vital questions.

- **What is the difference between a religion and a cult?**

- **What the difference between a destructive cult and one that is not destructive?**

- **How does the First Amendment apply to some of these "religious" organizations?**

Not everyone perceives cults in the same way. We have said, the problem is complex, riddled with "gray" areas without definite answers. Rather than prescribing specific answers, we are presenting a variety of views, both from experts and from individuals whose lives have been touched by the cult experience. We invite you to read what concerns you most directly, and to draw your own conclusions.

The word "cult" originally referred to any kind of ritual, ceremony or liturgy, a definition rarely used anymore. Current connotations give the word quite a different meaning. It has come to mean a teaching, group or movement which deviates from orthodoxy while claiming to represent the true faith. The media has added their own (not necessarily unwarranted) sinister overtones to the word. "Cult" often describes a group of people who are considered injurious, authoritarian, weird, or incomprehensible outsiders.

An Abundance of Definitions

In *Challenge of the Cults,* a report prepared by the Jewish Community Relations Committee of Philadelphia, the perspective is that of Jewish professionals looking at a "religious" but non-Judaic phenomenon.

Like many words in popular usage, the word "cult" means different things to different people. Webster's dictionary states that a cult can be formal religious worship or a system of religious beliefs and ritual, but few people who use the term today mean it that broadly.

For most people "cult" is a far more subjective word, and usually a pejorative one. It is used to designate a minority religious group, usually one whose beliefs or practices are unusual or esoteric in the eye of the judgmental beholder. This is obviously a highly relativistic definition, one that would make Baptists a cult in India and Moslems a cult in Indiana. A measly 1.5% of the world's population, the Jewish people, would by this standard be a cult virtually everywhere.

But even this definition does not really apply to the specific way the word "cult" increasingly is being used in America in the 1970s. Today it has become the label for a particular set of groups having unique characteristics that are not shared with other religious communities.

For the purposes of this report, we propose a definition of our own. It is not the only possible definition of a cult group, but it is what we will mean when we use the term for the remainder of this report.

According to our definition, a cult is a group that exhibits the following characteristics:

It is a group of people who follows a living leader, usually a dominant, paternal male figure, or occasionally a pair or a "family" of leaders. It is a group whose leader makes absolute claims about his character, abilities, and/or knowledge. A leader's claims may include any or all of the following:

- A claim that he is divine -- God incarnate, the messiah, etc.

- A claim that he is the sole agent of the divine on earth -- God's agent or emissary.

- A claim that he is omniscient and infallible -- the possessor of absolute truth and total wisdom.

It is a group in which membership is contingent on a complete and literal acceptance of the leader's claims to divinity, infallibility, etc., and acceptance of his teachings, doctrines, and dogma. It is a group in which membership is contingent on complete, unquestioning loyalty and allegiance to the leader.

It is a group in which membership is contingent on a complete and total willingness to obey the cult leader's commands without question.

It is then, a group that is, by definition, undemocratic, absolutist.

These characteristics are not offered as an all-inclusive and unvarying definition of all the groups that are popularly labeled "cults." Indeed, each group we examine in this report may vary in some significant degree from this overall definition, even as it conforms in most other respects. Consider the definition to be a barometer, then, of the "cultic" nature of any group.

In fact, most groups have some cultlike characteristics. Most groups have leaders, after all, and most leaders inspire confidence and trust. But few of them make the claims that characterize the cults. The difference is one of degree. Cults are not a unique species of human group; they are the endpoints on a continuum. To the degree that a group fits the cult definition, to that degree it is cultlike. If it fits the definition exactly, or nearly so, then it is a cult.

Before going on, let us examine a few of the implications of this definition.

One implication is that **many religions now popularly considered "established" or "respectable" might once, in their early history, have been considered cults but are clearly not cults today.** Judaism, Christianity, and Islam, for example, all have formalized religious doctrines and holy scriptures that may not be altered or rewritten arbitrarily by any one religious leader, no matter how high he or she might be in rank or esteem. Even the Lubavitcher Rebbe, for example, cannot alter the halakhah, the Jewish religious law, to put the Sabbath on Wednesday or permit the eating of pork by Jews. He certainly could not advocate willful deception (except in a life-and-death situation) or murder, as some cult leaders have, and claim that he was being consistent with the teachings of his religious group.

A second implication of our definition, is that **a group need not necessarily be religious in nature to be a cult.** A political organization or a therapy group may just as easily take on the characteristics of a cult, and on occasion they have.

A third implication of our definition is that it does not assume that any of the more objectionable actions commonly ascribed to cults are necessarily intrinsic to their nature. **To put it another way, the fact that a group is a cult does not necessarily mean** that it has to raise funds under false pretenses, recruit members through deception, counsel hatred of parents, distort the beliefs of other religions, violate the laws of the state, or forbid its members from receiving medical attention.

On the other hand, there is nothing intrinsic to a cult that would prevent any, or all of these practices from taking place; **in a cult everything depends on the leader.**

Challenge of the Cults

last sentence***

Cults, Quacks, and Nonprofessional Psychotherapies

In the following section from *Cults, Quacks, and Nonprofessional Psychotherapies*, **Louis J. West, M.D.,** Director of the UCLA Neuropsychiatric Institute, and **Margaret Thaler Singer, PhD.,** Professor, University of California Berkeley, take a historical/ psychological view, pointing out that cults proliferate during times, like our own, when previously established social mores are questioned. They clarify the difference between a commune and a cult, and point out three factors to distinguish the destructive cults from the benign.

Periods of unusual turbulence in human history are sometimes accompanied by the emergence of cults, both religious and non-religious. After the fall of Rome and the French revolution and during the Industrial Revolution, numerous cults appeared in Europe. The westward movement in America swept a myriad of religious cults toward California. In the hundred years after the gold rush, at least 50 well-defined and well-studied utopian cults were established here (Hine, 1953). The majority of these cults were religious and lasted on the average about 20 years; the secular variety endured only half that long. Most purported to offer health benefits of one kind or another. Of course, similar cults were established elsewhere in America, some becoming transformed by their own success -- for example, the Oneida colony and the Amana colony -- into enterprises far different from their founders' intent.

Some cult-like activities and the beginnings of a counterculture -- beatniks or the beat generation -- emerged in America in the 1940s and 1950s after World War II and the Korean War. A new set of disturbances in the American culture welled up during the 1960s with the expansion of an unpopular war in Southeast Asia, massive upheavals over civil rights, and a profound crisis in values defined by unprecedented affluence on the one hand and potential thermonuclear holocaust on the other. The youth were caught up in three rebellions: red (new left), against political and economic monopolies; black, against racial injustice; and green (the counter-culture), against materialism in all its manifestations, including individual and institutional struggles for power (West and Allen, 1968).

Drug abuse and violent predators took an awful toll among the counterculture's second generation (hippies) in the late 1960s. Many fled to form colonies, now generally called communes. Others turned to the apparent security of paternalistic religious and secular cults, which have been multiplying at an astonishing rate ever since.

Those communes that endured the 1960s or appeared during the 1970s -- perhaps 2,000 or 3,000 in North America -- can generally be differentiated from cults in three respects:

1. *Cults* are established by strong and charismatic leaders who control power hierarchies and material resources, but *communes* tend to minimize organizational structure and to deflate or expel power seekers.

2. *Cults* possess some revealed "word" in the form of a book, manifesto, or doctrine, whereas *communes* vaguely invoke general commitments to peace and libertarian freedoms and a distaste for the parent culture's establishments.

3. *Cults* create fortified boundaries, confining their membership in various ways and attacking those who leave as defectors, deserters, or traitors; they recruit new members with ruthless energy and raise enormous sums of money; and they tend to view the out-side world with increasing hostility and distrust as the organization ossifies.

    In contrast, *communes* are like nodes in the far flung reticulum of the counter-culture; their boundaries are permeable membranes through which people come and go relatively unimpeded, either to continue their pilgrimages or to return to a society regarded by communards with feelings ranging from indifference to amusement to pity. Most communes thus defined, seem to pose relatively little threat to society. Many cults, on the other hand, are increasingly perceived as dangerous both to their own members and to others.

L.J. West and M.T. Singer

* * *

What is a Cult?

Another approach to defining a cult is in **Ron Enroth's** pamphlet *What is a Cult?* Enroth is Chair of the Department of Sociology at Westmont College in Santa Barbara, an evangelical institution. He is the author of *Youth, Brainwashing, and the Extremist Cults,* and *The Lure of the Cults.,* among other books.

Enroth's concern is whether cult beliefs adhere to Christian dogma, whereas the JCRC emphasizes characteristics of destructive cults and their deceptive nature.

One could take at least three approaches in defining cult: a sensational or popular approach, a sociological approach and a theological approach. A sensational approach to cults is built on journalistic accounts in the popular press which frequently focus on the dramatic and sometimes bizarre aspects of cultic behavior. A sociological definition includes the authoritarian, manipulative, totalistic and sometimes communal features of cults. A theological definition involves some standard of orthodoxy.

Let's consider each of these three approaches before offering any tentative response to the question: What is a cult? It will soon become apparent that **any simple and precise attempt to delineate a cult must be viewed with caution,** if not suspicion, because of the common tendency to oversimplify a very complex phenomenon.

Most people gain an image of what cults are and how they operate through the news media. Journalists are frequently required to sacrifice in-depth research and careful analysis in favor of a story that sells, a story with human interest appeal. Cults often provide exotic material for the media. Accounts of bizarre behavior, including mysterious rites, promiscuous sex, occult practices and robes of white sackcloth, make for good copy. As a result, when the public thinks of cults, the images conjured up include flower-pinning Hare Krishnas at airports, zombie-like followers of a Korean evangelist who claims to have talked with Jesus and Buddha in the spirit world, and orange-robed disciples of a guru named Rajneesh cavorting in a cosmic encounter group.

On the other hand, new religious **movements like Eckankar remain largely unknown to the public because of lower visibility** and minimal media value, despite the fact that their membership is considerably larger than better known groups like the Moonies and the Hare Krishna.

From a sociological perspective, there are important differences between the categories church, and sect or cult. Churches are culture-accepting religious organizations; that is, they have accommodated in varying degrees to the dominant cultural and social realities. Sects and cults, in contrast, are culture-rejecting. Not only are their belief systems typically outside the Judeo-Christian tradition, but these groups usually exhibit great alienation from other dominant social structures and the prevailing culture. In the words of sociologist John Lofland, cults are "little groups" which break off from the "conventional consensus and espouse very different views of the real, the possible, and the moral." (1)

Basic cultic world views are, by definition, quite different from the dominant cultural perspective, we should expect that the new religious movements will experience difficulties as they engage in recruitment of new members, fundraising, indoctrination efforts and other aspects of their involvement in the often disapproving parent society. The sociologist, aware that the term cult retains disparaging implications, is interested in the social dynamics that relate to the labeling process as these groups interact with the larger society.

A comprehensive sociological definition of cult would include consideration of such facets as authoritarian leadership patterns, loyalty and commitment mechanisms, lifestyle characteristics, conformity patterns (including the use of various sanctions in connection with those members who deviate) and the many other features common to sectarian, elitist religious groups.

For the Christian, the most significant component of a definition of a cult is theological in nature. This is because basic issues of truth and error are involved. Unlike the secular sociologist who is unconcerned about the truth of a particular belief and unlike the typical person whose religious naivete precludes any serious interest in doctrinal matters, the Christian must be able to distinguish truth from error.

A theological definition of cult must be based on a standard of Christian orthodoxy, using the Bible's teaching as a focal point. Sire defines a cult as "any religious movement that is organizationally distinct and has doctrines and/or practices that contradict those of the Scriptures as interpreted by traditional Christianity as represented by the major Catholic and Protestant denominations, and as expressed in such statements as the Apostles' Creed." (2)

A theological analysis of a particular group's belief system would examine issues like the group's understanding of the person and work of Jesus Christ, its view of human nature and sin, its teaching regarding salvation, the Trinity, and the nature and role of the Bible, as well as many other questions crucial to the historic position of orthodoxy.

"... of all the approaches to defining a cult, the theologic or doctrinal is the one least addressed by secular analysts. The lack of interest in such matters is typified by a statement by the distinguished sociologist of religion, Brian Wilson." The sociologist is not concerned to test the "truth" of belief. He is not concerned with the efficacy of rituals. He does not attempt to judge between divergent interpretations of a tradition. He does not challenge the claimed legitimation for practices and ideas which religionists endorse. (3)

... While secularists may exhibit disdain for the theological side of the cult question, evangelical Christians have been guilty of focusing almost exclusively on doctrinal/theological concerns and have neglected the psychosocial aberrations of cults. As one concerned Christian layman put it (without suggesting that we abandon theological critique of the cults), *"I think there is merit in placing more stress on the other danger zones created by cults, such as the psychological and moral injury, disruption of family ties, impairment of scholastic and professional careers."* A more encompassing definition of what constitutes cultism would contribute to more effective rehabilitation as well as evangelization of those persons caught up in aberrational religious groups. Whether we are theologians or sociologists, philosophers or readers of the morning paper, when we hear the word cult we think of certain distinguishing marks. What features can we expect to find in most cults?

We will look at nine common characteristics. All of the cults have some of these features; not all cults have all of them.

1. **Authoritarian.** A crucial dimension of all cultic organizations is authoritarian leadership. There is always a central, charismatic (in the personality sense), living human leader who commands total loyalty and allegiance.

2. **Oppositional.** Their beliefs, practices, and values are counter to those of the dominant culture. They often place themselves in an adversarial role vis-a-vis major social institutions.

3. **Exclusivistic.** Related to the oppositional character of cults is their elitism and exclusionism. The group is the only one which possesses the "truth," and therefore to leave the group is endangering one's salvation.

4. **Legalistic.** Tightly structured autocratic groups operate within a legalistic framework which governs both spiritual matters and the details of everyday living. Rules and regulations abound.

5. **Subjective.** Cultic movements place considerable emphasis on the experiential -- on feelings and emotions. Subjectivism is sometimes linked to anti-intellectualism, putting down rational processes and devaluing knowledge and education.

6. **Persecution-Conscious.** Perceived persecution is one of the hallmarks of virtually all new religious movements.

7. **Sanction-Oriented.** Cults require conformity to established practices and beliefs and readily exercise sanctions against the wayward. Those who fail to demonstrate the proper allegiance, who raise too many questions, disobey the rules or openly rebel are punished, formally excommunicated or merely asked to leave the group.

8. **Esoteric.** Cultic religion is a religion of secrecy and concealment. Eastern spirituality, especially, has been described by Brooks Alexander as "split-level religion, with an inner truth (the real truth) and an outer truth (an appealing, but limited and somewhat misleading face). "This kind of esotericism, Alexander continues, "accepts the appropriateness (and practical necessity) of a deliberately created gap between the picture that is projected to the general public and the inner reality known to the initiates." (4)

9. **Anti-Sacerdotal.** Cults tend to be organizations comprised of lay people. There are no paid clergy or professional religious functionaries like those in traditional groups. That is not to say that cults do not have spiritual hierarchies or titles applying to specific roles.

We now see that when the word "cult" is used to describe a contemporary social phenomenon, it nearly always refers to groups seen as dangerous or destructive, and share these features:

- **A charismatic living leader.**

- **Claims of omniscience or divine descent for the leader.**

- **Absolute obedience to the leader.**

- **Social boundaries which separate and polarize members from mainstream society.**

Ron Enroth

* * *

(1)   John Lofland, *Doomsday Cult*, Page 1.

(2)   James W. Sire, *Scripture Twisting*, Page 20

(3)   Bryan Wilson, *Religion in Sociological Perspective*

(4)   Brooks Alexander, *The Rise of Cosmic Humanism*, SCP Journal 5 (Winter 1981-82), Page 3-4.

Are Cults Constitutionally Protected?

We frequently hear "cult" to describe religious activity. Although there are many non-religious cults in the United States, most cults consider themselves, and are considered by outsiders, to be religious. "Religion" thus becomes a key in determining whether counter-cult activity is appropriate. Many cults represent themselves as valid forms of religion, entitled to protection by the First Amendment to the U.S. Constitution, and exemption from taxation. While we do not claim ability to determine what is a "valid" religious belief, nor wish to establish "rules" governing what is valid religious belief, we want religions to follow all the laws governing the United States, not just laws which afford them special protection. How then can we understand the First Amendment as it relates to destructive religious cults?

We have presented viewpoints that religious organizations, although separated from the state, must conform to the laws that govern the state. There is an implied obligation that we, as citizens, must make sure that all laws are upheld, and that we do not allow ourselves to be blinded or frozen into inactivity by shouts of First Amendment protection.

The First Amendment and the Cults

The Philadelphia JCRC paper *Challenge of the Cults;* says that the Constitutional guarantee of freedom of religion does not imply freedom to violate laws, and that although individuals are free to believe whatever they choose, they may not act contrary to the law.

There are undoubtedly a great number of people in American Society who take violent exception to the activities of various cult groups but believe that there is no way to inhibit their activities because of the protection provided for religious groups under the "church-state clause" of the First Amendment. *("Congress shall make no law respecting an establishment of religion, or prohibiting the free exercise thereof . . .")*

We believe that such a total laissez faire attitude towards the cults -- indeed, toward any group or set of groups in our society -- is not only irresponsible but clearly unwarranted by either the requirements of the Constitution or the substantial body of church-state law that has been derived from its provisions. The constitutional guarantee of freedom of religion is simply not infringed by the enactment and enforcement of laws motivated by no anti-religious purpose and furthering a substantial governmental interest. The free exercise of religion does not give groups or individuals the right to violate such laws.

Regarding this type of "limitation" on the right to religious freedom, constitutional lawyer Alan Goldhammer made the point succinctly in testimony to a California legislative inquiry on cults:

> *"While every person is guaranteed freedom of conscience and freedom of belief, the freedom to act is not guaranteed. When belief is translated into action, a person may be required to conform to regulations . . ."*

We believe that this distinction between freedom of belief and freedom of action is a useful and valid one. We oppose most strongly any attempt to call into question the sincerity and/or legitimacy of any group in our society that claims to be a religion, no matter how unorthodox or personally objectionable to us its beliefs and dogma may be. At the same time we believe that law enforcement authorities must not be afraid to act when any group, religious or not, stands accused of violating the laws of the land through deception, fraud, coercion, or any other illegal means.

Challenge of the Cults

* * *

The Reign of the Religious Fanatic

Norman Cousins, a social thinker and former editor of the *Saturday Review*, offers a cogent criticism of how well-meaning Americans allow common sense and capacity for moral outrage to be paralyzed when confronted by anyone who claims to speak in the name of religion -- even when the "religion" is dishonest or destructive.

Government officials have acknowledged that they knew members of the People's Temple had been fraudulently exploited and were even in some personal danger. But the officials said they were helpless to intervene in view of the religious nature of the organization and the protection afforded it under the First Amendment.

Thus is revealed once again, the curious paralysis of American society when confronted with any knave or fanatic who wraps himself in the mantle of religion. Almost anyone can form a sect, prey on its members, collect money, use the cash for his own purposes, and apply for and receive tax-exempt status and benefits. Misrepresentation, deceit, chicanery, falsification of records, and even theft can be disguised as religious undertakings and carried out with immunity and impunity. All this becomes possible because of the mindless assumption in American society that anything calling itself a religion is deserving of special respect and privilege. We apply the term religious intolerance indiscriminately and promiscuously, laying ourselves wide open for any charlatan who uses the mumbo-jumbo of "religion" to accomplish his fraudulent and anti-social designs.

If a burglar broke into your home and made off with your valuables, police would spring into action and an alert would be sent out to track him down; but if a religious fanatic inveigles you into parting with your property or half your weekly salary, the law offers no protection and shrugs at your loss. If your child were kidnapped, federal, state, and city officials would run over one another in the attempt to get at the kidnapper; but if a religious racketeer brainwashes your child and causes him or her to leave your home and turn against you, the authorities say they are without means to help you. If someone were to imprison you in a private jail or concentration camp, the government would come to your aid; but if your jailors call their prison a religious commune, there is no clear way the government can help you because your captors can invoke the religious clause of the First Amendment.

Where did the notion originate that religious movements should be beyond the law? Certainly not with the American Founding Fathers. When they spoke about freedom of religion they had something in mind quite different from the position attributed to them today. The founders of this nation came here to get out of the clutches of state-sponsored religions that perpetuated all sorts of injustices and outrages against which the citizenry had no recourse under the law. When the Founding Fathers spoke about freedom of religion, they were speaking of the need to separate religion from political authority. Freedom of religion was intended to protect the individual in his right to believe or not to believe, to affiliate or not to affiliate, to worship in a church or to worship in his own home, or not to worship at all. Freedom of choice was what the First Amendment was all about. The Founding Fathers never intended that religious organizations or their representatives should enjoy exemption from the laws. They saw fanaticism as a denial, not an assertion, of spiritual belief. The notion that they would have tolerated the kind of venal exploitation and predatory assaults that, under the guise of religion, have disfigured this nation in recent years is poor history and even poorer policy.

In a way, the mass murder at Jonestown was inevitable. Sooner or later the freedom of half-crazed and evil men to mesmerize and manipulate people in the name of religion, brotherhood, togetherness, common sacrifice, and community was bound to lead to collective and hideous tragedy. "Fanatics have their dreams," wrote Keats, "wherewith they weave a paradise for a sect." But fanaticism also converts paradise into private prisons. It is irresponsible to think that society's indifference to or toleration of corruption and violence by fanatics, however heavily robed, will not reach a hideous culmination. Our reaction of shock and outrage over the mass murder at Jonestown will be a terrible waste of human emotion if we do not accept our own share of the responsibility for that monsterous event. By providing special dispensations to religious despots and demons, we set a stage on which they can play out their macabre plots.

And all the sorrow over 900 men, women, and children, whose corpses were so entangled that they could hardly be counted, will be meaningless unless we recognize that there is more than one Jonestown. The same dangerous nonsense is being peddled today by a dozen or more religious cults. The same opportunity offered by society and seized by Jim Jones is being effectively exploited right now by those who know how easy it is to get people to reach for a better life on earth and in heaven; who can readily turn to their own advantage the inherent desire of people to come together in the name of a common humanity; and who are quick to recognize the absence of spiritual fulfillment in the lives of so many Americans, especially the young.

It is not enough, therefore, to lament the mass tragedy in Guyana. So long as we are prepared to provide unlimited hospitality and give status and tax benefits to imposters and spurious organizations who call themselves religious, we must be prepared to deal with the horrors that are their natural progeny.

Norman Cousins

* * *

Is a Jewish Countercult Response Consistent with the First Amendment?

In the introduction, we mentioned that we would address ourselves to the cult problem as it relates directly to the Jewish community. The preceding pages address several of the issues involved in the First Amendment debate, primarily from a secular standpoint. Where does the Jewish community stand in this debate? How can it attack other "religious" organizations while staunchly defending its own right to independent survival?

> **Rabbi Stephen Robbins,** Former Chair of the Commission on Cults and Missionaries and currently the Vice-Chair of the National Cult Task Force of the Union of American Hebrew Congregations, favors the Jewish community actively protecting itself by counteracting the proselytizing efforts of cults. He shows the division between church and state has historically been based on reciprocal openness and adherence to mutually agreed-upon laws. Most important for Jews, however, is his assertion that the right to resist intrusive proselytizing is essential to freedom of religion.

The history of Judaism in America is really founded on the principle of freedom of religion in a pluralistic society. The history of Jewish attitudes toward the First Amendment has always reflected the Jewish community's belief that the First Amendment rights to freedom of religion must be protected in the most intense ways. The Jewish community has taken the position that it would protect First Amendment rights even when those being protected may have positions antithetical or inimical to those of the Jewish community.

However, we find ourselves in a new situation in which the First Amendment guarantees of freedom of religion in the United States are the cover for, not only direct proselytizing efforts to the Jewish Community, but also deceptive and manipulative attempts to convert large numbers of Jews without an awareness on their part that an approach has been made to convert them. **Thus, we face a different issue in freedom of religion.** That is whether or not the Jewish community exercises its right for freedom of religion to maintain the integrity of its own religious tradition and religious community. I believe that the answer to that question would obviously be yes, that we have as much right to protect and defend freedom of the individual and his right to religious choice within the Jewish community, as it must be protected in other religious communities.

Freedom of religion is not a license to behave in any manner one chooses to authenticate by calling it a religious belief. Internally, within the structure of religious organizations, there is freedom to practice religion within constraints that do not violate either civil or criminal law and the general social compact of American society. **When the operation of those religious organizations begin to produce aberrational or illegal activity, then society has a right to respond.** The response can be two-fold.

First, there can be a governmental response. In all cases where that has occurred, it has occurred as a consequence of illegal activity on the part of cult groups, not as a result of cult awareness groups speaking out against them. It is not an abridgement of their civil rights or freedoms for any religious community to educate its own members and/or enjoin a dialogue in the general community about what many perceive as destructive behavior on the part of organizations who claim protection under freedom of religion guarantees.

It would be dangerous if our concept of freedom of religion was a ban against dissent, disagreement or dialogue about the behavior of religion as it impacts individuals in society. It would be a greater travesty on the constitutional notion of freedom of speech to limit such behavior and discussion, rather than to permit it to go on.

Second, and most important, these organizations refuse the same normal procedures and activity that main-line organized religious organizations in the United States adhere to. They refuse consistently to participate in the body of American society in the same open and accepted manner as other religious groups. Since the concept of freedom of religion is built on the assumption of an openness both ways between religion and society, it is, therefore, assumed that the openness is somehow the hallmark of appropriate behavior.

As we see cult groups developing greater levels of secrecy in order to hide their activities, society as a whole becomes insecure and afraid of those activities since it is a violation of accepted behavior. If this fear were acted upon in such a way that it curtailed the freedom of these individual groups to exist, then that would be a violation of the Constitution. However, that has not happened.

The criticism of cult groups has never touched the issue of belief because First Amendment principles as understood by American citizens are that each individual person or group is entitled to believe what it wants, and to behave ritually according to those principles unless they violate the law.

It is important to note here that freedom of religion as guaranteed under the Constitution does not obligate one religion which is being attacked by another to be silent in the face of that attack. Nor does it obligate a religious community to stand by passively while there are direct programs of proselytizing aimed at its constituency. To respond to such acts as an intrusion into our community is, in fact, the essence of freedom of religion.

Rabbi Stephen Robbins

* * *

If destructive cults are permitted to thrive, these groups will eventually undermine individual rights. Yet those groups continue to enjoy legal and societal privileges afforded religious organizations. We know that there have been cults throughout history, as West and Singer mentioned, but why is it that cults have achieved such tremendous success today?

What is it about contemporary Jewish society and society in general that has led to this "exodus" of people into destructive cults? This is what we will be exploring in the next chapter.

Study Guide

For the Group:

1. Discuss the First Amendment* to the United States Constitution. Divide the group into halves, with one side arguing that religious freedom is of paramount importance. The other side will argue that government must protect the individual's right to freedom even at the expense of religious freedom.

2. Have the group establish guidelines for what constitutes religion as opposed to a destructive cult. Using this outline, "test" the religiosity of various mainstream and radical groups to see how they fall within the proscribed guidelines.

3. In a round-table discussion, have the group talk about their own religious background. If there are members of the group who feel no attachment to their family's religion, ask them to talk about why there is no connection, what would make the connection stronger, and if they are looking for a religion. For those who feel a strong attachment, have them talk about that bond.

For the Individual:

1. Does the set of definitions of "cult" included in this section make clear to you the difference between a cult and a religion? What more would you need to better understand the difference? (see *Resource* section, Part 10)

2. Does it appear to you that these are old established religions fighting off "new" religions? Should any new group be allowed to continue to exist because there might be a chance that this group could benefit people in the future?

3. What role do you think government has in protecting citizens from potentially harmful experiences? Should the government step in only when individuals have been hurt or does it have a responsibility to act before?

4. How many people does a cult have to harm -- psychologically or physically -- before you would consider it destructive? What if an equal number of people claimed the cult had helped them?

5. Who should make the decision about a group's harm or benefit to society? Should government or the individual make that decision?

FIRST AMENDMENT

Congress shall make no law respecting an establishment of religion, or prohibiting the free exercise thereof; or abridging the freedom of speech, or of the press, or the right of the people peaceably to assemble, and to petition the government for a redress of grievances.

PART 2:

ENTRY

PART 2: CONTENTS

PART 2:   *ENTRY*

How Could I, or
Someone in My Family, Join a Cult?

"How could my son become one of them? He had everything anyone could possibly want. He must have gone crazy. That's the only answer."

This kind of dialogue has become more and more common in recent times. Parents, spouses, and friends of bright, seemingly well-adjusted people are bemoaning the fact that their loved one has joined a cult. They ask themselves how this could have happened. What sort of magic spell could have been cast to turn them into "those weirdos we laugh at when we're at the airport"?

If you are among those people who say that it could never happen to *your* children or *your* friends -- they're too smart, too sophisticated to be caught up in this obvious con -- be careful. *It can happen!* Destructive cults are not composed of bumbling idiots stumbling through life. The leaders of these organizations know that all individuals go through periods in their lives when they are more susceptible to suggestion, and when these periods come, the cults are ready.

I Could Never Get Involved!

The following test was developed by **Judy Israel** now with the Bureau of Jewish Education in Boston. It emphasizes that those most confident they would never get involved in a cult, may be among the most vulnerable.

Stop for a moment and think about what you might expect to learn from this article. You have just done more thinking that most cult followers do in an entire day . . . month . . . or year.

If you are expecting to learn that you are not the type to be a Moonie, a Scientologist, or any other cult follower, read on, because you couldn't be more incorrect. Take a minute to take this test. Rate yourself (your child, a friend) as honestly as possible to determine if you may be the type to become involved in a cult.

Check those items which apply to you:

☐ I am considered bright in most things.

☐ I am a curious person about the world around me.

☐ I have been a leader among my friends at school, in my youth group, and/or in extra-curricular activities.

☐ I have been a member of a group and consider myself a follower.

☐ I have moments when I doubt myself and my ability to succeed.

☐ I am afraid of the future from time to time.

☐ I am considered idealistic by parents and/or some of my friends.

☐ I enjoy being liked by those I like, and I enjoy receiving compliments from them.

☐ I sometimes like taking risks.

How many of the preceding statements did you check? If you circled *at least three of these statements, you are a prime candidate* for a cult. **All that is missing is the right time, place and a recruiter from a cult.** People like you do not join cults because you want to be a member of that particular group. Rather, **the cult recruiter creates a need in you** that only the recruiter can fill. Imagine being in the desert for three days without water and the only way you can purchase some water is to exchange your soul for it. Is that too high a price for you to pay? Or is staying alive the most important thing to consider? The real point is how to stay out of the desert in the first place. The psychological desert where a cult takes you to is more desolate, more empty, more dangerous than any "real" desert in the world. This is where the cult leaders have the only maps to the oasis and the water. Once you accept directions from them, you are totally dependent on them.

The cult recruiter has turned on the heat by engaging you in an incredibly self-revealing discussion which is, in essence, a therapy session without a therapist. It is a conversation that is not kept in strict confidence and it is not with the aim of helping you. **The sole purpose of the discussion is to bring you in** -- nothing more, nothing less. Without realizing it, the recruiter will get you to talk about everything from your sex life to your family relationships to your dreams and aspirations. Once you open up to them, two things have happened: 1) You are now tied to them emotionally. 2) They have information about you that is powerful enough for them to use as "emotional blackmail" should the time ever present itself.

If you think that what I am telling you is too strong, or too unbelievable, or even incorrect, I urge you to read about cults and their practices, talk to knowledgeable people, and think about it yourself. I guarantee that those three activities will only be available to you while you are still outside the cult. The following is a list of eight items to keep in your mind (while you still have it):

1. **Know who you are** and why you are the way you are. Especially before you throw your identity away in favor of a philosophical group that does not encourage your questions.

2. **Find yourself a role-model** (a person you know, respect and admire) to help you through tough times and inspire you during good times.

3. You cannot ward off recruitment if you are deficient or unknowing about what the cult is selling. **Know issues like salvation, life after death, or messianism.** Try to gain an understanding of these issues *before* you start dialoguing with others about them.

4. **Be wary of people who want you to share intimate and personal things with them** without really knowing you first. Also be wary of those who love you immediately upon first meeting.

5. **Beware of groups that subtly separate you** from friends and/ or family and substitute that relationship with a peer family

6. **We are all vulnerable** because we all have things within ourselves that we do not like -- cults are superb at identifying those things and providing quick and easy ways of solving them.

7. **When you are thinking of rebelling** from home and parents, *do not* walk into an even more paternalistic group that allows no individuality or autonomy.

8. **Don't be cocky** and think *not me - I could never get involved,* because then your defenses are down and you are even more susceptible.

If your expectations have not been met by reading this article, read on in this book and in others. You have every right to have your questions about life answered. Do not ever allow yourself to have that right taken away from you.

Judy Israel

* * *

Why Do Cults Attract?

We started this book by explaining the differences between cults and religions, and discussing the various destructive aspects of most cults. Given the obvious drawbacks of surrendering one's autonomy to a destructive cult, we must ask: Why would someone be attracted to join? Boy's Town published *Cults and Kids* which points out: **The appeal of the cult depends largely on the weakness and vulnerability that all of us feel during key stress periods in life.**

There are times in anyone's life when events and pressures pile up and we experience extreme stress. Such times of stress are particularly frequent and painful when we are young. But such times occur to everyone, at every age.

It may be a time when one has moved to new, unfamiliar surroundings (one may have lost a relative or close friend) whatever the reason, in times of stress, we feel depressed -- lost, lonely, unhappy. At such times, a person is much more suggestible than would normally be the case.

Whenever a person is in a position or state of mind in which he or she is especially vulnerable to suggestion, that person is likely to be attracted by the skillful appeal of a cult recruiter. Loneliness, stress, depression all create fertile ground for the cult recruiter to fill.

> *Cults and Kids*
> Robert W. Dellinger, Boys Town Center
> * * *

Edward Levine, Ph.D. is a sociology professor at Loyola University in Chicago. A more specific, psychological analysis is found in Dr. Edward Levine's article: *Religious Cults: Havens for the Emotionally Distressed, Idealists and Intellectuals, and Strongholds of Authoritarian Personalities.*

Religious cults attract members with several strongly appealing incentives. First, cult leaders are individuals with authoritarian, charismatic personalities who exude, if for some with reserve and indirection, a determined and unshakable conviction in themselves and their religious views. They serve as authority figures with whom their converts identify and their views and pronouncements are presented as infallible. Next, each cult leader claims that only the religious views he espouses are true, as well as being the ideal and practical means of resolving the problems afflicting the world and those who join cults. The doctrinaire character of their statements provides converts with a clear sense of meaning, direction, and purpose for their minds and lives, thus dispelling the confusion, uncertainty, and self-doubt that are characteristics of many of them prior to their conversion.

Third, cults impose specific, demanding, and often ascetic and puritanical rules and regulations that govern most of the major aspects of converts' daily lives (e.g., the observation of religious rituals, diets, personal appearance, sexual codes, prohibiting drug use, etc.). Cultists perceive the religious views as true, encompassing explanations about the meaning of life and their role in it, and welcome the inflexible standards as concrete guides for their personal, inter-personal, and social behavior. Both provide them with an alternative of substance to the anomie culture that so bewilders them. Finally, those who join cults gain close, ongoing relationships with like-minded others of their age -- companionship and the feeling of being special, appreciated, and worthy. Their new-found companions also give them a special mission to bring their religious truth to others. Furthermore, these new friends assure the novitiates of the correctness and wisdom of their having converted.

... while most cult converts appear to be drawn to these incentives, additional reasons for their converting suggest differentiating them into three categories -- the "Emotionally Distressed," the "Idealists," and the "Intellectuals."

... For those who were **emotionally distressed** before entering cults, their reasons for conversion cannot be ascribed to careful deliberation and reasoned choice. They may be the most vulnerable of all who are contacted by cult proselytizers. Furthermore, conversion merely stabilizes their emotional and behavioral problems; psychotherapy is required to eliminate their causes, and cults neither provide this service for those of their members needing it nor send them home ..

These converts are bright, **idealistic** young people who have a compassionate concern for the well-being of the down-trodden and the needy. They share a genuine and deeply held interest in finding ways to help them and to improve the quality of life throughout the world. Articulate inheritors of a liberal-intellectual tradition who possess an admirable social conscience, they apparently join cults because they believe them honestly to be committed to the betterment of human beings and society. The Idealists are more apt to join Christian, rather than Eastern, cults since the latter express little or no interest in social activism.

A third category of cultists, apparently less alienated than the first and more so than the second, consists of those who seem to be drawn to cults, especially Eastern ones, because of an **intellectual quest**. The Intellectual's search is born out of a compelling need to find a more satisfying explanation of the meaning of the world and of their role, the role of human being, in it. Here, too, there is no indication that they have studied the tenets and scriptures of their own religions prior to their conversion as thoughtfully and extensively as they do their new religion subsequent to their conversion.

Dr. Edward Levine

* * *

Challenge of the Cults

The first thing that becomes clear in speaking with cult members about their "conversion experience" is that these people have often, if not always, joined the cults for reasons that have little or nothing to do with the specific content of the cult's teachings or even the particular charisma of the cult leader. In short, the purposes of people joining cults are not the same as the proclaimed purposes of the leaders in founding them.

The reason why people join cults can be broken down into several overlapping categories. We list them in what seems to be their relative order of importance.

1. **Loneliness and the Need for Friendship:** More than any other factor, the desire for uncomplicated warmth and acceptance seems to lead people into cults. Indeed, there is much evidence to suggest that the cults understand this need and work hard to fulfill it ...

2. **A Desire for a Transcendent Experience:** Jeff Oboler suggests that there is a "growing disillusionment with reason and science as vehicles to solve all our problems," and he is undoubtedly right. For many people today reason once again seems to require its once-discarded companion of faith in order to make sense out of an increasingly complex and morally ambiguous world [the cults] offer a kind of experience that is dramatically different from those offered by more conventional religious institutions, and most likely different from any other experience the prospective cult member has ever undergone, makes the cults' claim to offer a path -- they would say the path -- to the unfamiliar realm of transcendence all the more plausible. It stands to reason, after all, that if you are looking for an experience that you have never had before, you should look in places you have never before been to find it.

3. **A Need for Moral Authority:** Middle class parents often seek to over-shelter and overprotect their offspring. They want to give their children things they themselves were denied in order to "make them happy." In such circumstances young people often build up dependencies on their parents of which they are not aware until, at the end of adolescence, they are suddenly expected to take charge of their lives and become independent individuals ... it is not surprising that many young people find this sudden assumption of responsibility burdensome and confusing, especially in today's world ... this is where the cults come in. Like a moral McDonalds, they offer lifestyles that are prepackaged and highly structured, with very limited choices and very specific demands. For some such a security blanket is most inviting.

4. **A Need for a Sense of Purpose:** ... many young people today are still seeking a cause beyond themselves, a way of making a contribution to the betterment of society. ... Idealism needs a

sense of mission that can animate good intentions and channel them toward a specific purpose. True, the cults' purpose is ultimately only to promote and enrich themselves. In reality community service to others in need is virtually unknown among them. But by the time a cult inductee realizes this, it no longer matters. Once in the group, serving the master becomes the necessary and sufficient purpose for all activities, collective and individual.

Challenge of the Cults

* * *

Who Is Approached by Cults?

Both The Philadelphia JCRC and Dr. Levine present plausible explanations for what might attract an individual to join a cult. To see if these explanations fit the realities of cults as they operate in the community, we approached several members of the community who deal with cults, members, former members, and potential members almost daily.

Dr. Sandy Andron is the Youth Program Director of the Central Agency for Jewish Education in Miami, Florida. He agrees that there are particular periods in a person's life when he or she is most vulnerable to recruitment by a cult. He also finds that the cults target specific demographic groups.

The one common denominator that seems to be pervasive in this area (Florida) is that they (cults) seem to be approaching people in transition. We have them going to the high schools and the colleges. Going around at periods of anxiety, periods of alienation, periods of confusion, periods of loneliness. Getting to the youngsters at exam time, at graduation time, and at holiday time. We have them (the recruiters) going to the beaches, the fast food restaurants, any place where teenagers congregate. We have them going now and approaching the elderly who are also in transition periods in their lives. We have them approaching those from the lowest socio-economic levels to the highest levels.

It is my personal contention that they go after the very very bright and the very very wealthy for what I believe to be the two most obvious reasons. If I were going to start my own cult, I would want those kids who are bright, articulate, inventive or creative. Idealistic and articulate enough to go out and bring in other recruits, and to go to the very wealthy, who are not necessarily capable of standing on street corners selling flowers, but are capable of turning over trust and bank accounts, and those things which have been purchased for them by their families. **Cults exist for two things: people, and money.** They need people in order to get the money, because money represents the power that the organization is capable of garnering for its leadership.

Dr. Sandy Andron

* * *

Esther Dietz, a former consultant on cults for B'nai B'rith International, also points out that many cults now recruit older people; she adds that Jews are particularly likely to be drawn to cults based on the Eastern religions (Hinduism in particular).

The young 18-25 age group has been most often targeted by the majority of the cults though it now seems to be changing. We have reports of the Moonies and the Church Universal and Triumphant going after the over-50 age group, especially in retirement communities, Sun Belt, etc. Scientology also seems to attract older, working adults in their late 20s, 30s, and 40s, perhaps because their courses are so costly. The Rajneesh people also appear to have more mature members.

With regard to religious breakdown, the Eastern or Hindu-based groups seem to be most attractive to Jews and to have a relatively high proportion -- as much as 25-30% (Divine Light Mission, Hare Krishna, Muktananda, Rajneesh, T.M. would be included in this group). Personality profiles seem to indicate that cults want the intelligent and idealistic, not the losers of our society. Most who become involved are rather naive, middle or upper-middle class, many are seeking to improve the world and are searching for a direct, meaningful spiritual experience. At the time of recruitment, these people are often mildly depressed, in transition, and feeling somewhat alienated.

Esther Dietz

* * *

Cults appeal to people who might seem to be improbable candidates at first glance.

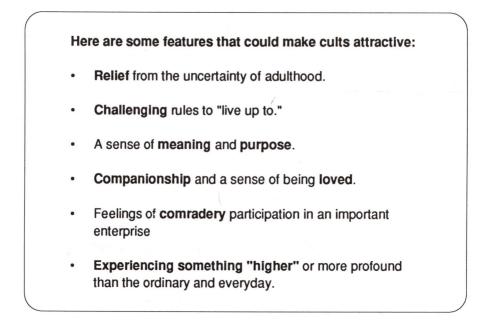

Here are some features that could make cults attractive:

- **Relief** from the uncertainty of adulthood.

- **Challenging** rules to "live up to."

- A sense of **meaning** and **purpose**.

- **Companionship** and a sense of being **loved**.

- Feelings of **comradery** participation in an important enterprise

- **Experiencing something "higher"** or more profound than the ordinary and everyday.

These could easily appeal to anyone who is in a period of insecurity or transition, depression, alienation, loneliness, or search for a deeper sense of purpose.

We can better understand why an educated, inquiring, successful person would join a cult when we see that much of what cults offer coincide with legitimate goals of a fulfilling life. Ironically, people searching to better contribute to society and to answer their own spiritual questions, may stumble into groups which ultimately rob them of the opportunity to do either.

* * *

Sydelle Levine, Former Director of Cult Awareness Network - New York/New Jersey, highlights the ways that cults explore the assets of particular target groups.

Those approached by cults can be placed in three categories. **One group consists of young intellectually gifted, idealistic people in a state of transition.** Vulnerable, lonely, facing a variety of decisions, and uneasy with ambiguity, they seek answers, frequently to philosophical or spiritual open-ended queries.

They have not become part of the mainstream professionally or economically.

These classic recruits are sought by the cults because they are a powerful source of strength. Investment in training and development provides the cult with a broad base of workers available for varied assignments. Young enough to withstand the rigors of physical work and to integrate new learnings, even foreign languages, they can proselytize in diverse environs.

When fully indoctrinated, satisfied that theirs is the sole route to world salvation, they project the image of true believers, possessing peace, purpose, and direction which eludes many of their peers (potential recruits).

As workers, they provide a steady source of income for cults whether engaged in cult-centered enterprises (solicitation, businesses) or by donating substantial portions of salaries earned in other pursuits.

A second group consists of those striving to improve the quality of their lives. They attend lectures, participate in workshops, and explore religions which promise to help them live up to their potential. Frequently, these programs are non-destructive manifestations of the human potential or religious movements. Attendees attempt to achieve tranquility. Seeking, and suffering feelings of uneasiness, they are easy prey for others who attend, recruiters, watching for the right moment to make an overture.

This group's value to the cult is two-fold. They are income producing, involved in career pursuits, and able to provide money for the cult coffers, and they are mature and professionally grounded, part of established society, not drifters. They supply an element of respectability.

The third group approached by cults consists of the elderly. They, too, are in a state of transition. Fearful of death, aware of waning physical prowess, they long for the safety and security of a loving family. Often, there is none nearby. Psychic bookkeeping, taking place as the end nears, points to glaring omissions in the areas of accomplishments and good deeds. The cult provides an area wherein the aged recruit, relieved of loneliness, can take pride in what are viewed as cult goals and achievements. An additional satisfaction, a quantitative measure of self-worth, is donations of social security and other income.

For the cult, the aged are viewed as a source of income and future bequests. It is easy to convince people, aware of increasing frailty, that the cult is all that is left for them and they should leave all to it.

Different groups do go after different target groups. The choice is determined by the method of operation of the individual cult.

Therapy cults are interested in recruits who are able to pay for sessions. Their constituency consists of wage-earners who turn over to the cult portions of their income for promised results. They are uninterested in drifters or those in a penniless state of transition. Entry into a therapy cult is on a "money up-front" basis.

Pseudo-religious cults, on the other hand, are willing to delay financial return, confident of a profitable long term gain. Young recruits who are articulate and physically active are potential proselytizers, income sources, and community builders. Once they are indoctrinated, they are ideal recruiters. They disarm their peers, seduce them, and propel them into the cult, swelling its ranks. Ideally, cult members marry each other and raise children to be cult members.

Increasingly, all cults are zeroing in on the elderly who succumb to varying approaches. They view a bleak and lonely future as old friends die and families are distant. Though they lack strength to work for the cult, they will donate well beyond their capacity, motivated by gratitude for a group that accepts them and from the fear of being ousted from the group. Social security checks, savings, and bequests, are substantial profits accruing to the cult through the involvement of the elderly. The aged are an eagerly sought plum.

Sydelle Levine

* * *

Dr. Sandy Andron shows demographic changes of cults which recruited derelicts and addicts in the 60s, but more recently target the mature and successful.

If you go back, for example, to Jim Jones, you saw him going after the lowest socio-economic strata. In the early days of the cult phenomenon in this country there were drug addicts that were being solicited, and there were the have-nots of society who were being offered a free meal as an enticement to come in and find out what the group's philosophy was. This situation is basically changed. Following Jonestown, Meg Greenfield, in an article in *Newsweek*, made the comment that the strange metaphor of Guyana is that the jungle is just across the street, and I think in making that suggestion what she was saying was that humans are capable of returning to the jungle but that we don't really have to look to the have-nots of society or the jungle communities to find where these groups are doing their operating. And I think you can see very clearly with the

Patty Hearsts, with the young women that were involved with Charles Manson, that the reality is that it's not necessarily to those areas that the cults seem to be going. Now all we have to do is look to the more recent Bhagwan Shree Rajneesh and we find that it's really not the young at all, but the middle-aged person, those who are already established financially, those who have businesses, professional, blue and even white-collar workers, who are being enticed into these particular groups.

As to why they target different groups, I think the answer is as clear as the entire cult phenomenon, and that is that if each one of these groups targeted the same population, there's a question as to whether or not there would be enough people around to be able to fill the needs that each cult requires for its own existence.

Dr. Sandy Andron

* * *

Why Are Jews Over-Represented in Cults?

Studies of cults suggest Jews are overrepresented in many psychological and Eastern oriented groups. Is there something making Jews a primary target of these cults, or is there a psychological weakness making Jews more susceptible to the cult's "sales pitches"?

Rabbi Stephen Robbins offers this answer:

This question must be understood in relationship to the context of middle class, white, educated society in America because that is the place from which most cult members come. Since cults tend to be a white middle-class educated phenomenon, Jews fit that niche in American society in greater numbers proportionately than do other religious and ethnic groups. Consequently, for example, when we see that the majority of members go into cults from college campuses, it is not because the Jews by themselves are more susceptible, it may be because there is a higher concentration of Jews in the university setting. That higher concentration may make for a greater level of susceptibility.

Another correlate seems to be relatively true and that is that those people who are more vulnerable to cults tend to be more highly secularized and farther along the track of assimilation or dilution of some form of specific cultural, religious or ethnic identity. This is also a valid description of the Jewish community which is more secularized in America and much farther along in comparison to other ethnic groups on a track of assimilation. Their distance from commitment to some form of traditional culture and cultural values make them, I believe, more vulnerable to individuals attempting to provide some form of religious experience.

Rabbi Stephen Robbins

* * *

A further discussion of Jews in cults can be found in the *Interview With Rabbi Yehuda Fine* at the end of Part 2.

Where are the Most Common Places to be Approached by Cults?

Understanding the targets is but partial defense against cult recruitment. Knowing the most likely recruiting sites can help avoid entrapment too.

. . . approaching takes place anywhere where teens congregate . . in the streets passing out literature . . . at fast food restaurants and fast food markets...high school and college campuses . . . leaving literature at places that teach yoga, the martial arts . . . sometimes even receiving solicitation through the mail. It is also not uncommon to have them coming to the door, ostensibly selling some kind of product..or a business where they can have racks of literature available for people to pick up. . . I think it's safe to say that the cults do their homework. They do demographic studies on where people are. They make sure that at those places and at the times when there is the greatest frequency of movement that they have recruiters out missionizing.

Dr. Sandy Andron.

* * *

Clearly recruitment is not random. Cults deploy members to where they will find their most likely prospects. Since college students are considered excellent prospects by cults, campus organizations are used as fronts for recruitment. **Arthur Dole, Professor at the University of Pennsylvania** in the Department of Educational Psychology, points out other recruiting spots.

The Unification Church, through its front group, CARP, the Collegiate Association for the Research of Principles, proselytizes on high school and college campuses through meetings and study groups, leafletting and dorm visits. Some groups, such as the Way, offer a free rock concert. Hare Krishna and Divine Light Mission sometimes sponsor movies. Hare Krishna and the Unification Church leaflet at bus stations, airports and train stations, where they can approach unwary young travelers. Cult recruiters attempt to frequent large gatherings of young people such as political rallies. Cults may take advantage of academic freedom on large university campuses and set up booths. Among others, Hare Krishna were present at the New York Peace March on June 16, 1982.

Arthur Dole

* * *

The most common places to be approached by cults seeking new members are:

- **Airports, train and bus stations,** where people, frequently young people wearing backpacks, are on the move.

- **College campuses,** where a concentration of intelligent, inquiring minds can be found.

- *How to ...* **lectures,** which suggest methods for improving the quality of one's life.

- **Religious meetings,** persons engaged in a spiritual quest are often experiencing dissatisfaction, a feeling of purposelessness.

The above listed places are selected by cult recruiters because they are populated, to a great extent, by those engaged in inquiry. Values clarification and establishing goals result in sifting thoughts. The mind, like the body, is weakest when in a state of transition. A rueful comment made in retrospect by former cult members is, "If they had spoken to me one month before or one month later, I never would have fallen for it."

Sydelle Levine

* * *

Challenge of the Cults points out that cult recruiters frequent places where travelers or anxious students might be found.

. . . Recruiters are especially active during stressful times of the year: the first week of classes on the college campus, for instance, when new students are often feeling alone and disoriented in a strange new environment. Other favorite times for recruiting are finals week and graduation time, when many students are feeling a great deal of pressure and uncertainty about the future . . .

. . . Vacation spots are especially popular with cult recruiters. One of the Moonies' main headquarters is in Berkeley, a mecca for young travelers. According to one source, Moon's recruiters are especially encouraged to strike up conversations with people carrying knapsacks and guitars, since these people are particularly likely to respond to the offer of a free meal or a free weekend in the California countryside. Krishna people annually pilgrimage down to Fort Lauderdale in the winter to recruit for much the same reason.

Challenge of the Cults

* * *

The Most Common Approach Techniques
-- Do They Work on Everyone?

Arthur Dole reminds us that the cult recruiter's initial contact usually involves some deception, and that once a prospect has let down his or her guard, more overt brainwashing techniques may be used.

Cults use a large variety of deceptions and intensive persuasion techniques, first to gain the attention and time of the prospective member and then to convert him or her. When cult recruiters behind a stand at the Berkeley campus invite a lonely traveler to come to visit the Creative Community Project and have dinner with a great bunch of people, they may deny that they have anything to do with the Unification Church or with religion. Recruits who wander into a Scientology center and sign up for a course on personality improvement are not told that they will be pressured to take just one more course and then just one more course, until they are completely converted. Similarly, the smiling sincere young people who invite the college acquaintance to drop by for some serious
of the Bible may not reveal that they are members of the Way. The first

approach, common to many cults, emphasizes friendliness, intense interest in the prospective recruit, love bombing in which the recruiter goes out of his or her way to show how much he or she appreciates the fine qualities of the prospect.

I know of very few hard statistics on the effectiveness of cult recruiting. In times of social disturbance and instability, large numbers of people become susceptible to brainwashing. Consider, as an example, the Nazis' control over the German people. Some former Moonies have estimated that one out of every four individuals who visited Booneville, the Unification Church's commune in northern California, was converted. It is certainly true that the probability of conversion is much higher if the cult is able to gain control of the individual's environment and communication channels.

Arthur Dole

* * *

The Cult Awareness Network (formerly the Citizen's Freedom Foundation), a national organization founded by parents of children involved in cults, expands the answer.

Cult recruiters have honed techniques to a fine and effective edge. They often use a warm one-to-one approach, involving much eye contact and expressions of warmth and fellow-feelings. Recruiters often ask vaguely worded questions to which no negative response could be considered—for example, "Would you like to improve the world?"

Contact with the recruiter frequently ends up with an invitation to dinner, to a study group, or to a workshop. The recruiter may (or may not) reveal the actual identity of his or her organization.

Remember: in general, individuals do not seek out cults; it is the cults which actively seek out new members!

CAN

* * *

Sydelle Levine explains how the recruiters adapt to "make friends" with the potential member:

The most common approach appears completely innocent; an overture based on a shared interest or perceived need. Associations and friendships, from earliest childhood on, have the same origin. Indeed, with the exception of formal introductions, it is difficult to envision social interaction starting differently. Small wonder, then, that the potential recruit is unaware that anything ominous accompanies the outstretched hand offered.

Cults make excellent use of knowledge of human experience when engineering an approach. Meeting a young person carrying a backpack and learning that he is alone, drifting, and seeking direction, the recruiter will describe a group of people, new to the community, who have settled and achieved a warm, friendly extended family-like household. The potential member will rise to the bait of an invitation to visit.

Noticing a young person carrying an instrument, the recruiter will refer to his or her own interest in music and the similar interest of others in the group he lives with. If the potential recruit is attending a religion-centered gathering, the recruiter will refer to his own spiritual quest and how his own needs have been met by the "church."

The approach works with most people. Relieved at the prospect of having his needs met, the recruit fails to probe to learn more about the recruiter and the group he represents.   Sydelle Levine

* * *

Dr. Sandy Andron adds that forging a false common bond works best when the potential member is alone and unhappy.

I think that probably the most common technique is just that friendly approach where you say, "Gee, I've had that kind of problem, or dealt with the same kind of issue, or I know where you are coming from," or "I've had a day that's a bummer as well." This leads to establishing a relationship where the recruiter invites the person to one of dozens of home-based direct approaches. I think if there's a common approach, probably the approach is that they almost always try to establish a one-to-one contact. It is rare that a person would come over seeking your soul, seeking your involvement in a group and talk to two or three people at the same time. Usually there would be reinforcement from the group saying let's get away from here, this is not our thing.

This technique certainly works with people who are lonely, it works with people who are seeking, it seems to have made its best, most potent response to people who are in transition. I think it would be safe to say that the approach does work in a positive way because it appeals to the nature of people in general, that nature which likes to be loved and which likes to be appreciated.

Dr. Sandy Andron

* * *

What Personality Type Makes a Good Recruiter?

Cult missionaries vary tremendously in their recruiting skill. A relatively new convert will tend to be zealous, rigid and inflexible. On the other hand, an intelligent, experienced and convinced missionary becomes adept at studying recruits and adapting his or her techniques to their vulnerability. Certain powerful charismatic leaders like Jim Jones are exceptionally clever and can skillfully adjust their techniques to situations and personalities. A large number of books, especially by former members about the Unification Church, suggest that Reverend Moon and his associates run the church much on the lines of a large business in which prospective "customers" are carefully studied and sales techniques adapted to the circumstances.

Dr. Arthur Dole

* * *

I have no doubt in my mind that recruitment is taught as a specific job, certainly former members have shared with me experiences of how they have been taught, of how those things which are designed to look spontaneous are very carefully and repetitively done over and over so that the spontaneity looks spontaneous. This is true, not only on the street corners, but at the recruiting centers as well. I guess so far as personality is concerned, a good recruiter would be someone who is a good listener, someone who is empathetic, someone who could appear very sincere, concerned, interested, idealistic. Painfully, I have to say almost all of those qualities that we look for in bright, gifted children, and all the qualities that we try to teach in our gifted programs are the same things found in a good missionary.

Dr. Sandy Andron

* * *

What If You Are Approached by a Recruiter?

Here are some guidelines for people who meet cult recruiters. **This is not meant to dissuade anyone from meeting new people and making new friends.** Though difficult for us to say, in today's world, a bit of skepticism is necessary when new friends or experiences seem "too good to be true."

Beware of Recruiters

Very few people ever set out to become cult members on their own. If they do not meet a recruiter, there is little likelihood of their "joining" a cult, regardless of how vulnerable they may be.

- *Beware* of people who are excessively or inappropriately friendly. **There are few instant friendships.**

- *Beware* of people with simplistic answers or solutions to complex world problems. **There are no easy answers.**

- *Beware* of people with invitations to free meals and lectures. **There is no free lunch.**

- *Beware* of people who pressure you because "everyone else is doing it." **Think how much harm is done, or how many wrongs are not righted because of peer pressure.**

- *Beware* of people who recruit through guilt. **Guilt, induced by others, is rarely a productive emotion.**

- *Beware* of invitations to isolated weekend workshops having nebulous goals. **There is no reason for a person to be vague** or evasive unless he or she has something to hide.

> **The two basic principles of psychological coercion are:**
>
> 1. If you can make a person *behave* the way you want, you can make that person *believe* the way you want.
>
> 2. Sudden, intense changes in environment lead to a heightened suggestibility and to drastic shifts in attitudes and beliefs.

Remember: Cults are not interested in helping you, but in helping themselves. Cults want your free-time, full-time, life-time commitment as a recruiter, worker and fundraiser. *What's in it for you?*

Are There Means to Stop Recruitment in Public Places?

There are a number of ways of stopping or discouraging on-site recruitment. Many airports now have prominently placed disclaimers directed against cult solicitation. Similar warnings could be posted in public areas where recruitment occurs. Notices should go up on college dormitory bulletin boards alerting students to recruitment practices and offering information about recorded entrapments in the institution. Cults suffer from exposure.

The most effective way to prevent on-site recruitment is to have someone identify, intervene, and engage in illuminating questioning in the presence of the potential recruit. A few such unrewarding encounters would serve to discourage recruiters from frequenting the site.

Sydelle Levine

* * *

I would certainly not deprive cults of their constitutional rights to free speech, freedom of religion and freedom to attempt to convert. But I do support "sunshine" regulations. Thus recruiters should be required to identify themselves and their organization. They should be restrained from harassing the public in airports and other public places. At the educational institutions, they should conform to well-designed regulations to control their activities. At the University of Pennsylvania, where I teach, the cults are permitted to use University facilities provided they identify themselves and observe procedures of open expression. Krishnas have been required to admit anti-cult protesters to their meetings. In my opinion, the best means of stopping on-site recruitment is publicity and preventive education.

Dr. Arthur Dole

* * *

Henrietta Crampton, as Founder of the Cult Awareness Network and parent of a former cult member, offers an approach to stop recruitment.

An effective means of stopping on-site recruitment would be for teams of young people to confront recruiters on campus. On-campus programs to discuss destructive cults would help. Concerned people could confront the cults at airports and public places. Mr. [Morris] Yanoff and his team of people at O'Hare airport cut down both recruitment and solicitation by the Hare Krishna. Unfortunately, people who are not in cults lack the drive and incentive to volunteer for activities such as counter-cult work on campus. Perhaps through student clubs, interest could be developed along this line.

Henrietta Crampton

* * *

Nearly all of the cults' membership comes through recruitment. It is unlikely that a person would walk into a destructive cult's meeting and say, "I know what this group is, and I want to join." People at vulnerable points in their lives are talked into joining, and then may find it almost impossible to get out. It is obvious from the fact that destructive cults still exist that some recruitment techniques work, but we do not know how well they work.

How Effective Is Recruitment?

How many people must a recruiter approach before finding one who will become a convert? Have efforts to counter cult recruitment techniques been successful? Has preventive education about cults paid off?

Unfortunately, the secretiveness and often deceptive claims of the destructive cults make controlled statistical studies near impossible. However, there is some evidence that enrollment in some groups has begun to wane, largely because of adverse publicity. Rather than fade out of existence due to a low growth rate, destructive cults have chosen new techniques for enrolling members. Sometimes, cult leadership will change the name of the organization and disavow any connection with the "old" cult. Other cults have taken to targeting people who either have not heard of that particular cult or who have not yet been exposed to preventive cult education. Although we may not be certain what specific cult awareness measures have succeeded, we know that if potential members are more aware of what lies behind the recruiters' promises of redemption and love, they will be less likely to believe them. Let us hope that as cults find new recruitment techniques, the cult awareness movement will have the foresight and tenacity to counteract those methods.

Study Guide

For the Group:

1. Have everyone take the "I Could Never Get Involved" test. Discuss the results, particularly if someone marks three or more, and still doesn't feel they are susceptible to cults.

2. Discuss ways in which different people have been approached by cults. Look for effective ways to avoid becoming targets for cults.

3. Discuss the difference between the right of the cults to express their philosophy and the deception used in attracting new members.

4. "Every young person must undergo his or her own spiritual search. Becoming part of a cult is part of that search. It may lead to spiritual fulfillment." Discuss this view and its inherent dangers.

For the Individual:

1. Why do you think people join cults? Are you vulnerable to joining a cult?

2. Have you seen cults trying to recruit new members? Are you attracted to them? What has kept you from joining?

3. If your salvation could only be achieved by getting other people to join with you, would you lie to get them to join?

4. The next time you are watching television, look closely at the techniques used in commercials to sell products. Do you see any similarities between television advertising and the pitch made by cults?

Supporting Article

Interview: *Update Magazine*

Rabbi Yehudah Fine is the Executive Director of Choices for the Jewish Family, headquartered in Brooklyn, New York. He is associated with the Manhattan-based Jewish Community Relations Task Force on Missionaries & Cults and is a spokesman on new religions for the larger Jewish community.

Update: *Let's start with some background material. Why did you become interested in new religions?*

Fine: In a nutshell, I became interested because I was living and working as a high-school principal in Mendocino, California where there was a lot of cult activity. Whereas I was concerned about all of my students, I was most surprised that many of the Jewish students were joining these groups, and I, a Jew, had no appreciable impact on them. I was aware that they were experiencing personality transformations and were radically altering their lifestyles. That was the milieu and context of California in the early 70's.

Update: *Why did you develop a professional ministry to new religious movements?*

Fine: I took a vacation to Jerusalem and, while there, I decided to make a radical change, a career switch, in my life. Until then I had invested seven or eight years in public education. Vacationing in Jerusalem, I realized that as a Jew I was living in an extraordinarily historical time; my people were back in Israel after centuries of exile. I felt that I wanted to contribute my skills to Jewish causes, so I became a rabbi. I left my job, studied in Jerusalem, and when I came to New York, the work with cults began to happen naturally. Because I was giving classes on the new religions, other rabbis, families, and family services began calling me. Various people, including those in the cults, were coming to me, and I began to counsel and redirect them.

Update: *Does your counseling have a distinctively Jewish character?*

Fine: I began my work with a true sense of mission, of reacquainting and reawakening in Jewish people their own rich spiritual heritage. I approached it from that angle, a Jewish perspective, and that approach has been both popular and successful.

Update: *Why have young Jews been attracted to the new religions? Some researchers would suggest that an inordinate percentage of Jewish people belong to some of the new religions. Is that true?*

Fine: There are a disproportionate number of young Jews in certain groups, definitely. One very obvious reason for that is that 85% of Jewish kids go to college where recruiting by the new religions takes place. They also come from upwardly mobile families who send their children away, out of town, to school. A third factor is the breakdown in Jewish family life. Jews have always had a very strong family tradition; not necessarily a religious one, but nonetheless a very influential, ethnic-oriented tradition. What we're seeing is that, within one generation of intellectually oriented kids who have not really had any religious and spiritual upbringing in their lives, those traditions have ruptured. Jewish young people haven't grappled with life and meaning questions, although the whole basis of questioning is built into the family. Add to that a divorce or any of those kinds of vectors that make kids vulnerable emotionally, besides their going off to school, and you have all the ingredients for somebody getting involved in one of the new religious groups.

Update: *Those factors don't seem to be distinctively different from the rest of the population, or are they?*

Fine: Well, I think they are very different because Jews are not part of the mainstream of societies in the United States or Europe. They are a minority group. Joining a new religion is often a form of cultural assimilation, a going away from Judaism. It's different for a Protestant kid in midwestern America who gets involved in a Bible cult. That's a modest shift from likely religious activity at home. But for young Jews, they wonder, what does it mean to be a Jew, rising out of the ashes of the holocaust? What does it mean to be one of 3.5% of the population in a non-Jewish culture? Those considerations affect Jews as individuals. They cause a person to question and wonder. And when men and women question and wonder inside of themselves, internally they seek resolution. The new religious movements, of course, provide that resolution.

Update: *Are there some new religions whose beliefs lend themselves to attracting Jews?*

Fine: I think the Eastern groups do. They have the universalist pitch -- we will accept and bring in everyone -- which fits in well with a loss of liberalism, and it also solves a lot of unique Jewish concerns instantly. You can still be identified more or less (mostly less) with your Judaism, but acceptance is for everybody.

You don't have to deal with any of those historical or minority problems because the solution is "we are one" to begin with. If you take away the diversity of all individuals and say there is unity, then you don't have to deal with any particular issues that raise distinctions.

Update: *Are you specifically thinking of guru groups?*

Fine: Yes, Jewish kids are attracted to guru movements. And those movements have, accordingly, tailored their proselytizing to address a Jewish audience. For example, I've seen poorly written materials in the Hare Krishna movement that are a psycho-spiritual textual attack on Judaism. Those commentaries to prove Krishna consciousness are handed out to Jewish disciples to deal specifically with Jewish questions. Some of the Bible groups approach it from a completely different angle. They manipulate and monopolize the tensions that have always existed between Christian and Jewish communities and seek to bring about a resolution of that tension for the Jews within their group. During the recruitment of a Jewish kid, if he maintains his Jewish identity, that tension is always discussed.

Update: *How has the Jewish community organized itself institutionally in response to new religious movements?*

Fine: Well, I think its true that we are way ahead organizationally of Christian institutions. But in terms of the new religions, they are still far outdistancing us. In the United States there is a growing national Jewish response that is centered in New York, primarily through the active Jewish Community Relations Task Force on Missionaries & Cults. We have a clinic in New York, and other cult clinics are springing up through Jewish family services across the country. We've trained many seminary students as well. There's an ongoing network of exchange of information and seminars through Jewish family services. The biggest thing we've done to make a broad-based statement as a religious community, besides our own Jewish efforts is to form an interfaith coalition in New York City. The archdioceses, the council of churches, and individual representatives from Greek Orthodox, Episcopalian, United Church of Christ, etc. denominations meet and conduct seminars that will affect clergy across the country. Our goal is to help them deal with the common, value-based issues raised by new religious movements and to develop programs that will affect Jews and Christians alike.

Update: *What value-based issues are important to that committee?*

Fine: Basically, cultic religious groups are so successful today because they supplant the natural family. Family and community identities are decomposing, and I think a theological perspective is critically important in supporting those identities. I think we've run out of gas in looking at the growth of new religions from a purely psychological perspective. One must have a family and community to come back to, integrate and grow in. I tell parents, what good is it to talk with your son and help him get on track again if he just assimilates into the culture and disappears? What good does it do for our whole journey down through history?

Update: *What do you offer a Jew who is coming out of a new religion?*

Fine: Through the Jewish Community Relations Council and other groups we work with, particularly in New York and Philadelphia, we're building communities--supportive places where individuals can grapple with the deep questions which the new religions raise. Whereas we're genuinely trying to work towards that, we're only in the development stage.

Update: *What do you offer, religiously, theologically, to Jews who are in new religious movements?*

Fine: Let me give you a little scenario of what happens here almost continually. By coming to my house, people encounter a major paradox. Why is that? Because they encounter a strong, spiritually oriented, religious family that is also autonomous. We are a community who is willing to engage their religious value structure. I care what individuals believe in, especially how they acquired that belief. So we will talk theology. They also encounter a community of people who are caring and support independent growth. A former Rajneesh devotee came here one Sabbath afternoon as we were singing and worshiping. She walked in and said, "My God, I'm back in Poona." Now that's just crazy on the one hand, but on the other hand, that doesn't happen if you're picked up by a coercive deprogrammer.

Something else happens here. Kids tell me that when they come out of groups, they have a lot of deep, God-related questions they wonder about. They want to talk about the kinds of values that we as human beings cherish. Where are they going to find that? This house is a place that is different from the average synagogue or church. Former members of the new religions will say, "You know, for the last few months I've really been scared to open up my heart again and to even think about any deep, spiritual questions, I've been afraid to do that. But here, I feel safe because it's mine."

Update: *How is your intense community distinctly Jewish?*

Fine: We maintain what we call religious rituals in our family life that are part and parcel of who we are and what we do. Those religious acts have the spiritual consequence in the family of drawing people together. In an open kind of atmosphere, a person can have an ultimate encounter with God. Come here some Friday night, for example, and watch my three-year-old daughter light a candle and tell me that you don't feel something. There is a special meaning beyond the mere lighting of the candle. If I look at it psychologically, lighting the candle brings light into the world, and that's a nice symbol. But if the lighting ushers in the Sabbath, a sanctity is brought down into the world. We can step out of our secular world for just a moment to remember who we are. It's more than just rehabilitation, more than just psychological counseling. It's an encounter with eternity.

Update: *Are there new religious movements in Israel?*

Fine: Yes, it's wild. They're all over there, too. Scientology, The Way International, Divine Light Mission, the Hare Krishnas. Nearly every group is present in Jerusalem, a prized piece of turf to acquire members in. To be able to recruit and train Israelis who will then come to the United States or Europe is obviously a tremendous plus. To be on ground that is acknowledged as the holyland is a very important thing. Israel is ripe. It's not easy to live there. How much tension, how much war can people take? How much suffering can they bear in a highly technological society? It's beautiful but nevertheless hard. That provides a fertile ground from which people listen and convert to new religious beliefs.

Update: *After exit-counseling, we assume a person leaves and becomes reoriented. Do you feel a religious worldview needs to be part of a person's reconstruction?*

Fine: Our counseling is not distinctly religious. I certainly hope non-Jewish clients come out of the groups. There's no doubt about that. In dealing with people who grew up in the Catholic Church, for example, I refer them to professionals I know who they can contact and engage in dialogue. I do that.

But I don't want to talk now about people who are the casualties of the new religions, because they need special kinds of counseling and attention. Let's talk about a "normal" recruit. Some of them may have come from wounded environments to begin with, but they are nonetheless functional. But because everybody brings their own kind of cultural baggage and fears into an exit-counseling situation, kids are not often encouraged to seek it out.

Based on conversations I've had with kids who have sought me out, however, I believe that even in the most perverted sense, in just about every group, there was some encounter with the divine. (That's looking at it from a somewhat mystical perspective, I realize.) Something happened to the person. You cannot just label it thought reform. No matter how perverted it was, it ripped that person into another reality that lies at the bottom of things--a reality in which they were not capable of functioning before. Good or bad (I don't want to say that most of it is bad), something was awakened in a funny way; a religious or spiritual awakening, whatever word you want to use. But that poses a very big question. Every kid wants to know what happened to them in the group. Most counselors say, here's Lifton (author of *Thought Reform and the Psychology of Totalism*). That's what happened to you. But that's not what happened. Something happened inside the person's heart and mind. How are you going to get at and understand that? How are you going to integrate that, because there is much confusion in that ongoing process that needs to be resolved.

Update: *Are there theological criteria by which you evaluate new religions?*

Fine: Yes, certainly, there are criteria. I'll speak Jewishly. Judaism says there are basically three criteria. I'll tell you a story to put them into context.

There was once a great Hasidic master named Reb Nachman of Breslov. His students are still around today. The story goes that one of his students was praying, swaying back and forth, and nothing special happened. But the next day when people came in, he was on fire. He was able to understand everything they asked them and to repeat the Rebbe's teaching. So they went to the Hasidic master and said, "You must be proud of your disciple. He explains your teachings and your stories, and when we see him pray with such fire, we become ecstatic ourselves." The Rebbe looked back and said, "No, when he gets over all of that experience, let's see if he really learned anything. Let's see if he has a better life."

So the three criteria address the question, How do I know what I'm doing is good and right? First, you have to ask, Am I hurting anybody? Second, Am I adding to what is here? Although there is an intuitive experience in Judaism that is private, personal, and indescribable, you should be able to speak about it in a rational way. Not the experience, but the effect of that experience. Third, is a positive action modality present in my life? Can I see that I am a better husband, that I'm not as angry, I'm more compassionate, more caring? Those are very powerful value statements. The Jews have ways of serving God which include all kinds of improved interrelationships and interactions. If the quality of life improves after a religious experience, then something true has happened. That includes the affirmation of family and community values.

Update: *What is your starting point in exit-counseling?*

Fine: I begin examining the theology in terms of the group's action modality in the world. Once you have a rapport with an individual, there are lots of ways you can enter into their theology. All groups have either a millennial or universal-saving-the-world component which operates only within the perimeters of the group. Those components never really reach anyone else apart from witnessing for the group to enlist new members. If you can get to the point where critical thinking begins, then ask members, what do you really want out there?, What is that for?, How is that tied into what you are taught? Glaring problems exist in most groups. Nothing is really happening except in the members "own little world." They're not really doing anything. Ask them why? What in their theology says that? Why is what they are doing so self-limiting?

Update: *The main editors of Shambala publishers wrote an article for Publishers Weekly that described how the new age market for belief and meditational books is withering. Consequently, they're now printing books and articles on how to be active in your environment; for example, new age ecology, energy, childbirth, cooking, medicine, community relations, etc. In that sense, I wonder if you see a potential change with new religious groups? Would your criteria of action modality change?*

Fine: No, I believe those movements are of such an unusual nature that if they were to adopt positive actions toward society and culture, they would dissipate. The social controls for maintaining membership would break up, and members would slip into mainstream culture. I would argue that once controls were eased, narrow and limited theologies would not attract members or provide a positive basis for positive social activism. By the way, I'd love to have consumer legislation in all religions--let's talk about what we're all about.

Update: *That's not really consumer protection, though. It's legislation directed at religious belief. But theoretically, how would you like to see that legislation applied? For example, if you join the Unification Church (UC), you should be told that you will probably be married within five years; your spouse will be selected for you; you're likely to work for the UC and, although they won't demand that you turn your paycheck back over to the church, you'll be a better steward of your monies if you do; that you will come and live in UC centers; if you do come to work for the church and stay for 15 to 20 years, a retirement program will not be provided for you; you won't have medical coverage, etc. Is that the kind of thing you would like recruits to hear?*

Fine: Yes. Why should we be afraid to talk about those things? Why shouldn't I be able to ask you about my retirement plan in the UC? Why shouldn't the freedom exist so that, when I ask the question about marriages, I'll get an answer?

* * *

PART 3:

STAYING PUT

PART 3: CONTENTS

PART 3: *STAYING PUT*

... the recruit is maneuvered into attending the first meeting. There is little discussion of a religious nature; the leader's name may not even be mentioned. Instead, there is a rousing but nebulous lecture, followed by cheery talk, sincere smiles, eye contact, hand holding, and general expression of great affection.

Dr. Louis J. West and
Dr. Margaret Thaler Singer
Cults, Quacks and Non-
Professional Psychotherapies

We see how easy it is to accept an invitation from a charming and skilled recruiter to attend a "first meeting". More difficult to believe is someone's rapid transformation into unquestioning acceptance of a belief system, one which may seem bizarre and antithetical to anything he or she has believed in before.

How could this person completely turn around in such a short period of time? What so powerful, could have happened to make this person totally disconnect from his or her family? No element of the cult phenomenon has been so widely misunderstood as the indoctrination process. There is much popular sentiment that the only way to induce radical changes in someone's behavior is to use physical force and torture. Such coercion rarely, if ever, takes place in destructive cults, if physical coercion is used, it is only a reinforcement for other, more powerful, forms of persuasion.

What is Cult Indoctrination?

In *Cults, Quacks, and Non-Professional Psychotherapists,* **Drs. Louis J. West and Margaret Thaler Singer** outline ten key points to cult indoctrination:

Like the political indoctrination studied by Schein (1961), successful indoctrination of a recruit by a cult is likely to include most of the following elements:

Indoctrination Elements

1. Isolation of the recruit and manipulation of his/her environment.

2. Control over channels of communication and information.

3. Debilitation through inadequate diet and fatigue.

4. Degradation or diminution of the self.

5. Induction of uncertainty, fear, and confusion, with joy and certainty through surrender to the group as a goal.

6. Alternation of harshness or leniency in a context of discipline.

7. Peer pressure, often applied through ritualized struggle sessions, generating guilt and requiring open confessions.

8. Insistence by seemingly all-powerful hosts that the recruit's survival -- physical or spiritual -- depends on identifying with the group.

9. Assignment of monotonous tasks or repetitive tasks, such as chanting or copying written materials.

10. Acts of symbolic betrayal or renunciation of self, family, and previously held values, designed to increase the psychological distance between the recruit and his previous way of life.

L.J. West & M.T. Singer

* * *

Information Disease

Flo Conway and Jim Siegelman have studied the cult phenomenon for years. An extensive excerpt from the January 1982 *Science Digest* article here describes how the force-feeding of certain information, combined with the withholding of other information, accompanied by physical stress can actually "snap" a person's mind.

Our nationwide survey of former cult members, the first of its kind, reveals that in their recruiting and rituals, many cults are using a new form of mind control -- a sweeping manipulation unlike anything ever witnessed before in our society.

Comparisons with brainwashing are misleading. The method of thought reform, first observed in the early Fifties in Chinese and North Korean prisons and "reeducation" camps, rests firmly on the principal fact of physical coercion. In America's cults, participation almost always begins voluntarily. From the first contact to conversion and in daily cult life, control is achieved not by physical coercion, but by an even more potent force: information.

For the past six years we have been studying the communication techniques that some of America's cult leaders use to gain control over people's minds. Most rely on the use -- and abuse -- of information; on deceptive and distorted language, artfully designed suggestions and intense emotional experiences, crippling tactics aggravated by physical exhaustion and isolation.

How is it done? Most groups actively seek out new members by using slick sales pitches: glowing images of easy pathways to ecstasy and personal encounters with God, Jesus or the group's own living messiah. Once an individual has been drawn into a cult, there is usually a single moment of conversion, an intense experience engineered through the skillful manipulation of information. A vivid example: the Hare Krishna's arti ka ceremony, in which new recruits, led by older members, perform a feverish, jumping dance amid flickering lights, heavy incense, loud, droning music and pounding drums until they are physically and emotionally overcome.

Next, most cults step up the indoctrination process, inculcating the group's beliefs and values at a time when the new convert is highly receptive. More importantly, at this stage group leaders begin to sow the specific suggestions that lie at the heart of the mind-control process. Calls to "surrender," to "turn off the satanic mind" or merely to "let things float" act as covert hypnotic suggestions. If heeded, they can place the new convert in an on-going trance.

These simple self-hypnotic rituals close off the recruit's mind to doubts, questions, and disquieting memories of family and the outside world. They also produce a kind of "ecstasy by default," a numbed, mindless high that many interpret as the attainment of their ultimate spiritual goal. But the price of this bliss may be incalculably high. It is here that the cult experience departs from what has always been respected as a valid religious or spiritual experience.

The most startling effects of all were the bizarre disturbances of awareness, perception, memory and other basic information-processing capacities. Former cult members complained of disorientation and of "floating" in and out of altered states; recurrent nightmares, hallucinations and delusions; of instances of bewildering and unnerving "psychic" phenomenon; and -- widespread among former group members known for their intensive repetitive rituals -- of an inability to break mental rhythms of chanting, meditation or speaking in tongues.

No term exists in medicine or mental health to describe this new kind of illness that is infecting America's cult members. In our 1978 book, *Snapping: America's Epidemic of Sudden Personality Change*, we introduced the term **"information disease"** for what may represent a disorder of awareness caused not by germs, drugs or physical abuse but by the manipulation of information feeding every sensory channel of the nervous system.

. . . without exception, the most compelling acts of cult life were the intense daily ritual or therapeutic practices required by every group. These methods varied widely according to cult: meditation in the Divine Light Mission, the Moonies' act of "centering" on the teachings of Rev. Moon, the "tongues" ritual in The Way, Scientology's "training regimens" and "pastoral counseling," the Krishnas' chanting of their familiar mantra. Our respondents reported spending from three to seven hours per day practicing one or more of these techniques. Members also reported spending time each day in group rituals, including sensitivity sessions, psychodramas, guided fantasies and a variety of emotion-filled confessional activities. Moreover, nearly all our respondents reported spending an additional 20 to 30 hours per week at lectures, seminars, workshops or required private study of cult doctrines.

This grueling schedule of devotional activities adds up to **a numbing 40 to 70 hours per week** (average time: 55 hours per week) spent in various mind-control practices.

Flo Conway and Jim Siegelman

* * *

In *Destructive Cult Conversion,* **Dr. John Clark** of Harvard Medical School's Department of Psychiatry and his colleagues, Langone, Schecter, and Daly, describe how cult conversion differs from the methods often used by traditional religions. He shows a process that begins when the new member is suggestible ; gradually he or she is trained to think in polarized terms ("us" versus "them," the cult leader's notion of "good" versus the rest of the world, which is "evil"), until previous logical thinking becomes distorted. Clark points out that while trance induction has been used by many religions to induce altered states of awareness in followers, they, unlike the destructive cults, make no attempt to keep their followers in permanent altered states of consciousness. Unlike destructive cults, they encourage these states briefly and only for particular purposes.

Conversion can begin in earnest once the prospect is in an especially receptive state of consciousness. Supported by marathon classes and intense devotional or confessional activities calculated to maintain and strengthen the convert's receptivity, the proselytizers attempt to effect a thorough ideological reform. By inducing the convert to repeatedly espouse and practice the cult's beliefs and sanctioned behavior, they lead him to a full and unquestioned adoption of the cult's world view. In time, the cult's way becomes the convert's way, and his old world view becomes a distant memory, partly forgotten and partly cut off (that is, dissociated) from his day-to-day consciousness.

One result of this reeducation is to polarize the convert's thinking, to lead him to believe that the cult represents all that is good and necessary to his needs, and that non-cult associations are harmful, even evil, and either to be avoided at almost any cost or manipulated to serve the convert's new needs. This simplification, in which the ambiguities of the new member's past life fall away, exaggerate prior alienation from many new aspects of the individual's pre-cult existence, and he becomes antagonistic toward them. He begins to recoil at the "heretical" beliefs about religion and society from which he is disengaging himself, and he will practice deception in his dealings with the hostile non-cult world because the sanctified ends justify the means. No longer able to evaluate beliefs and perceptions about those associations according to the proven common sense criteria which he formerly used, the convert now makes judgments which tend to conform to the cult's precepts and vision.

Parents are often the chief subjects of this polarizing thought reform when young people are involved because they provide the strongest link between the youthful convert and his old way of life, a link fraught in any case with emotional difficulties stemming from the weaning process. But rather than simply help the convert to "leave home," as it were, in order to establish a separate yet reasonable healthy existence, the cult provides a new family which becomes the focus for relationships previously sustained by kinship links. Parental affection and concern often become for members of most cults demonic attempts to maintain the corrupting controls responsible both for the convert's problems and for the sad state of the world. One group, for example, encourages the transfer of positive thought from the old order to the new by inculcating a distinction between "biological" parents, who bore and raised the convert, and "true" parents, who turn out to be none other than the leader(s) of the new "cult" family.

In the same way, the initiate's notions about what is good or evil, about what can ensure health and well-being, are skewed or totally revised by cult curricula which recognize the essential connections between language, thought, and action. Members of ISKON, for example, reportedly learn first that gambling is wrong, but in due course it is hammered home that gambling is akin to "speculation," and finally that speculative thought, independent thinking not guided and informed by the cult's concrete and simplistic world view, is both evil and dangerous. Similarly, Unification Church members' loyalties are redirected by a calculated confusion between the initiates' new "father" (already a revised definition of the term) and the "heavenly" father (God himself) whose authority should not be questioned. Thus "heavenly deception" in the marketplace can become a way of life literally because God seems to sanction it for the greater good of the victims and for the very salvation of the deceivers.

Distortions of familiar terms and symbols are especially effective when they are incorporated into old, familiar songs and idioms. This helps further to clinch the convert's break with the past and bind him to his new existence.

As indoctrination proceeds, the cult vividly conjures up the specter of supernatural sanctions for non-conformity. Redemption and salvation will only come to true believers and practitioners, while damnation and misery await the heretic. This fate, moreover, is reserved not only for the backslider or apostate, but for his benighted family, who do not yet believe as he does. The antipathy toward parents nurtured by the cults is thus mitigated, as perhaps it must be, by the convert's new compulsion to save his family, and friends, by reforming them. His mind is now filling with terrifying thoughts, perhaps last experienced only in normally suggestible childhood years, the convert strives passionately to make the cult way his own. He joins wholeheartedly in continuous self-evaluation by cult standards. Past experiences, values, powers of discrimination, become so well suppressed that he begins to manipulate, both in self-defense and to achieve fulfillment, the simple, concrete, and magical universe which the cult has revealed to him.

In effect, the convert's mind seems to split. A factitious second personality (the cult personality) begins episodically to achieve a certain autonomy as it struggles with the old one for position in the forefront of consciousness. The stress on the individual here is, of course, very great, and can be relieved only by giving in to the new self. Indeed, converts in most destructive cults learn special dissociative techniques (meditation, chanting, glossolalia) in order to suppress impure and, therefore, stressful thoughts, or to deflect outsiders' equally stressful challenges to their beliefs and life-styles.

... it should be emphasized that the induction of trance states, even in something like the manner we have outlined, is nothing new, and certainly not the mysterious invention of contemporary cults. The achievement of a state of uncritical receptivity has always been a prominent feature of both Western and non-Western religious practice. Great and good divines, as well as harmful ones, have depended upon gaining such receptivity to help inspire changed attitudes and new lifestyles among the congregates, while Christian faith-healers, like their analogues on every continent, still use their appropriate devices to treat all sorts of afflictions. But unlike Jim Jones and other destructive cult leaders, these relatively benign practitioners have not, as a rule, maintained supplicants in radically altered mental states long enough to produce the deadening syndrome elaborated here. Quite the opposite. The African villager who has submitted to the dissociating ritual of affliction in order to cure an illness, like the ecstatic recipient of the Christian healer's touch, soon returns to his familiar, everyday world, perhaps on the way to recovery, even spiritually uplifted, but essentially unimpaired in his mental functioning. Indeed, the experience is geared to help the individual adapt in some integrative way to the wider society whence he came for help. And the same can be said, we think, for the results of monastic training and similar disciplined, devotional regimes, where the history of a person's involvement does not usually result in a drastic attenuation of mental processes or personality development. Such malignant effects are, however, the hallmarks of many contemporary cults which have "rediscovered" the age-old folk art, refined it, and carried it to an uncharacteristic extreme.

Clark, Langone, Schechter, Daly

* * *

How Do Cults Differ in Indoctrination Techniques?

Dr. Arthur Dole points out common features of destructive cults. He notes that in both indoctrination techniques and basic philosophy, they have a disturbing similarity to totalitarian governments.

Many cult watchers have noted the parallel between the approaches to totalitarian governments and the cults. What is perhaps most characteristic is the deprivation of freedom of thought. "I am your mind, I will do your thinking," is the message of the cult leaders. **Criticism, analytical thinking, free exchange of opinion, and the opportunity to verify facts are replaced by cult dogma.** The dogma may differ from one cult to another but in all, members regress to a state of childlike dependency, according to cult theorists. The cults do differ somewhat in their techniques of member submission. For example, Hare Krishna and Divine Light Mission appear to use chanting more frequently than other cults. The Unification Church and the Divine Light Mission depend heavily upon confession which is used to induce guilt. In the Unification Church, as in Scientology, cult members exist in a state of great fear and apprehension because they feel that the world is filled with evil forces. Cults such as the Unification Church preach that injuries, accidents and illness may be punishments for past misdeeds. The members are frequently threatened with consequences to themselves and their loved ones, if they deviate from the cult demands.

Dr. Arthur Dole

* * *

In *Destructive Cult Conversion*, **Clark, Langone, Schecter, Daly** describe that what keeps the new member attached is often a skillful effort by the cult to control the environment, so that the new members' mental and emotional stability gradually crumble.

Speaking generally of destructive cults, they have the unique capacity . . . to cause harm (stemming) from the central activity of all cults: the sudden conversion through aggressive and skillful manipulation of a naive or deceived subject who is passing through or has been caused to enter a susceptible state of mind. Through highly programmed behavioral control and in a controlled environment, the subject's attention is narrowed and focused to the point of becoming a trance. Within the totally controlled atmosphere provided by each group, this state is maintained during several sleep periods until it becomes an independent structure. The loss of privacy and sleep in a bizarre new atmosphere, change of language, and continuous control of excitement level amount to an onslaught of information that sustains the continued state of dissociation; throughout this period of focused attention, new information is absorbed at an accelerated rate and rapidly becomes integral to the available mechanisms of the mind. As a result, the convert becomes dependent on this new environment for definitions of reality. From this stage the group controls not only the forms of action but also the content of thought through confessions, training, and conditioning. To think for oneself is suspect in many groups; to think wrongly is satanic and punishable by psychophysiological reactions such as migraine headaches, terror and panic, sharp depressions, or gastrointestinal symptoms . . .

Clark, Langone, Schecter, Daly

* * *

What is Mind Control?
-- What is Brainwashing?

Is there a difference between them?

This excerpt comes from *Challenge of the Cults*. Although lengthy, it sums up the ideas of **Robert J. Lifton's** book *Thought Reform and the Psychology of Totalism*, and discusses differences between political thought reform and "religious" cult indoctrination.

The American people seem to have a hard time believing that there are techniques by which one person can coerce another into doing his or her will without the use of physical force. For instance, polls show that the public generally approved of the guilty verdict handed down by the jury at the trial of Patty Hearst. University of Pennsylvania Professor Martin Orne, who appeared as a witness for the defense at the trial, is convinced that Hearst was convicted "because no one could be convinced she was actually brainwashed."

Orne believes that there is such a thing as brainwashing, or "coercive persuasion," as he prefers to call it. He has studied the literature coming out of the Chinese civil war and the Korean conflict in the fifties, books like William Sargant's *Battle for the Mind* and Robert J. Lifton's *Thought Reform and the Psychology of Totalism.* Orne is aware of the techniques by which the Communist Chinese were able to "reprogram" their Nationalist Chinese captives so that after only a few weeks of indoctrination they were prepared to fight alongside the Communists against their formal allies.

At a conference, Orne outlined the procedures by which the Communists retrained these enemy soldiers to fight on their side. Preconditions for this coercive conversion, he explained, were complete control of the captive's environment, a real and credible threat of death, complete control of all sources of information and of overall rewards and punishments.

In his book on mind control and ego destruction, Robert J. Lifton lists eight elements that he found to be intrinsic to the complete involuntary conversion of a person to a new and absolute philosophy, a process he calls "totalism."

---

1. **Milieu Control:** The purposeful limitation of all forms of communication with the outside world, sleep deprivation, a change of diet, control over who one can see and talk to.

2. **Mystical Manipulation:** Teaching that the control group has a special (read "divine") purpose, and that the subject has been chosen to play a special role in fulfilling this purpose.

3. **Need for Purity:** Convincing the subject of his/ her former impurity (before joining the control group) and the necessity of becoming pure or perfect as defined by the group.

4. **Confession:** Getting the subject to let down his/her barriers and openly discuss his/her innermost fears and anxieties.

5. **Sacred Science:** Convincing the subject that the control group's beliefs are the only logical system of beliefs, and therefore must be accepted and obeyed.

6. **Loading the Language:** Creating a new vocabulary, by creating new words with special meanings understood only by members of the group, or by giving new and special meanings to familiar words and phrases.

7. **Doctrine Over Persons:** Convincing the subject that the group and its doctrine take precedence over any individual in the group or any other teaching from outside it.

8. **Dispensing of Existence:** Teaching the subject that all those who disagree with the philosophy of the control group are doomed.

Robert J. Lifton wrote his description of the components of ego destruction and mind control in 1961, based on his study of coercive persuasion techniques in China and Korea. He was not knowingly describing any of the cult groups that were to emerge in America many years later. Yet it is remarkable to note how many of the conditions he outlined are found, to a greater or lesser degree, in most of the cults we have been examining. Obviously there are some differences. The most obvious is that the cults, with few exceptions, neither imprison their subjects nor threaten them with bodily harm. But the similarities are too great to simply be ignored.

For his part, Martin Orne suggests that while cult indoctrination is not the same as Korean coercive persuasion, it unquestionably borrows some of the same elements. Parke and Stoner, in *All God's Children,* question whether cults need to use all of the elements of Oriental brainwashing in order to gain the same effect. They point out some significant differences between the situation of neophyte cult members and subjects of Korean and Chinese brainwashing methods:

"Cult recruits have already volunteered their time and presence to the group. Unlike the independent businessmen, landowners, and others who opposed Chairman Mao's takeover in China, or the Allied soldiers in Korean POW camps, they don't need to be threatened. These young people are idealistic and frequently searching for a goal, a purpose, and sense of community, so the promises of the cults appeal strongly to them.

Unrelenting group pressure, combined with a young subject's inherent need to conform, produce the same result as imprisonment. The potential convert's complete and undivided attention is in the hands of those who wish to control him."

Preying on the new cultist's willingness to submit to indoctrination, many groups never make clear to the prospective convert the full extent and nature of their intentions. In some cults, particularly the Unification Church, there is often a deliberate attempt to mislead the newcomer, entrapping him or her in a more serious commitment to the group than had been intended through a dishonest game of bait and switch.

Challenge of the Cults

* * *

Mark Roggeman, an exit counselor in Colorado, believes the cults do have the eight characteristics described by Lifton of brainwashing. Roggeman offers additional qualities he has found in the indoctrination techniques of destructive cults.

Mind control is the result of several different techniques used to achieve absolute control. Using Robert Lifton's eight steps from his book (*Thought Reform and the Psychology of Totalism* - Chapter 22) as a guideline, every technique used by the cults seems to contain all eight steps. What I have found is that in all techniques, one step may be used more strongly or more frequently than another but all are present. For example, one group may totally control the environment of a recruitee, while another controls (the recruitee) with fear.

Brainwashing is a way to bring someone under mind control. In my opinion, brainwashing would be the control of one, physically, leading to the control of the mind. Examples of this might be POWs, Patty Hearst-type cases, hostages, etc., which in many cases have the physically captive siding with their captors. When a person is held like this; 1) there is total control of the environment, who you talk to, what you eat, when you sleep, and where you go; and, 2) the only information one hears or is allowed to see is what the captors want you to see. After a period of time, the mind has no other choice but to accept the information that is being made available. The information is repeated over and over, and, eventually, the captive will begin to take on the thought pattern and start talking in the same way. The third factor in this type of control is outward intimidation with possible physical abuse leading to a constant state of fear. All of these (factors) put together would definitely cause one's mind to snap.

When it comes to cult groups that control people, the term I like to use is thought suppression, which also results in mind control. In cult groups, members are not usually physically (captive). I have found that in most cases, cults are not honest in their recruiting about who they are and what they really believe. They choose [recruitment sites] which are far from church settings, usually in areas where the people congregating are not local residents, i.e. bus stations, airports, parks, college campuses, tourist spots. When a person is approached under these circumstances, he or she is not thinking or searching for religion at the time. The best way for me to explain it is to share my own experience:

In wanting to learn (exactly) what happens, I went down to the bus station and was recruited by a cult. When I was approached, I was sitting down and a male member sat down one seat away from me. The conversation started with, "where are you from, where you going," etc. We began talking about world problems, hunger, communism, my beliefs. He was very agreeable with almost everything I said. He began to tell me how he was involved in helping the community and he lived with some others who were doing likewise. I asked him if he was involved in a religious group of some sort, and he said "no". I was asked if I would like to have dinner and so I went.

The people there all seemed very happy, very loving and appeared genuinely interested in me. They complimented me on my looks and on how profound and inspiring my words were. Later in the evening, I was invited to spend a couple of days with these people in the mountains, to talk and play games, (and I accepted).

Everyone is up early, lots of volleyball, singing, chanting, lectures and discussions. We went to bed at 2:00 AM and woke up at 6:00 AM. Still there was no mention of who they were. I've talked to former members from this group who were in from two weeks to three months before they were told who their leader was.

Following are some steps of bringing someone under control based on the groups that I have studied and others that I have infiltrated.

1. **The "emotional pull" of other people is very strong.**

   When I went into these groups I felt this pull, and would feel guilty about checking them out. They say that everything is based on what you experience and feel -- this plays on the emotions. You're looking for emotional highs because these feelings have become equated with spirituality.

2. **Commitment is stressed by guilt.**

   - Are you going to leave your (new) friends?
   - After what we did for you, are you going to leave?
   - Are you going to walk out on God?
   - If you leave something terrible is going to happen to you, or you'll be lost forever.

In some groups commitment is stressed by money you may have paid rather than guilt. You paid this money to become a better person and you can't waste it.

3. **The disassociation of the past,** relatives, friends, and your own past identity.

This is accomplished very subtly, but I believe it to be the most important step in maintaining control. Little by little you are told that your parents are to blame for our poor condition and the world's poor condition. You must pray for your past friends and relatives, but don't contact them. They are controlled by Satan and they couldn't understand the beautiful new truth you have. Those people will even try to make you denounce your new truth. Any thoughts or questions you may have in your mind come from your evil past, from Satan.

After a period of time, the mind has become controlled very effectively, and will only allow in what the group has dictated. The mind stops logically analyzing facts and becomes totally dependent on the group and the group's leader for all its decisions. Independent thought ceases.

. . . I would say that the control becomes stronger over time in more cases than less . . . the reason it becomes stronger is because during a long period of isolation (the cult member) develops a fear of being able to make it outside of the group. Any additional programming about the evil of the outside world would add to the fear of leaving it.

Mark Roggeman

* * *

**In short, remaining in the strict mental and social
confines of a cult for even a short time can have the
following disastrous effects:**

- Loss of free will and control over one's life.

- Reduced capacity to form flexible and intimate relationships.

- Poor capacity to form judgments.

- Hallucinations, panic guilt, identity confusion, paranoia, and dissociation in some groups.

- Occasional neurotic, psychotic, or suicidal tendencies.

- Involuntary, de facto slavery.

Cult Leaders -- Why Do they Do It?

Are these "leaders" maniacal despots out to subjugate the world, or are they misguided individuals whose only goal is to "save" the world from destruction? A partial answer is found in this excerpt from **Dr. Edward Levine**'s *Religious Cults: Havens for the Emotionally Distressed, Idealists and Intellectuals, and Strongholds of Authoritarian Personalities.*

The incentives adopted by cult leaders to win converts and the mounting body of evidence indicating how they deliberately manipulate, subjugate, and exploit their members expose the former as authoritarian personalities bent on fulfilling their aggrandistic needs to dominate others and, secondarily, for material gain by using converts to work for them with little or no compensation. The various and deep-seated needs of gullible young people render them susceptible to those whose personalities compel them to prey on the weak. As the lives of cult converts evidence, cults are settings for the classic symbiosis of sadistic and masochistic personalities. Appearing to provide the assurance and affirmation so greatly needed by the young people drawn to them, the domineering personalities of cult leaders and their assistants enable them to capture and control the minds of those they successfully proselytize. Their false, if inspiring, promises of personal fulfillment and peace of mind through completion of prescribed stages of religious growth and understanding tantalize even those who are reasonably self-confident, for surely such are the quest of many of their generation.

There is little that is genuinely religious about cult leaders and their organizations if the word "religious" is used to incorporate only the second five of the Ten Commandments and to mean a genuine, active concern with the well-being and fulfillment of the individual, encouraging his use of reason, respecting and supporting his independence of thought and action, and a companion concern for the welfare for the family and society. Cult leaders' actions belie their facade of spirituality, for they have drawn off and placed in subservience some of the best and brightest of our young people, the loss of whose contributions to society is an enormous cost to us all. And there is ample evidence that many unscrupulously induce converts to use devious and morally reprehensible means in their fund-raising, proselytizing, and other relations with the public . . .

. . . Cultists are "true believers" who are given a false sense of self-sufficiency, and whose identities and sense of well-being are contingent upon their accepting the status of passive-submissive followers of those who derive gratification from their subservience. This may be the ultimate moral degradation, for their conversion costs them their individuality, their unique sense of personal identity. It is not the habit of authoritarian personalities to reveal their true motives or to admit to them when they become evident. Unfortunately, cultists remain unaware of them and are prevailed upon to believe what their leaders tell them is truth. In fact, their values are facades masking their propensity to seek to dominate those in search of meaningful values.

Dr. Edward Levine

* * *

Indoctrination is essential to maintaining each member's unquestioning obedience and long-term contribution to the cult. But would it be possible for a cult to continue to exist without using a process that requires mind-control? Other organizations, both religious and non-religious, seem capable of sustaining themselves without using these destructive techniques: Could cults do this? If so, why are they not doing so already? Perhaps the use of these techniques defines the greatest social harm of these organizations. If cults could exist without these indoctrination techniques, would they still pose a threat, or would they become benign, out of the mainstream religions?

It is our opinion that without these mind control techniques, many cults would survive, but in a much reduced capacity. Their appeal would be the same, but the binding force would have been removed. We believe their drop-out rate would be substantially higher. If the thinking of a member had not been disrupted during indoctrination, the inconsistencies of the cult as it related to the outside world, the leader and, the doctrine would eventually drive many members back into the non-cult world.

> **Dr. Marvin Galper**, a clinical psychologist in San Diego who treats former cult members, says that the long-term effects of cult involvement may depend on how much support the individual receives from family and friends outside the cult, and on the individual's personality.

A cult member who has an empty life in the community outside of the cult with no real warm personal support either from family or friends -- and who feels that his life outside the cult has been bleak and isolated -- will tend to immerse himself more completely in the cult environment. As he does so, the depths of his indoctrination in the cult ideology and belief system will tend to increase. Other kinds of situations involve cult members who happen to be unusually strong and able people, and who as a result of this rise to a position of leadership in the cult leadership hierarchy. Such persons then, because of their much greater freedom of operation, are much more involved in the outside community, often in public relations capacity. Because they are less immersed in the control environment, they have more opportunities for interchange with people who have different points of view. On occasion, a person of this type will become freed up from the brainwashing effects and leave the cult because he has been able to recognize the destructive effects as a result of the greater freedom of thought permitted to him. Nonetheless, I suspect that such people continue to be troubled by feelings of guilt after they leave the group unless they receive professional counseling subsequent to their exit.

Dr. Marvin Galper

* * *

How Do Long-Term Members Simply Walk Away?

Some cults become looser in their organization and as a result of weakening of their control over the membership, the intensity of the indoctrination effects and the psychological coercion becomes weaker. As an organization becomes more open in this fashion or more disorganized, people have more opportunity to think freely within the cult and use their own rational abilities. When they can therefore communicate more openly with each other about critical thoughts regarding the cult, this sometimes results in a reinforcement of their healthy judgment, eventually leading to an exit from the cult.

In my opinion also, there are variations in the extent to which each cult is a closed social system. The Unification Church, for example, is a much more closed social system in my opinion - for example - than the Divine Light Mission. As a partial result of this, I would suspect that the defection rate from the Divine Light Mission is as a result higher than that of the Unification Church. The answer to your question is a highly complex one, and there are many factors involved.

Dr. Marvin Galper

* * *

The people we questioned agreed that certain factors are usually found in the process of indoctrination into destructive cults, but they cautioned treating this process "globally" rather than on a cult-by-cult basis. We agree that in each cult, we see aspects of indoctrination specific to that particular cult. We offer an overview of cult phenomena in *Resources / References*, Part 10 for more specific information on individual cults.

Study Guide

For the Group:

1. Are there any group members who do not believe in brainwashing (in regards to cults). Have them explain the behavior of cult members who cut off all ties with their families for the sake of their "new families". Allow the group to discuss their explanation, keeping in mind how commercials help us buy things we might not need.

2, Discuss cliques. How many people feel they belong to a clique or a special group of friends that others might call a clique? How does it feel to be among tightly-knit friends? How does it feel to be excluded? How far will you sacrifice your individuality to continue ties? How does that differ from being in a cult?

3. Refer to the excerpt from *Challenge of the Cults* in this chapter and find out if any of the group members have experienced aspects of "totalism". What were they? How did this make the group member feel?

4. Would a cult grow if it were no longer able to use an "indoctrination process" to keep its members? What is the difference between this indoctrination process and the ones used at schools and at businesses?

For the Individual:

1. How well do you know yourself? Could you survive a cult indoctrination process? The vast majority of former members of cults say it is impossible to do so; if you believe you are immune, what makes you different from them?

2. If an organization has worthwhile goals and sets about to achieve them in an ethical manner, then why would it need to deceptively indoctrinate its members?

3. If the goal of a group is worldwide peace and harmony, then is any means used to reach that goal acceptable? When does the ends justify the means?

4. If you wanted something very badly that someone else could provide, how far would you go to get it? If they did not want to give it to you when you told them your desire, would you try to get by lying?

PART 4:

ON THE OUTSIDE . . . LOOKING IN

PART 4: CONTENTS

Supporting Article

PART 4: *ON THE OUTSIDE...*
... LOOKING IN

To have someone you love in a cult is like a living death. I compare it to the grief of watching a person die knowing there is a cure and being unable to use it. To see the physical and mental health of one you love and be helpless is more than most people can tolerate. To add to this frustration there are the articles and books by so-called experts who support destructive cults.

Henrietta Crampton

A person's decision to join a cult is not made in a vacuum; it affects others, including parents, siblings, spouses and friends. Although removed from the intensity of the recruitment and indoctrination, the family and friends of a new cult member usually react to the decision to join with surprise and shock. If they know what a destructive cult is, it seems as though the new member has taken leave of his or her senses (which may not be far from the truth); if unaware of the nature of the organization involved, it may seem like a simple act of rebellion, a temporary "growing experience" which will end with increased maturity and insight. Even these parents usually realize in time that this "phase" is more serious and potentially dangerous than ever realized.

Eventually, someone realizes there is a serious family problem. Such realization could take weeks, months, or years. This chapter discusses what happens after the realization comes.

How Does It Feel?

One **Mother of a former member of the Unification Church** writes this poignant account of her experience:

Most parents have a philosophy of child rearing which embraces their relationship with their child throughout (the child's) growing years. Ours was one of encouraging the development of independence and adventure, building toward self-reliance with responsibility to self and society. When our daughter first told us she was moving to a commune, eight years ago, we were very disturbed.

Her first letter home assured us that "I have never done anything to harm myself or others and I will not now."

Should we have intervened at this point? With hindsight, perhaps. At the time, no. We respected her independence and cults were an unknown entity. We were not the kind of parents who planned a strict way of life or direction for our children.

Would I act differently today? Yes, because I believe I have some options where I saw none then. Eight years ago - when we asked a rabbi what to do - he said, "she could be doing worse things like learning to throw grenades with the Jewish Defense League." We asked a psychiatrist. He said, "Its just a stage. She has some unfulfilled needs. When she out-grows them, she'll come out."

We asked the local leader of the cult who met with us willingly over breakfast and told us our daughter would have a chance to go to school, marry, and lead a life. He denied any relationship with a well-known cult leader -- which was an untruth. Although we expressed our disapproval to our daughter, we did see her as happier, more out-going, with a new bigger purpose to her life. But eight years ago -- the Rabbi and the psychiatrist knew as little as we knew. Cults were an unknown entity. Our daughter had a great many needs, some of which were being satisfied by the cult community. Our daughter was already under mind control and we did not even acknowledge that there was such a thing.

Today: I would intervene immediately- because I know (as does the world) so much more. I would still respect her independent choice but I would be more forceful in having her examine alternatives now available. I would have her talk to former cult members, religious and professional people. Hopefully, I would do this soon enough after exposure so that she would still be thinking clearly enough to make a wise choice.

Waiting six years, as we did, required a forceful confrontation. Confronting the situation immediately (now with hindsight and the assistance of qualified help) could at least provide a setting where there might be open choice rather than blind acceptance.

Mother of a former cult member

* * *

Accounts by the parents of cult members express the feelings of shock, loss, and the fear of permanently losing a child, more clearly than any theoretical discussion. Here is **a Father's account.**

Initially, I didn't think of the organization that my daughter joined as a cult; just a group of nice kids looking to do some good in a community environment. This evaluation was confirmed after talking intimately with those who seemed to be running the group. I asked the assistant leader, "Is this what a smart young man like you expects to be doing the rest of your life?" and he assured me that in a short time the members would carry the message of hard work and exemplary behavior to wherever they settled down. Then they would marry and have families. I tried to console myself into believing this was one more adventure on the road to maturity for my daughter and might prove to be a helpful education in relating to people and experiencing difficult living situations.

I was in for a series of shocks: the discovery of a direct connection between the organization my daughter belonged to and the Unification Church; her mouthing as fact the irrational so-called religious beliefs and weird interpretations of the Bible; having to accept the dangers to her health from lack of sleep, poor diet, and a strenuous fund raising regimen; and finally, her request that we not see each other for at least a year. After each one of these shocks, I would find some rationalization to help absorb the pain. Any reason, from "its an adventure" to "its just a passing phase" would suffice. And each one of these rationalizations was supported by the professionals we consulted; psychiatrists, rabbis and knowledgeable lay people.

Early on, I tried to discuss with my daughter the doctrine and beliefs of this cult. Not only did I find her ill-informed about the cult writings, but what she had learned of the cult and its teachings contained obvious fabrications which could be refuted with simple logic.

There were times when I would try a playful jab, as I had done when she was a child, and say, *"Come on, do you really believe that?"* This only caused her to be more resentful and she would refuse to discuss her beliefs any more.

The shock of her not wanting to see her mother and me for a year, and the progressive reduction in contacts created strong conflicting emotions. Sometimes I was filled with a longing to be with her, kid around with her, and see her infectious smile. At other times, I would say "to hell with her! She is causing her mother and me too much pain, better to get on with our lives and devote our energy to other interests and commitments."

Everyone we talked to, professionals, ex-cultists, wise laypeople, unanimously agreed that we must keep the channels of communication open. *We must not allow contact to be broken off completely.*

The telephone was practically the sole method of maintaining this contact. It was an inadequate substitute for being together. To avoid losing contact and to encourage phoning, my wife insisted that conversations be pleasant and positive and non-confrontational. For me, the phone call represented *my only opportunity to attempt to make my daughter think*, to question, to respond to some of my questions.

The dual objectives, plus the time constraints of a long distance call, created not only conflicts within myself but also emotional conflicts with my wife whose focus was completely on maintaining harmony.

Other emotions come clearly to mind. One was the unsettling and frustrating ambivalence as to whether we should try forcible removal from the cult environment in order to get her to pay attention to rational arguments. This was coupled with the frustration of the problems and lack of competent assistance to accomplish this, if we could bring ourselves to do it.

To conclude on a happier note, the pain was more than offset by the joy of our daughter returning to our family and society. If it involves your child or someone you love as deeply as your child, **take heart, a way to bring them home will be found.**

Father of a former cult member

* * *

Marilyn Malek is the mother of a young man who has been a member of the Church Universal and Triumphant since Fall 1978. She has devoted enormous effort to learning more about how cults function. Here are excerpts from a letter she wrote a newspaper.

Learning to understand the frame of mind of a Church Universal and Triumphant member and how it differs from a non-member is not easy. But there can be some understanding which might alleviate some of the confusion and bewilderment created by CUT...

...I would like to be able to touch the minds and hearts of the members of CUT, especially our son, as well as the community, but my understanding is based on the ability to reason, and therefore limits the audience I can reach. CUT teachings destroy the ability to reason . . .

If a member's transformation is upsetting to their family, they must be able to break the bondage of family ties disruptive to their path. They supposedly chose their parents before birth to give certain souls another chance to know the "light" (illumined source of wisdom). Reincarnation is central to CUT teachings.

They believe that where there is the greatest light, there will be the greatest attack by the fallen ones. Criticism then becomes a reinforcement of their beliefs and the issues (confronting them) are left unanswered.

Love the members and understand them if you can. In my opinion, they have all been sorely deceived to think that God Almighty will justify deceit in His name, but with the tools or reason destroyed, how can they know the difference? The distinction of reason and the appearance of reason are not always clear.

Marilyn Malek

* * *

Dr. Marjory Zerin, a private practitioner in marital and family counseling, lists common responses parents have when their child joins a cult:

Parents vary in their reactions depending upon their relationship with their child and the interpretation that they attach to the fact that he or she is involved with a cult. If they are indifferent, detached, or hostile toward their offspring, that is one thing; however, if they are emotionally attached to their son or daughter, they may experience a range of emotions from puzzled and anxious to frustrated, resentful, angry, guilty or sad. The following are some of the reactions reported by parents in my research group.

Pleased, at first, then worried and scared: It sounded like a clean-cut, idealistic, Christian movement. Then I read about cults and realized that I might have lost my child forever!

Ambivalent: I thought he seemed so much more comfortable with himself now that he was part of something. I was uneasy about his activities, but I only objected a little bit.

I was so eager for him to make a clean break from his drug habit and depression, that I actually took him to the ashram. It hurt me later that he became so confused, withdrawn and distant. I didn't know what to do!

Shocked: I don't know . . . when I think what could have happened if he had stayed in, I think it might almost be better to know that your kid was dead than not to know where he was or whether or not he was alive!

Furious: I wanted her to get the hell out of there right away! I demanded that she leave and come home at once!

We wanted to know what he was doing and where he was doing it. We insisted that he call us once a week on the phone. After six weeks and some advice from cult experts, we went up there and pulled him out!

Regardless of how strained the parent-child relationship might have been, no loving parent wants to believe that the group his or her child has joined is evil or destructive.

Dr. Marjory Zerin

* * *

How Can You Be Sure an Organization is Truly a Destructive Cult?

Cults vary on a continuum in terms of destructiveness to the degree to which they (a) demand total subservience to an authoritarian leader and (b) practice deception in their recruitment and membership maintenance programs. For a very helpful and comprehensive guide to destructive elements in an organization, I recommend "Finding the right path," a flyer by Richard J. Israel. It is very difficult to maintain an attitude of detached observer when one is passionately caught up in a social group and especially so when the social and psychological environment is being systematically manipulated by the group's management. On the other hand it is very important to at least listen to opposing opinions, whether or not one agrees with them. Another important thing to do is to conduct discrete tests to determine how willing members of the group, and particularly its leaders, are to hear new and different ideas from (the cult member) . . ."

Dr. Marjory Zerin

* * *

Groups: *Proceed with Caution*

Do some critical thinking about your involvement with group movements.

- In this group, are you pressured to change your beliefs as proof of personal commitment and progress?

- Are you prohibited, discouraged, or made to feel bad, if you:
  - express doubt?
  - hesitate to do something you really don't want to do?
  - retain contacts outside the group?

- Does this group speak in terms of them - versus- us? Are they the exclusive possessors of the "Truth"?

- Is there a revered leader whose teachings and practices are not subject to critical questioning?

- Do you know where the money goes?
  Can you prove it?

- Does this group make you feel:

  Accepted - (based on group conditions?)
  Secure - (incapable of independence?)
  Important - (specially "called" for a great cause?)

- Do members speak of lifetime commitment? Are you a failure if you leave? Will they still be your friends?

- Is it possible to feel trapped in this group?

Organizations which exhibit these characteristics can prove to be harmful.

FOCUS - Los Angeles . . . Former Cult Members

Finding the Right Path

Richard Israel has created a useful checklist when one is perplexed about a new group.

You may have begun to feel that your life has not had sufficient meaning, that you want to reach toward values that are really important. If you are thinking about taking up a totally new life style, or have recently joined a new religious group, these are some questions for you to consider:

1. In the group do you find yourself without enough private time? Enough nourishment? Enough sleep?

2. Does the group make it difficult to place phone calls, receive letters, visit with old friends, or discuss your thoughts with people you trust who are not in the group?

3. Do they demand your entire life, without even small corners left belonging only to you?

4. Is the group reluctant to accept you as you are? Is it essential for you to transform yourself into a totally new person and to suppress thoughts you previously believed acceptable?

5. Does the group view all aspects of your former life as bad?

6. Is it proper to deceive people for the sake of the group?

7. Is it wrong to deviate from the teachings of the leader or the group, even in small ways? If you are to remain within the group, must you view the teacher as always right about everything? Do they make you feel guilty if you have doubts about their teachings?

8. Is the group's teacher reputed to do miracles? Are they revealed only to the initiated?

9. Are you uncomfortable with the group's attitudes to women?

10. Are the rules for the group's leaders different from the rules for its followers?

Breaking with your past in some significant ways could mean a healthy change for the better. Joining a new group may help, and all groups try to impose some values on their members. But, if you answer yes to more than a few of these questions, you should think hard about what you are doing. You should be particularly careful if you became interested when you were lonely, depressed, or detached from your family. You may be losing control of yourself to people who have their interest in mind more than yours. Though Truth may be absolute, our knowledge of it seldom is. Those who claim to have it all should be suspected. It is right to try to make yourself into a better person. You may be far from perfect, but you aren't all bad either. Neither are your friends, family, or former values, even if you now feel that you need some distance from them. As you continue your new explorations, try not to dig yourself into a deeper hole than you can climb out of. Don't irrevocably sever relationships that you may one day want to restore.

Richard J. Israel

* * *

What Can Parents Do When Their Child Becomes Involved in a Cult?

The first response was written by **Dr. Michael Langone,** Director of Research for The American Family Foundation, in his book *Destructive Cultism: Questions and Answers.*

There is much they can do, but all the intelligent alternatives involve much uncertainty, anxiety, and effort. Parents should realize that:

- Not all cults are necessarily destructive.

- "Rescuing" a convert from, or persuading him to leave, a destructive cult is not always possible or even advisable (e.g. because the group may provide a refuge for a troubled person, or because of disunity within the family).

- A "recipe" for persuading a convert to leave a destructive cult does not exist - each case must be treated individually.

- There is hope for parents.

After parents understand this, they can try to conduct (with professional assistance, when appropriate) an informed, reasoned investigation of their possible course of action.

Alternatives

1. Accept a child's conversion to a group as a long-term, if not lifetime, involvement.

2. Tolerate, but disapprove of, a long-term involvement.

3. Tolerate a cult involvement while attempting to persuade a convert to make an informed reevaluation of his commitment to the group.

4. Tolerate a cult involvement in order to facilitate a "rescue" attempt (i.e. forced deprogramming).

5. Cut off communication with the child (i.e., disown him).

Although space permits only a superficial analysis, consider briefly each of these alternatives.

Alternative 1:   **Acceptance.**

This is generally rejected by parents of a child in a destructive cult, although it may often be the wisest course of action for parents whose child belongs to a benign group. Therefore, it is imperative that parents collect well-tested data to assess the destructiveness of the group with which their child is affiliated and if parents want to respect their child's autonomy, they may find themselves in the uncomfortable position of trying to accept and understand a lifestyle of which they disapprove.

Alternative 2:   **Tolerate, but disapprove**

This is often the only course of action open to parents who are unable or unwilling to pursue other alternatives. It can sometimes be a very trying course, for parents may feel helpless and bereft. In such cases, professional assistance can be helpful, for the parent must come to grips with a seemingly interminable grief, as well as its accompanying anger and guilt.

Alternative 3: **Promote voluntary, informed reevaluation**

The parent who chooses this alternative must: a) devise an ethical strategy for maximizing his influence over the convert and b) develop the requisite self-control and awareness for implementing, evaluating, and revising the strategy as needed. Although the former task is difficult, the latter is usually even more trying, as well as easier to neglect. Parents following this course are advised to seek help from a variety of sources, including other parents of cultists, ex-members, reading material, and professionals with expertise in this field.

Alternative 4: **"Rescue"**

Although many former members have publicly supported forced deprogramming as a necessary means of freeing people from cult enslavement, the procedure, nevertheless, is legally and psychologically risky. Its failure may sometimes cause irreparable damage to a parent-child relationship and may even result in lawsuits. Hence, parents who select this alternative ought to do so only after careful deliberation. Although many people consider forced deprogramming to be the only way to "rescue" a person from a destructive cult, increased understanding of the cult phenomenon has led to a greater appreciation of voluntary methods for facilitating a convert's reevaluation of his cult affiliation.

Alternative 5: **Disown child . . . ?**

Disowning a child is a form of "blocking out" an unpleasant reality. Although many persons seem to be able to function adequately while denying "bits" of reality, the depth and significance of the parent-child bond make this alternative impossible to follow without paying a severe psychological penalty, even when disconnection is less distressing than intense, continuous, and unresolvable family conflict. Hence, *parents who seriously consider this alternative are advised to seek professional assistance.*

Dr. Michael Langone

* * *

Cults and Kids discusses three options that parents of cult recruitees have: keeping communication open until the cult member agrees to talk to a third party about leaving the group; requesting to be made the legal guardian of the adult cult member; and forcible abduction.

Margaret Singer, Father Burtner, and (Jean) Merritt believe that parents must keep in mind that cults see the world through polarized glasses: everybody inside is good and everybody outside is demonic or, at least, influenced by Satan. If parents tip their hand too early by coming out openly against the group, the recruit will often go underground and may not be seen again for years. To counter this, the three counselors tell parents to keep lots of "love messages" going to their kids.

Parents who have had their children drawn into cults have three basic options. By keeping communications going, they can try to get their son or daughter to talk with a former member or local cult authority. Sometimes this third party, by providing critical information about the group, can break the cult's hold.

...Some parents go to the courts when their children refuse to listen to the "other side." There are two connected legal remedies: conservatorship-guardianship and a writ of habeas corpus. Through conservatorships-guardianships, a state places an adult in temporary custody of another adult. Although state laws differ about the grounds on which these legal orders may be granted, the most common reasons include being harmful to oneself and others, physical infirmity, or mental incompetence. But civil libertarians argue that it's an unconstitutional form of legal kidnaping, and many magistrates are reluctant to issue these orders. If a judge decides that the cultist does need a conservator-guardian, a writ of habeas corpus is then issued to gain custody of the person. Most conservator-guardian decrees specify a time period in which medical and mental health evaluations must take place. At the end of these days or weeks, the judge reviews the case.

The last alternative, the forcible abduction and restraint of the cult victim, is illegal. And although some judges have been sympathetic to parents who take this course of action, these kidnapings have been prosecuted at every level of the criminal justice system ...

Cults and Kids

* * *

Henrietta Crampton provides practical suggestions for family and friends of someone involved in a destructive cult:

Avoid panic. As in any crisis situation a cool head is necessary.

Investigate the group. Obtain the leader's name, the address and phone number of centers, other names the leader may have, names of others associated with the group.

Assess the group. Is it destructive and to what extent? Get factual information from former members, news accounts, investigative reports, books, organizations who specialize in cult awareness programs.

Learn to communicate with a cult member. Traditional means of communication just don't work. Cultists have changed meanings of words and speak in a jargon of their own. If a cult member has doubts and reservations about the group, he will suppress them through thought-stopping techniques that are triggered when issues are raised that cause him to question. Chanting, meditation, speaking in tongues are often used to block out any doubts. Programmed responses are ready to answer questions you may ask. When you visit the cult member, always be loving, talk about happy things, don't get into a controversy. Do not tell lies. Admit you have read or heard unfavorable things about the group and you are concerned. Say what specific things concern you but don't argue. Don't play games. When you write, send pictures of family, home, friends, pets, etc.

Let the cultist talk if you are able to visit. Remember, you will probably not be allowed to talk to your child alone. Don't argue theology. Leave that to the theologians. Do not accuse, threaten or act angry. The cult has already conditioned your child to believe Satan works through his parents. He is told that parents will be angry and mean and want to destroy the cult and the victim's peace and right to study the religion of his choice. Do not act the way they expect you to act. Go with love, not hate. Treat everyone kindly. Other cultists have parents, too, who love them. Show you have more love and concern than the cult. Earn their respect. Look and listen to everything if you are allowed to visit the cult center. Make mental notes. Be calm and cool. Observe books read by members, their dress, use of words, names, belief system (astrology, Eastern religion, Christianity, space travel, etc.), diet, anything unusual. Don't believe everything you are told by your child or other members of the cult. Listen and use your critical judgment. Look at what they do, not what they say they do. If you have been able to leave your first meeting on good terms you have set the stage for another meeting. If your child should invite you to attend the cult, go at once. *Watch for turning points, highs and lows.*

After you have written your first letters or made your first visit to your child in a cult, you should start your journal*. Put down on paper the mental notes you made during your visit. Record everything. Names mentioned, events, front groups, suspicion of illegal activities associated with group leaders. File news items. Keep all letters from your child and even make copies of letters you send so you will know if he answers. Often mail is censored or not even delivered. Relate to the entire family. In your anxiety over your child in the cult don't forget the needs of the entire family. Involve all the family in a letter writing campaign. Even if the mail is censored, some will get through. Don't allow brothers or sisters to go visit the cultist in an effort to bring him out. Too many families have lost second children from such actions. Don't give money or things of value to the cultist. It only gets turned over to the leader. Provide for the security of your estate so that the cult will not become beneficiary in the event of your death.

Intervention. Not to be attempted until all facts are learned. Talk to former members, seek references from other parents, and professionals who do exit counseling on a volunteer basis, not coercive. Do not give large sums of money to anyone who claims they have the perfect solution to your problem. The degree of control the cult has over your child can vary, even with people in the same cult. You need to evaluate your child's situation. Former cult members can be very helpful at this. Some might even know your child. The length of time in the cult, his mental condition, the kind of person he was before joining, if he is married or has a partner in the cult, all these elements need to be considered before intervention. Don't do anything in a hurry. If you have learned to communicate you may be able to keep in contact until intervention seems possible. Don't be afraid to join with other parents in efforts to combat the cult influence. Become an activist not a passivist. Speak to your friends, neighbors, church groups. If parents, who have accurate first person knowledge, don't speak out, how can we blame the public for being ignorant on the issue? Parents who hide the facts about their child's cult involvement hurt themselves. The support, knowledge, advice, and the care that comes from discussions with other parents, especially those who also have children in cults, is the best help you will receive. **Don't give up hope.** If you or some member of your family has kept in good contact with the cult victim, he will know he has a place to go when he finally calls for help.

---

* *When you start your journal, notebook, file, or whatever record keeping method you decide upon, you may be asked to share information with others or to send to a lawyer or mental health professional. Never send originals. Make copies of anything you decide to send to others and send the copies. Continue to keep up to date on all activities of the cult. Read books, do your homework.*

If you are grandparents you should consider attempting to gain custody of grandchildren or at least the visitation rights. If a group has a known record of child abuse, such as the Children of God, every effort should be made to locate grandchildren and gain custody. Courts are recognizing grandparents rights for visitation and in many instances have granted them, even when child abuse is not present.

If a friend becomes involved in a cult, you should investigate, assess, learn to communicate with the cult member, contact parents of the cult member, and let them know what you have discovered. Visit your friend in the cult only after you have read some books to understand how cults recruit and do not go alone. Cooperate with parents. If the parents can not be reached, don't give up on your friend. Write to him or her, let them know your care so there will be contact with someone outside the cult that he or she can talk to if they decide to leave.

Although the above suggestions vary, one point remains constant: *Open lines of communication are the key to eventually helping a loved one get out of a destructive cult.*

Henrietta Crampton

* * *

Are Destructive Cults Physically Dangerous?

Dr. Harold Scales, a private physician in Teaneck, New Jersey, describes physical harm which cult members suffered, directly or indirectly due to cult involvement.

Much has been written about the psychological deterioration of cult members, but not enough of the threat to physical health and death.

Threats, beatings, and solitary confinement were the rule in Jonestown. The same can be seen in other totalitarian cults with absolute leaders. Jim Jones turned the power of love to the love of power and was corrupted.

Certainly, growth, maturation, goals, and education become a wasteland in destructive cults. Robot members are driven to bring in even more members and money to feed the insatiable appetites of the leadership. This kind of pressure takes its toll. Their frenetic 18 hour a day activity leaves little time for sleep, reflection, or adequate nutrition. The diet is high in carbohydrates and low in essential proteins. Suicides and psychotic breaks result from the pressures of rejecting their satanic nuclear family and embracing "Father" who is corrupt. Father lives in luxury and his members live below the poverty line.

Dr. John Clark, Psychiatrist at Harvard Medical School and Dr. Stanley Cath at Tufts Medical School examined cult members after conversion and find signs, symptoms, and EEG finds characteristic of Temporal Lope Epilepsy. This spells danger (to cult members) since pressures on Temporal Lope Epileptics could drive them into schizophrenic breaks. A mother whose daughter has Temporal Lobe seizures controlled on Dilantin and mesantoin has been unable to locate her daughter in the Divine Light Mission for the past years.

A young lady from Westchester, NY had a detached retina with gradual and progressive loss of vision in one eye. The Moonie leader told her to work and pray harder to drive Satan out of her eye. Fortunately, she checked into a hospital in Boston and doctors were able to salvage some of the failing vision in that eye.

There are cults that pray over serious infection and broken bones. The Children of God forces women into prostitution for money or new members.
The Way cult has a three week fast and purge program combining laxatives, detoxificants, green life vitamin tablets, water and occasional fruit juice. This regimen combined with high colonics makes the Way member more vulnerable to indoctrination because of physical and mental exhaustion.

English pediatricians in the *British Medical Journal* (C 1:296, Feb.3.1979) and the *American Journal of Diseases of Children* (133:141, Feb.,1979) reported nutritional rickets, multiple nutritional deficiencies such as anemia and B 12 deficiencies, etc., and malnutrition in children with severely limited cult diets. They reported marked depression in rate of growth in pre-school children.

. . . doctors strongly recommended that when food faddism and nutritional cultism put these children at risk, the state social services must step in and provide adequate treatment as in abused children.

Dr. Harold Scales

* * *

Cult Clinic

Fortunately, there are now a few places in the United States that provide families with a place to go for help: one such place is the Cult Clinic of Jewish Family Service of the Jewish Federation Council of Greater Los Angeles. **The program is non-sectarian.**

The Cult Clinic is a comprehensive support system to help individuals and families distressed due to the involvement of family members in cults. The clinic is composed of staff social workers and volunteers including parents of former cult members, and former cult members themselves.

In addition to family and individual counseling, the Cult Clinic offers a support groups for both families and former cult members where individuals share experiences, gain perspective, and explore options.

The Supporting Article following the Study Guide shows the innovative approach the Cult Clinic Jewish Family Service in Los Angeles has taken.

Study Guide

For the Group:

1. Have one person assert that the"moon is made of green cheese." Have everyone else try to convince him or her that the statement is incorrect. The "green cheese" believer will say this "truth" is not based on logic but on a higher truth that comes from within. Ask each member of the group to describe how they feel about their inability to break the cheese myth. Expand this into a discussion of the feelings of a parent "dialoguing" with his or her cult-involved child.

2. Discuss the questions, "If you were the parent of a cult-involved child, how far would you go to get him or her out of the cult? Do the bonds between parent and child go beyond the laws of society?"

3. *a)* Learn if there is a cult clinic in your area. Arrange for a spokesperson from the clinic to talk to your group about mind control, personal experiences with cults, or exit counseling.

   b) Learn if there is a cult-awareness center (such as a local chapter of the Cult Awareness Network) in your area. Arrange for a speaker to talk to your group about the cult phenomenon.

For the Individual

1. Do you know anyone in a cult? Are you comfortable with that person remaining there? Do you feel responsible to let that person know the danger they may face?

2. Imagine that one of your family members is in a destructive cult. Compose a letter to that person explaining how you feel and why you think they should come out. Compare your letter with the suggestions of the parents in this chapter.

Supporting Article

The Cult Clinic Helps Families in Crisis

Marsha Emmer Addis is the Chair of the Commission on Cults and Missionaries and Deputy Director of UCLA's Jonsson Cancer Center in Los Angeles, California. **Judith Schulman-Miller** is the former Coordinator of the Cult Clinic, Jewish Family Service, Los Angeles, California. **Meyer Lightman** is District Director at the same agency.

Families losing children to cults experience severe stress that traditional therapeutic approaches do not address. The Cult Clinic offers counseling and educational services to these families, and has developed techniques to treat related family dysfunctions. Their article is based on a paper presented at the meeting of the Academy of Family Psychology, Sixty-fifth Annual Meeting of the American Psychological Association, Anaheim, California, August 1983.

Since the early 1970s, when refugees from cults began seeking psychological and psychiatric treatment for problems resulting from their involvement with these groups, there have been numerous professional attempts to understand and explain the mental health, sociological, religious, and legal perils of cults and the psychological factors involved in cult recruitment and indoctrination. In recent years laypeople and ex-cultists have developed sometimes controversial "deprogramming" and rehabilitation programs for cultists, but few mental health professionals have set about to provide treatment (or "reentry counseling") for cult members.

The most evident victims of cults are the members themselves. But in the rush to understand and help these victims, clinicians have often overlooked the special problems experienced by relatives of cult recruits. This article addresses the counseling and educational needs of these troubled families and describes techniques developed by the Cult Clinic of the Los Angeles Jewish Family Service to meet these needs.

The Problem: Signals to parents that their child is involved in a cult include a sudden personality change, a drastic change in goals (such as dropping out of school or leaving a job without notice), sudden attempts to transfer funds or personal possessions, or, more dramatically, the child dropping out of sight. Subsequent trauma to the family can be similar to that experienced by relatives of a prisoner of war. As with the POW, the cult member appears to be a captive of a hostile force, is not allowed freedom of action or communication, and his or her location may be unknown to the family. Resulting hazards to the cult member are now well known; the potential for stress and pressure upon his or her family is massive.

Parents' Reactions: Generally speaking, the response of family members to a relative's cult membership runs the gamut of frustrated behavior: from the impulse to rescue their child, to ineffective attacks on the cult, to passive resignation. Parents may feel helpless, frustrated, rejected, desperate, or shocked. Bewilderment is often followed by anger and hostility. Parents may feel resentful toward their lost offspring (blaming the victims) and try to argue with them to point out the error of their ways. They may be furious at the cult for stealing their child. Feelings of guilt are also prominent, and the overwhelming sense of loss and frustration results in depression. Sometimes parents suffer physical consequences of the stress they are experiencing. The intense pressure may cause heart attacks or severe psychosomatic reactions, as well as uncontrollable crying or irrational outbursts.

Siblings' Reactions: Brothers or sisters are especially affected by a sibling's cult membership. Some parents are so obsessed about the child in the cult that the family becomes focused solely on the cult-involved child and the other siblings may feel ignored, neglected, excluded, or rejected. A mother and father who had made two unsuccessful attempts to rescue their daughter from a destructive cult described the consequences on their eleven-year-old son. "He went from a very happy, good student to a very troubled child socially and scholastically. He's angry with us because he says that if we had never tried the deprogrammings, his sister would still be here; she'd come to visit and we'd know where she is."

Threat to Family Structure: Cults often demand that members reject the technology, education, science, and rationality respected by their parents. Acceptance of the cult frequently means recruits must reject their families and their traditions, sanctions, and values--values integral to the child's earlier growth and development. Cult membership, therefore, often interrupts the normal developmental process that leads to the establishment of a healthy adult identity. Parents see a frightening and powerful influence usurping the authority of the family, threatening the very fabric of family life.

Various members of the family may react differently to a relative's cult membership. One parent may be terribly upset and express concern, while the other may appear passive or disinterested. Some members of the family may be inclined to resist challenging the child's autonomy; other members may feel compelled to protect the convert; still others may be paralyzed with indecision. Like many stressed families, in their frustration parents may begin blaming each other for their child's behavior, thereby inflicting severe damage on marital relationships. Siblings may also suffer if parents become overprotective because of fears that the same thing will happen to their other children.

Family members feel helpless when unsympathetic friends, relatives, and mental health professionals suggest that some familial pathology must be responsible for the problem. Their social contacts may dwindle because they are embarrassed by questions about their lost child. Futile attempts to gain information about the cult or advice on how to deal with the situation result in the realization that there are few, if any, resources for help. Without outside expertise, the family often flounders in a sea of psychological, legal, religious, and financial problems.

When Parents Have No Contact: Some parents have no contact with their cult-involved children for long periods of time, sometimes years. These situations are particularly stressful because it is difficult for parents to maintain hope when they do not even know if their child is alive or dead. A husband and wife may differ drastically in their ability to handle their loss, and the very core of their relationship may be threatened. Their grief may be similar to that experienced by parents whose child has died. However, after the death of a child, parents can complete the mourning process and reconstitute their lives. When a child is lost to a cult, reconstitution is extremely difficult because the child seems neither dead nor alive.

Unique Treatment Issues: The Clinic's clients, with few exceptions, have had histories of normal psychosocial development. The cult-related problems that these families present do not fall within the usual clinical orientation. Therefore, these special problems require the use of several nontraditional therapeutic approaches.

Ordinarily, when a clinician is consulted by non-cult-involved parents about the behavior of their adult child, he or she is likely to treat the parents' apparent symptomatology. The clinician may conclude that the parents are overprotective, thereby inhibiting their child's emancipation. He or she may assume that the adult child is rebellious and is struggling legitimately with separation-individuation issues in an enmeshed family environment. Given these hypotheses, the clinician's work would be to help the parents "let go" of their adult child and to develop separate and positive identities for themselves. The clinician would help the parents understand the need for their child to make his or her own decisions, might validate and reinforce the adult child's ability to choose an independent life-style, and would encourage the parents to reduce their overprotective and intrusive behaviors.

These interventions are ineffective and sometimes counterproductive when dealing with families of cult-involved children. The sudden and pervasive personality change that a cult-involved person undergoes is the distinguishing factor. Unlike people who are consciously choosing an alternative life-style, cult-involved people are often converted and held by powerful and subtle techniques of which they are unaware and that impair their abilities to think critically and to be self-directed. The clinician attempting to help such a family must understand these cult-related phenomena.

Clinical interventions in these situations must help families understand cult characteristics that have diminished their adult children's mental functioning and have reduced them to childlike dependency. In this respect, the therapist must be a more active participant in the process than is usually the case, acting as an educator as well as a therapist. Having helped the family understand the causes of the child's behavior, the clinician should focus on interventions that help the family reconnect with its child.

A Response: The Cult Clinic

The Cult Clinic developed because traditional therapeutic approaches did not address the unique problems faced by cult-involved families. No comprehensive treatment model to help strengthen these families was available anywhere in the United States. The first clinic group session was held in February 1979, just three months after the Jonestown tragedy. The treatment goal of the clinic is to help families gain perspective and control of their situations by giving them education, options, and hope.

The Cult Clinic works by helping families:

- Learn about mind control and cult recruitment techniques.

- Learn communication skills to enable them to reestablish relationships with their cult-involved children.

- Develop effective strategies to encourage their children to reevaluate their cult involvement (if that is the parents' desire).
- Explore family issues and crises that have contributed to or are exacerbated by cult involvement.

The clinic also:

- Provides a support system for families that are unable to extricate their children from the cults.

- Provides information on strategies for locating children lost within the cults.

- Provides information on legal issues surrounding cult membership.

- Helps parents to recognize emotional blocks (for example, anger, guilt, apathy) that sabotage their relationships with their children.

- Enables parents to realize that they are not alone in their suffering.

Thirteen families utilized the clinic's services during its first month of operation. Since then more than four hundred families have been seen in the clinic. Clinic staff have also been consulted by more than one thousand other families by telephone. At present the clinic operates full time for individual sessions and holds two evening group sessions each month. A family may be represented by either parent, both parents, siblings of the cult member, or a combination of family members. Some families come only once; others have been attending, off and on, since the clinic opened. Most families live in southern California, but the clinic also has helped families from Australia, Israel, South America, and Europe.

Intake Procedures: When a family contacts the Cult Clinic, an initial intake interview is set up. At this time a psychosocial assessment is conducted by the clinic coordinator. This includes: *1) obtaining a family history from the cult member's birth to the present, 2) assessing family dynamics, 3) assessing the level of family functioning past and present, 4) determining the family's psychosocial resources, and 5) assessing whether family pathology exists.* After the assessment is completed, the coordinator discusses with the family options for treatment -- individual counseling, family counseling, group counseling, or a combination of the three. If severe psychopathology is suspected either in the family or in the cult member, individual or family rather than group sessions is recommended.

Clinic Group Program: Several factors determined that group counseling was a vital part of the program and that volunteers were essential to its success. First, as Theodora M. Abel and her colleagues point out, "when several families work together, various positive factors emerge that seem superior to those operating in the treatment of individual families. These factors include quicker reduction of tensions, a recognition that other families have similar problems, learning through identification, reduction of scapegoating, modeling, and emotional support." Second, while there was no money to support this service initially, qualified volunteers (including psychiatrists, social workers, attorneys, ex-cult members, parents of present and former cult members, and a mental health administrator) were available. Third, the magnitude of the problem was large enough to require different types of expertise and a system that could handle a large clientele. In addition, group counseling has proved to be particularly helpful to some parents who must resolve issues of competitiveness and resentment. The theoretical framework of the family group sessions draws upon both the family life education (FLE) approach to counseling and the concept of an ongoing emotional support system. Unlike traditional group therapy, FLE groups may contain as many as twenty to twenty-five clients. Work is problem-focused, that is, it is centered around specific issues rather than individual or family pathology. FLE employs a strong educational component that includes role-playing and modeling to teach specific skills. Each family is expected to use the information and the understanding obtained through the group experience to decide what is best for its own situation. Family life education group leaders act as facilitators or resource persons rather than as therapists.

Clinic Group Process: Staff members meet together before the group session to review each family situation. During this meeting, they share information about contacts they have had with families between sessions, insuring that continuity is maintained from one session to the next.

Each session begins with introductions, first by the staff, then by each family member. Parents are asked to describe their concerns. As each family relates the particulars of its situation, common issues emerge, and families begin interacting with each other. These interactions are the core of the work within the group.

Cult recruitment and the resultant change in their child's personality is a standard topic of family concern. As discussion progresses, staff ex-cult members describe their own cult experiences, explaining how they were recruited, what their lives as cult members were like, and how their perceptions and judgments were altered by the group. Families share feelings of difficulty in coping, and the staff members who are parents of cult members describe their own experiences: their feelings of despair and helplessness, how they were initially overwhelmed, how they gradually developed knowledge about cult life, and, finally, how they learned to reestablish communication with their children. They discuss both failures and successes encountered during this process.

A recent session exemplifies this activity. A family expressed their distress about a visit with their cultist daughter, with whom previously they had a close relationship. After traveling two thousand miles to see their daughter they found her to be distant and aloof. She insisted that they wait three days to see her and limited their visit to an hour and a half. This left the family feeling that they were inadequate and had failed. A staff member who was formerly a member of the same cult was able to share a similar experience when her family visited her while she was in the group. She told of the intense conflict between her feelings of family love (which the cult labeled as selfish) and her group loyalty (which encouraged no family contact). As she described her feelings, the family was better able to understand the daughter's distant behavior. This insight helped them to see their daughter as a victim, a person not in control of her situation. As a result, their guilt feelings were ameliorated and they were better able to mobilize for the future.

At the end of sessions, the coordinator sums up the discussion. To encourage a sense of continuity, she includes in the summation information about future sessions and how to contact staff members between sessions.

Specific Objectives and Interventions: Families seeking help are in crisis. To deal effectively with this crisis, the clinic's objectives are to help them: *1) gain perspective on the situation, 2) understand what strategies and options are available to them, 3) mobilize themselves, and 4) attract the cult member's attention.* These objectives represent a process, the elements of which may occur concurrently or independently, depending on family situations and the particular issues being dealt with. To accomplish these objectives, families must understand how their own behavior and emotions may impede rather than promote action.

Gaining Perspective: The first objective, as John G. Clark, Jr. and his colleagues suggested, is "to create a supportive . . . atmosphere in which parents feel safe expressing emotions and perceptions or beliefs that seem very strange to . . . them." This enables them to confront their guilt and rage -- emotions that may lead either to passivity or impulsivity. One way to lessen guilt is to explain how cults use powerful techniques to control and manipulate their followers. This helps families realize that they are not primarily to blame for what has happened. Once relieved of this guilt, they become less immobilized. Reading relevant materials, and having discussions with other parents and ex-cult members from the same cult to which their offspring belongs, are extremely useful in helping families to understand their problem.

A woman, attending a group session for the first time, began to express rage at her daughter (who is in a cult where couples live outside the group) for having married a man the mother considers an "ignoramus" and for associating with people she believed were far beneath her. According to the mother, a professional woman, her beautiful, "brilliant" daughter had abandoned all intellectual pursuits, selecting instead a life totally committed to homemaking. The mother was so enraged by her daughter's apparent rejection of her own values that she shook with anger. Attempts to help her understand that her daughter might not be making these decisions for herself were met by derisive sneers and comments such as "You just don't understand what I'm saying." An hour later, after hearing other parents describe their reactions to similar rejections from their offspring, the mother was able to put aside her abrasive anger. Through her tears she expressed some sympathy and concern for her daughter.

In situations where parents have not had contact with their children for long periods, the clinic offers an empathetic, supportive environment in which parents can express grief, interact with other parents who have successfully retrieved their youngsters, and thereby gain some sense of hope.

Soon after the clinic opened, a couple who had not seen or heard from their son for a year and a half attended a session. The last time they had talked with him, he told them that his guru had died. They were concerned that he and his cult associates might elect to follow the guru to the grave. The mother reacted to the situation by hoping to find her son; the father, who could not deal with the loss, considered his son dead and rarely spoke about him. The couple had turned their frustration into anger against each other, endangering their own relationship.

The clinic staff was able to help the couple to understand their different reactions to grief and to realize that both their reactions were normal. They were put in contact with resources that could help them try to locate their son. The couple attended the clinic three or four times and then stopped coming. Several months later, they reappeared to share with everyone their joy at having effected a reunion with their son and their new grandson, of whose existence they had previously been unaware.

Understanding Available Strategies and Options: The feeling that there is nothing a parent can do about the situation is a major cause of frustration.

Through the Cult Clinic, families learn that possibilities for action do exist. After gaining some perspective, families are ready to look at various alternatives. However, the staff is particularly concerned that families, in exploring their alternatives, not rush headlong into poorly conceived and impulsive acts. The entire process of exploring options is oriented toward one goal: to provide information so that families can make their own decisions based on the most knowledge available.

Most families want to help their children reevaluate their cult involvement. In discussing various ways to accomplish this, staff explore with them the family's role in reconnecting with their child. The strengths and weaknesses of family members and outside resources are assessed -- for example, who communicates best with the cult-involved person? If parents are in conflict with each other about strategy, they will be less effective in influencing their child. Families must realize that there are no guarantees that any intervention will work. They should also understand that leaving a cult is just the first step in their child's reintegrating into the mainstream of the family and society. Family problems that existed before the child joined the cult may arise again after the child's return. Additionally, the transition to noncult life can be traumatic and the cult experience can have many residual effects. Help for ex-members is also part of the clinic's comprehensive program.

Some families decide that they are not able to help their children leave the cult situation. When parents choose this path, they are encouraged to keep up the positive communications so that, if and when their children leave the cult, they will know that their parents love them and are available to help.

Mobilizing the Family: To deal with a relative's cult membership most effectively, a family must be a cohesive unit. Members must stop blaming each other for what happened and understand the resentments that lead to competitiveness rather than collaboration. Siblings must receive the attention they require, but at the same time feel and acknowledge their own and other family members' concerns for the lost relative. While acknowledging the problem at hand, each family member must continue to function as an individual, rather than suppress personal interests in favor of the needs of the cult member. Family members are encouraged to pursue normal interests and relationships as ego-enhancing activities at the same time that they gather information about, and build rapport with, the offspring who has joined the cult. The group format can be very helpful to families that face these tasks. However, when there are severe tensions between parents, or when family members have unrealistic expectations, the Cult Clinic's individual and family therapy program is recommended.

Attracting the Cult Member's Attention: Cults attempt to alienate members from their past experience and history. Therefore, before a family can help a child reevaluate the situation, it must reestablish contact with their child.

A large amount of time is spent in individual and group sessions helping parents develop new, nonargumentative communication techniques. They must learn how to listen to what their child is saying despite their own possible discomfort with the content. They also must learn to control their own negative emotions when talking with their children. Learning these techniques is crucial because, even though parents may not find cult behavior acceptable, they want to maintain contact with their offspring. Sometimes parents share in group sessions the drafts of letters written to their children in order to receive constructive feedback. Discussion of the content of one mother's letter helped her recognize how angry she was at her daughter. The mother softened her letter, sent it, and for the first time in years, received a letter back from her daughter. Although the daughter still is in the cult, she and her parents communicate regularly and she allows her parents to visit occasionally. Once contact has been established, one more task remains--creating a healthy tension within the cult-involved person by planting seeds of doubt. This process is essential in order to reawaken the offspring's critical thinking abilities necessary to reevaluate their situations.

Doubts can result from: *1) information presented about pleasant things outside the cult structure, 2) alternative interpretations of the cult doctrine, 3) the realization that independent decisions and questioning are not allowed by the group, or 4) information about the cult to which the member does not have access.* All this information must be presented without putting the cult-involved person on the defensive or implying that he or she is stupid.

Families have devised highly creative ways to plant these seeds of doubt. One parent, for example, whose son has been in a cult for eleven years, sent a diary to him as a birthday present. On the cover the mother pasted pictures of all the family activities the son had enjoyed in his childhood years, in order to stir up pleasant memories of his family and his precult experiences. Another parent, a nutritionist, explained to his child that her "euphoria" was not of spiritual or psychological origin (as the cult has said) but was the result of a physiological process that occurred after taking cult-prescribed vitamins. In another situation, the parents provided indisputable evidence to their child of her group's stockpiling of arms and ammunition; it helped her bring to question the validity of other information her group presented to her. And just observing that "It's too bad you can't decide for yourself when you visit us" has been used by other families to create a healthy tension in their childrens' minds. Establishing and maintaining contact with their children gives families something to do to combat frustration and to counteract the sense of helplessness and despair. During one of the group sessions, when a parent was feeling particularly discouraged because his efforts had not yet resulted in separating his son from the cult, the volunteer staff parent buoyed him up by reminding him: "Keep up your acceptance and lack of criticism of him. In his present state, your son's ears can't hear what they used to hear, and his mind can't accept what the cult has told him to reject."

Effectiveness of the Clinic: Used by more than 1,400 families so far, the Cult Clinic has produced the following results:

1. Parents have become better educated about their childrens' cult involvement and have gained an understanding of their childrens' behavior.

2. Mental health functioning of these parents has been substantially improved, as evidenced by their diminished need to ruminate about the cult situation, greater involvement in ego-enhancing activities, increased self-esteem, and a better communication between spouses. As a result, parents have been able to mobilize to help their children.

3. The majority of parents have modified their communication styles to develop more appropriate relationships with their offspring who remain in cults. Among this group are parents whose rage at cult involvement previously had alienated them completely from their offspring.

4. Because of appropriate interventions learned by families at the clinic, some children have left cults.

5. The knowledge base developed by the clinic has been shared with other service agencies, resulting in the establishment of several similar programs throughout the United States.

6. As families have met with success and more cult-involved youth have left their groups (many on their own accord), new services for ex-members (including individual, group, and family counseling) have been added to the clinic's program.

The Cult Clinic, addressing a problem for which no help had been previously available, demonstrates that breakdown of the family unit under stress can be prevented and families can be helped to reestablish relationships with their cult-involved children. Nevertheless, such a clinic represents only one approach to the problem. It is time for mental health and legal professionals to work on preventive strategies. They must share with the public their knowledge about causes of vulnerability, cult recruitment techniques, and possible legal remedies. By making this information widely available to students, educators, legislators, parents, and the public at large, young people may be less susceptible to deceptive recruiting tactics, and related family stress may be ameliorated.

Addis, Schulman-Miller, Lightman

* * *

PART 5:

GETTING OUT

PART 5: CONTENTS

Supporting Articles

PART 5: *GETTING OUT*

Help from the mental health care system is usually necessary to help the brainwashed person readjust to his usual environment after the brainwashing experience

Comprehensive Textbook of Psychiatry

Removing a member from a cult raises many legal issues, and is both emotional and controversial. Voluntary or involuntary, by covert or overt action, one or more of the parties involved is likely to allege violation of their rights. Some civil libertarians deplore actions taken by the parents who wrest their children away from cults, but few are callous enough to tell those parents to forget their children. When pressed for alternatives, few can provide parents constructive suggestions.

We speak here of "getting out" of cults. If you need to get out of a situation, the implication is that you are being held, usually against your will. Why then do we see cult members walking freely down the streets of our community, apparently capable of walking away from the cult at any time -- and not doing so? In preceding chapters we showed how someone's control of his or her own destiny has been taken away, or, at least, "guided" into a direction chosen by the cults. This guided "destiny" conforms to the collective cult mentality, and this is why a person may *seem physically capable* of walking away from a cult, but is *psychologically unable to leave*.

Few parents can sleep well at night knowing that their child is in a cult, but what can they do? "Deprogramming" is usually the first option that comes to mind.

Deprogramming:
How Does It Apply to Cults?

The Comprehensive Textbook of Psychiatry defines deprogramming as follows: The therapy offered is supportive in nature, with emphasis on reeducation, restitution of ego strength that existed before the trauma and alleviation of the guilt and depression that are the remnants of frightening experiences and the loss of confidence and confusion in identity that results from it.

This medical definition does not offer a clear understanding of what happens during deprogramming. It may well be that deprogramming is more art than science.

As **Dr. John Hochman,** a psychiatrist in Los Angeles and Former Vice Chair of the Commission on Cults and Missionaries of the Community Relations Committee of the Jewish Federation Council of Greater Los Angeles, writes,

Deprogramming is essentially a nonprofessional cluster of psychotherapies that have sprung up because professional psychotherapists have poorly understood the cult problem and have not risen to meet the challenges it presents. Although people have remarked about the sophistication of mind control techniques that cults have used, it's been my impression that a good deal of their recruitment methods have been based on trial and error techniques that have turned out to work.

Deprogramming is a similar product of trial and error method; rather than being mental health professionals, its pioneers have been people who are naturally gifted with persuasive abilities and who are "street-smart", quickly being able to see through cult hypocrisies and double talk that seems to be making sense to intelligent but naive cult indoctrinees.

Dr. John Hochman

* * *

Well-known "deprogrammer" **Galen G. Kelly** of Dale System Inc. states his goals for a successful deprogramming:

Deprogramming is in the eye of the beholder. What it entails, how it is accomplished, and the goals are very different, depending upon who is providing or interpreting the information. Therefore, it is very difficult to describe or discuss or even arrive at a definition that can generally be applied to the term "deprogramming".

Having been involved in several hundred deprogrammings since late 1975, I have, of course, my own interpretation and opinion. I feel that deprogramming is a counseling process that is designed to bring a person to a neutral place, in an intellectual and unemotional manner, where the subject can make an informed decision on whether or not to maintain affiliation with what is perceived by the deprogrammer and the family of the subject to be a destructive cult.

Just as "brainwashing" has many definitions and takes a variety of forms, so does "deprogramming." There is a vast difference between a deprogramming in a guarded "safe house" without escape for the cult member and a counseling session that occurs in the office of a religious leader, mental health professional, or a trained counselor. "Deprogramming" is really used as a catch-all word for a number of techniques to ease the exit of a member from a cult.

The cult member's family also can take no action to remove their relations from the cult. This decision may be motivated by various perceptions :

1. The group appears benign and the cult member's lifestyle is non-offensive to the family.

2. The family decides to wait and see what happens.

3. The family believes if the child really wants to leave he or she will come out voluntarily.

4, The family feels "frightened by the consequences of trying to remove my child and failing."

5. The family lacks knowledge about the problem and its possible solutions.

Are parents wrong to hope that their children might "see the light" and walk away from the cult? We cannot determine the correct approach parents should take with a cult-involved child, and there is certainly evidence to support some parents' hesitancy to take action. Although some cult-involved children leave on their own, we must emphasize that family love and support can tremendously affect a member's decision to voluntarily leave the cult.

Galen Kelly

* * *

Exit Counseling:
Does it Differ from Deprogramming?

A term often found with the word "deprogramming" is *exit counseling*.

We have explained that, deprogramming has come to be a catch-all term for techniques in removing individuals from cults; it now has both positive and negative connotations. Many now use "exit counseling" which lacks the controversial associations of deprogramming.

The distinction made generally refers to whether the counseling is *coercive* or *non-coercive* counseling.

Galen Kelly

* * *

There appears to be a real desire of "non-coercive exit counselors" to separate themselves from deprogrammers. They want to bring about a "voluntary deprogramming"; to do this they must be able to divorce themselves from bad press and from cult teachings that have frightened cult members of deprogramming. Several practitioners of non-coercive exit counseling were themselves deprogrammed in a less voluntary way when they were coming out of a cult. They see voluntary deprogramming as less stressful, and allowing for an easier readjustment to everyday life.

For the parent of a cult member, a discussion of the merits of one term over another is not useful. Their primary concern is if it works not what it means. Can we compare effectiveness of different techniques? Unfortunately not. Those cult members who underwent a particular exit-counseling and broke the cult's hold might have done as well through a different process; or they might have returned to the cult more convinced to remain there than ever before. Scientific studies are not possible. Experience shows advantages and disadvantages to all the different forms of counseling. Concerned families must learn as much about each method as possible. If you are a parent or concerned friend of someone in a destructive cult, the more you talk to individual counselors, the better able you will be to judge your ability to set the action in motion and follow through with it. Research both the cult and the potential counselor carefully before taking any action!

Now that we have taken away any hope of a quick and easy decision about deprogramming and exit counseling, we must also warn the person looking for help that deprogramming / exit counseling does not always work.

Why Would Deprogramming or Exit Counseling Fail?

The principal reasons might be as follows: a) the subject leaves the deprogramming environment either by walking out in a voluntary situation or by "escaping" during an involuntary situation; b) the deprogramming is terminated for external reasons such as: the arrival of the cult, arrival of the police, or extraordinary circumstances; c) the person is psychologically unstable to the degree of borderline personality or true psychosis; d) the person "burnt out" in the group, e) the person is not under any form of coercive persuasion or mind control and is in the group for his or her own reasons of entrepreneurship; or f) the person finds something too devastating in the outside world to deal with.

Galen Kelly

* * *

Another approach, by **Dr. John Hochman,** shows particular personality characteristics of cult members which may have a bearing on the success of counseling.

First of all, it is my impression that a very small minority of cult members suffer from serious mental illness, i.e., they are psychotic all or part of the time. If psychotic, they may have been this way before they joined the cult, or they may have become psychotic while in the cult. A cult for various reasons might not want to part with such an individual, and this individual would have great difficulty entering a meaningful relationship with an exit counselor or deprogrammer.

Some cult members, while not psychotic, may have had held some eccentric beliefs before they joined the cult (part of whose doctrine validated their own eccentricities). Such cult indoctrinees would reject attacks on the cult's doctrine, which a deprogrammer might not realize would also be an attack on beliefs that the indoctrinee cherished before they joined the cult.

Similar to the eccentric, are cult members that have antisocial trends; these people may identify with manipulative "beyond the law" attitudes of the cult leader -- a deprogrammer would be unsuccessful in attempting to educate such a person about the cult leaders' hypocrisy and their traits.

Deprogramming/exit counseling could also fail on individuals who are better "put together" psychologically. If the cult indoctrinee has built up a strong network of peer relationships within the cult and harbors strong pre-existing antagonism to his family of origin (where the antagonism might well be deserved) the odds for success of the deprogramming go down.

Deprogramming and exit counseling are essentially nonprofessional forms of psychotherapy where the cult indoctrinee is confronted with changes in his condition, educated about aspects of cult life of which he was unaware, re-encouraged to use thinking and reasoning capacities, and confronted with old relationships that he has attempted to put out of his mind. Poor skills of relating on the part of the deprogrammer, accompanied by failure to understand and empathize with a cult member, would lead toward failure as well.

Dr. John Hochman

* * *

The preceding excerpts are not optimistic but keep in mind that both Dr. Hochman and Mr. Kelly were asked why the process sometimes fails. Therefore we emphasize that both mentioned these "failure factors" come into play only a small part of the time. Verifiable statistics are unavailable, but Mr. Kelly estimates that **85% of those who undergo exit-counseling make a decision to disassociate from the group.**

The Legal Aspects of Deprogramming

There are more risks involved in deprogramming than just the cult member not leaving the cult. Sometimes, parents of cult members have chosen deprogramming methods which are illegal. In addition to researching deprogramming and exit counseling, parents considering action to free their child must consider legal ramifications. Families that break laws may be sued, prosecuted, or damage the link to their child. Laws regarding these matters are under review.

Richard Delgado, Professor of Law at the University of California, Los Angeles, discusses this:

Voluntary deprogramming, or "mutual reassessment" is not illegal, and the parent or family member who meets with a cultist in an uncoerced situation has little to fear. The same is true of a counselor, religious advisor, or a deprogrammer who sits in on or participates in such a discussion. A recent federal court decision (Weiss v. Patrick) held that such freely entered into conversations generate no liability on either side.

Legally-aided deprogramming, usually carried out pursuant to a court order of conservatorship or guardianship, is also relatively safe. Unless the parent obtains the order by means of false affidavits or evidence or commits a similar flagrant abuse of the judicial process, or else goes beyond the powers enumerated in the order, there should be no legal liability. The willingness of the courts in various parts of the country to issue such orders varies widely; a local attorney experienced with such litigations is essential.

Involuntary deprogramming carried out without a court order does generate legal liability for all concerned, parent, deprogrammer, driver of escape car, etc. One can be sued by the child for civil damages, for violation of civil rights, unlawful imprisonment, and possibly other torts (civil wrongs) as well. In addition, criminal prosecution for kidnaping and unlawful imprisonment is possible; these are serious felonies and can carry long prison terms. Many parents and deprogrammers have escaped conviction because the police or prosecutors looked the other way, or have been acquitted under the "defense of necessity" (choice of evils defense). Parents have also been found guilty but given a suspended sentence on condition that they stay away from their son or daughter. No responsible lawyer would advise a parent or family member to attempt an illegal deprogramming.

                                        Prof. Richard Delgado

* * *

What Factors Influence
Voluntary Departure From a Cult?

Incomplete suppression. Total suppression of undesired thoughts and tendencies is quite difficult. Frequently, a trace, however nebulous, of that which is suppressed lingers in consciousness and evokes anxiety. This anxiety may lead to psychiatric symptoms or to a chronic, fatiguing distress. Eventually, that which is suppressed may break through into consciousness or the person may become so debilitated that his function within the group is seriously impaired. The resulting skepticism or group pressure to improve his performance may motivate the convert to leave the cult, however unhappy he may feel about his decision.

Fatigue and boredom of tedious work. Selling flowers or soliciting at an airport 18 hours a day, week after week, can become a "drag", even to a devoted member. Furthermore, such work can often be so enervating that the convert feels inadequate to the task and leaves the cult, usually feeling like a failure.

Habituation. Many pleasures lose their glitter over time, even perhaps, love-bombing, sharing, witnessing, and so on. If this happens, the group loses its appeal to the individual, who may be tempted to leave. However, the disenchanted convert's dependency on the cult - i.e., his lack of replacements for the formerly wonderful "highs" provided by love-bombing and other cult-activities - makes it very difficult for him to leave or causes him to be anxious and guilty should he gather the courage to walk away.

Contacts with outside world. If destructive cults weren't so intent on making money, their attrition rate might be lower, for their members would have less opportunity to bolt and less contact with doubt-eliciting stimuli. But so long as members fund-raise and proselytize, contact with the outside world is unavoidable. And since total acculturation takes much time, most members will from time to time be shaken by criticisms by others, newspaper articles that they happen upon, and charged memories that are unleashed by, for instance, an old song on a jukebox or a letter from home. Such experiences are like cannonballs pummeling the "armor" in which the cult has encased the believer. If the armor is weakened for some reason, or if the fusillade is heavy, the cult may lose its hold on a member.

Clark, Langone, Schecter, Daly

* * *

In summary, by the time parents reach a decision to intervene in their cult-involved son or daughter's life, they are probably very anxious and frustrated that our legal system allows cults to control the minds of their children. To a person in such distress, any action, even illegal, may seem better than doing nothing. We have shown that if a situation has several options, one need not choose first the most radical or risky. See also: *Legal Issues*, Part 8.

Fifteen years ago, "cult awareness" of communities across the United States was practically nil. Today that has changed dramatically; no parent need make a rash judgment regarding the welfare of his or her child. There are people across the country whose life's work is to assist parents in making informed and practical decisions. If you are the parent, sibling, or friend of someone involved in a cult, check the *Resource Section* in Part 10 to find professional assistance nearby.

Study Guide

For the Group:

1. Discuss: Kidnaping is a crime. Are there any circumstances which justify kidnaping an individual?

2. Couldn't it be argued that the process of deprogramming is really the process of reprogramming. Society determines the "proper" behavior for an individual and if they deviate from that, they need to be reprogrammed.

3. How much free will and self determination does an individual really have? It appears that given the proper circumstances an individual can be made to do anything. Is there an inner core of being which truly knows what is right and what is wrong?

4. Why do you think exit counselors prefer not to be called deprogrammers? Is it just to avoid bad publicity or is there a difference in style and substance to their technique?

5. How does a family determine when the use of deprogramming/exit counseling is necessary? If you were in the same situation, how would you decide?

6. Why do you think so many deprogrammers/exit counselors are former members of cults?

For the Individual:

1. It has been said that no one knows until the time comes, but if you were the parent of a cult-involved child, would you be able to make the decision to have your child deprogrammed? Why do you feel that way?

2. If you chose to do something which your parents felt was terribly wrong and they threatened to have you "deprogrammed," how would you react? Is there any difference between this scenario and one involving a cult?

3. Where do you think the line is drawn between non-coercive and coercive exit counseling?

Supporting Articles

We realize that extricating people from cults is controversial. No aspect of cults has been less understood then deprogramming / exit counseling. The "horror stories" have discouraged people from investigation and thoughtful choice. To give a more personal view of deprogramming and exit counseling, we have included an interview with Rabbi Maurice Davis.

An Approach to Non-Coercive Exit Counseling, Hillel Zeitlin and Gary Scharff, and *Exit-Counseling: Working to Undo the Shackles of Cult Mind Control,* Steve Hassan offer detailed descriptions by exit counselors of the processes they use.

I Don't Deprogram Kids. I Rescue Them

Rabbi Maurice Davis,*Westchester Illustrated,* June 1979

We met Rabbi Maurice Davis in his office at the White Plains Jewish Community Center. He has been involved in deprogramming young people for the past five years. During that time, he has helped persuade 128 of them to leave religious cults.

What kind of a deprogrammer are you?

Let me say that I am not a professional deprogrammer. I am a rabbi of the Jewish Center in White Plains. That's my job. When people come to me for help, I do as much as I can. I've never had any other desire in life than to be a rabbi.

Where do you begin when you are faced with a young person who has been a member of a cult?

When a youngster is brought to me, there can be no restraint. He has to be there of his own free will. That doesn't mean he wants to see me. Maybe he has been persuaded by his parents. He may be belligerent. Certainly, he is uncooperative. Nonetheless, he is in a room where he can get up and walk out if he wants -- I make that very clear. Then, I begin. I say, "I have nothing against you. I would like to get to know you better. But I'm going to tell you what I think about the group to which you have attached yourself and I'd like to show you why I feel this way."

Then, I bring out some evidence, some material. I try to reawaken the values that you had when you walked into the group. I know that 99 times out of 100 you walked into it without knowing what was wrong. I keep probing until I find something to which you will react. Once you react, then a dialogue can begin.

You must understand that if you were such a person, and you and I were meeting for the first time, you would probably just sit there for the first two or three hours and look at me, and maybe smile, and maybe hum, but not answer me. Then, somewhere along the line, you would answer, and we would have established communication. Then I could ask you questions about your life and what you're running away from and what you're trying to find. And I could show you that you're not going to find what you're looking for where you're at. Then, I'd try to find some area in which your sense of values has been appalled.

To find something, you have to have in mind a kind of profile of the person you are dealing with, the type of person who gets caught. The profile goes something like this -- white, middle class, 18-25, of a warm and loving nature, a good kid, someone for whom the world is a little too complicated, someone who is searching.

Knowing that, I begin to talk. What has happened to you as a thinking person? What happens to anyone who abdicates the right to think? You become an automation. What happens to your soul if you become a person who can no longer stand up and say no? What happens to you when you are manipulated? This is the approach.

What qualifications make a good deprogrammer?

First of all, he has to know the cult he's dealing with. If I was to try to rescue a kid out of a group that I didn't understand, there could be no meaningful dialogue. Secondly, he ought to have heavy experience with teenagers and young adults in other areas. I've lived my life with this age group, so I think I have a handle on it. It would be great if someone had a good social or psychiatric background or religious background. Most of all, you have to really feel deeply that you are involved in saving these kids.

How did you first become involved in deprogramming?

I guess you've noticed that you keep saying "deprogramming' and I keep saying "rescuing," because I'm not really sure what these words mean. I got involved on a Friday morning six years ago when I received back-to-back phone calls from two members of my congregation. Each had the same story to tell. And I never had heard that story before.

One was about a son and the other was about a daughter, both of whom had been caught by the Moonies up in Albany State College. They asked for help. I didn't know how, because I didn't know anything, but I stumbled through. The boy came home. I talked to him and he dropped out of the thing. The girl had already gone through her indoctrination in Tarrytown and I was unable to get her out of the movement.

But I became so angry at what I witnessed that I began doing research. And that research was used in a sermon that I gave to my congregation, which was picked up by the Times and Time magazine. All of a sudden, people began writing to me and asking for help, and I didn't know how to help them.

Finally, in desperation, I sent them all postcards asking them to come and talk. About 150 people came and we pooled our knowledge and we pooled our ignorance and we met some kids who had dropped out. Gradually, we developed into an organization called CERF - Citizens Engaged in Reuniting Families.

Our job wasn't to rescue kids, but to get the American public to be aware of the danger, to get Congress to move, to help counsel parents whose kids are in, and to help kids who were coming out. I ran CERF until two or three years ago.

Tell us about some specific cases that made an impression on you.

There are a lot of them. There was one boy whom I rescued three years ago. He was searching for something he hadn't found in his youth, thought he found it in the Moonies, and I showed him that what he had found . . . was counterfeit. He turned back to his own faith and began studying it and now he is preparing himself to be a rabbi.

There was a boy from a neighboring state. I went to him. After I worked on him all day and deprogrammed him, he said he wanted to come and live with me. He lived with me for two weeks, while the Moonies searched for him in his own city.

There are some wonderful stories about some truly beautiful people. The kids that get caught are the vulnerable ones. But their motives are good. That's what makes the cults so dangerous. I know where these cults lead and the last line is Jonestown.

Do you think all cults are dangerous?

The word cult was originally a neutral term, but it has taken on a meaning. So I try to evaluate. What I'm talking about when I use the word cult is: One, a dictatorial leader, or charismatic -- someone who has absolute and total control over the destiny of its members and is answerable to no one. Two, a following that has given up the right to make value judgments. These are kids who have sold their souls for the security of slavery. Three, unlimited funds. Four, the most dangerous doctrine that I know, "The end justifies the means." Five, the teaching of fear, hatred and suspicion of everything outside the group. The Nazi Youth Movement, or the Unification Church or the People's Temple, they have all these five characteristics. So that's what I mean by the word cult.

Do you think that someone who enters a cult has to want to give up the right to think?

No! No! That's the price he pays. In joining one of these things, you've gone to visit and you've been "love-bombed" and made to feel important. It's your desire to belong that helps you to convince yourself step by step. You don't give up thinking all at once. You give it up a little at a time. In the beginning when your faculties are high, the information they feed you is low. It's only as your critical faculties are reduced that they begin to feed you more. Finally you stop thinking and become accepting.

How do you feel about deprogrammers who use restraint?

I don't use any kind of restraint. I wouldn't feel right about it. But first, anyone who says physical torture is used is just outright lying. It's not done. What would be done is that someone might be brought into a room and the door locked. This is only done in the presence of the parents, so that the deprogrammer is acting in locus parenti. While I wouldn't feel right about it, I know their intentions are good. They want to help. Remember, I get the easy cases. I get the kids that are still willing to walk through that door. But what about the kid who won't come talk to me? Someone else gets him and that's a different case. I don't condemn those that use restraint. They see it differently than I, but their motives are just as pure.

Is there something missing from our society? Is that why kids join cults?

Yes, I think teenagers in this country are the loneliest people in the world. I compare their lives with my life when I was their age. I grew up in an extended family: these kids grow up in a nuclear family. When I grew up, everyone in the neighborhood belonged to the neighborhood gang. Today, they don't even have neighborhoods. When I grew up, the temple was the center of everything.

Today, the temple and the church are the center of nothing. Where do these kids belong?

Parents are another problem. They don't think kids are real. They think they're something in transit. Then they go to college. In the 1950s and 1960s, the colleges had causes. They were alive. There were protest marches. They marched on Washington. They marched with Martin Luther King. And every time they marched, they had cousins believing in the same things. Then they killed Martin Luther King and John Kennedy and Robert Kennedy. Johnson lied to them, and Nixon tricked them, and now there are no more causes. What is there now? TM Yoga. They're inward turnings. They only enhance the feeling of loneliness.

* * *

An Approach to Non-Coercive Exit Counseling

Gary M. Scharff and Hillel Zeitlin
Options for Personal Transition

Recent years have seen an increased interest in voluntary or "noncoercive" methods for assisting individuals and families harmed by destructive cults. While many people have expressed strong appreciation for those who developed forcible intervention as a means for rescuing individuals from the confinement of cultic mental influence, changes in prevention and response to the cult problem, as well as changes within some of the cults, have stimulated exploration of noncoercive approaches. Increasing difficulties - legal, financial and ethical - associated with forcible deprogramming have also encouraged development of voluntary forms of exit counseling.

Our office, Options for Personal Transition, or OPT, represents an effort by two former cult members to combine experiences, training and skills to provide effective assistance to cult-disrupted families and individuals in a non-coercive setting. When the office opened in Berkeley, California in early 1981, Gary Scharff, a former Unification Church member, was completing graduate work in religious studies, emphasizing the nature of religious conversion. Hillel Zeitlin, former Divine Light Mission devotee, was a clinical social worker with a broad background in counseling. Both had worked previously in assisting individuals and families affected by cults, providing family preparation, exit counseling, and post-cult rehabilitation and re-entry support. We opened OPT to create a model for professional service that could effectively respond to the range of needs arising from cult involvement while operating within the law and professional ethics.

OPT's approach to counseling proceeds from the assumption that responsible decision-making stems from freedom of choice, and that the freedom to choose requires that a person know the significance and consequences of a given option. By employing social pressure and thought control techniques to interrupt and divert individual direction, cults can "short circuit" the process by which people can explore and evaluate. The milieu of a destructive cult is designed to limit and disqualify all of a recruit's options except the choice to obey.

But cults do not step into a vacuum. Each recruit brings a unique personal history that includes character, life aspirations, and family background, as well as distinctive qualities of development and maturation. Many cults are skilled at assessing these subtleties and tailoring an enticing approach around them. Through cult indoctrination, a person's sense of self is often drastically altered. Recruits are likely to have internal experiences they cannot explain. They frequently form intense new friendships, and assimilate a new language as well as new beliefs and mannerisms.

The changes resulting from cult indoctrination can leave family and friends frightened and bewildered. The respect and mutuality which normally sustain their bonds with the recruit are often ruptured by the cultist's new identity. Familiar and habitual patterns of communication no longer seem to affect the cult member. This often leads families to feel that "programming" has replaced the individual they once knew.

How is it possible to deal with such communication breakdown, particularly in a noncoercive situation where any substantive communication may seem (and often is) so precarious?

The Need for Information: At OPT our concern has been to develop a flexible model for helping with the four principal human elements of the cult-disrupted family situation - the cult member, the family, the cult and the web of relationships by which these are all connected. Specific information in all these areas is crucially important. Individual, family and cult all have particular backgrounds and circumstances influencing their relationships to one another.

Social control techniques also have a distinctive character. Current research has enabled mental health and religious professionals to articulate more refined perceptions of the intrusive control processes employed in destructive cults. New findings in communications theory suggest that "naturalistic" hypnotic processes and "information disease," especially when adroitly mixed with partial or largely untestable deception, intense but conditional affection, and carefully orchestrated isolation and social pressure, lead to a serious loss of personal autonomy. Knowing that this occurs is a familiar fact to many a disrupted family and former cult member; knowing better how it occurs in terms of the specific methods for disrupting choice provides new possibilities for reversing such influence. More recent interactional views of cultic recruitment convey a degree of precision, complexity and applicability which earlier concepts of "brainwashing" and "mind control" - derived from other historical and cultural contexts - could not.

An effective therapeutic strategy seeks to utilize specific information to match the resources alive within individual, family and circumstances to the shifting requirements of a given situation. Our goal is to help the cultist "re-engage" previously demonstrated skills for evaluating, testing and reconsidering relationships to oneself, family, cult and world according to one's own criteria for responsible conduct.

Four Steps: Our model for attaining this goal involves four steps.

1. **After initial contact by a distraught family member, we plan an in-depth session to exchange information.** Counselors and family bring into focus the specific circumstances, intentions, possibilities and difficulties which characterize this particular family, individual and cult involvement. This session normally has three parts. First, counselors learn about the individual personal and family background, as well as his cult history. Next we discuss cultic control patterns to identify how communication between individual and family has been altered. Finally, counselors work together with the family to build a strategy to match resources and communication strengths with the needs of the cult member which are not likely to be adequately cared for within the cult. This plan for developing communication enables old areas of more meaningful relating between individual and family to be re-established, and new areas to be carved out.

2. **Next we pursue this strategy for developing communication.** We assist the family to establish a pattern of contact with the cultist of a hopefully more human and less ideological tone and substance. By demonstrating their care and respect for the cultist, the family works to build an atmosphere of trust in the face of disagreement, and a willingness to care and respond to the other despite

disappointment. As a two-way street engendering a sensitivity for the feelings of others in the relationship, this process, even by itself, can often have the healing effect of easing tensions and enabling each side to acknowledge the other's positive motivations.

In some cases, if the individual has been struggling internally in his allegiance to the cult, this approach with the family may be enough to open a door out of the group, as the cultist discover his family has not rejected him and that there is indeed life outside the cult. In many cases, however, the individual will attempt to develop a connection with his family alongside his cult allegiance; juggling these two loyalties, he may need to withhold from the group the extent of his growing bond with his family. He may then develop with someone in his family an intimacy which provides a sense of personal affirmation and value beyond what the performance-centered lifestyle of the cult can supply. This can lead to a greater willingness to acknowledge and feel for - rather than abruptly repudiate - his family's anxieties, even as the cultist continues to doubt the validity of these anxieties.

3. **The family works toward an eventual appeal to the cultist to come home and engage in a serious dialogue in which their concerns about his cult involvement can be expressed and discussed in an atmosphere of trust, honesty and respect.** He is not "set up" for a deprogramming in which he will be held against his will. Rather, he is invited to accept that respect and trust imply a willingness to take some responsibility for the effects one's behavior has on the lives and feelings of one's family. As the cultist may have requested that his family learn about the cult from other cult sources than himself, the family now requests that the cultist also engage respectful counselors and/or former members whose awareness and critique of the cult may exceed the expertise of the family even as it articulates family concerns.

The cultist is challenged to explore different interpretations of his cult involvement, including a review of the process by which his initial allegiance developed. He is asked to measure the consequences of that allegiance against his own criteria for responsible behavior and to explore with his family the confusing changes in communication and conduct perceived by family members since his encountering the group. He is challenged to explain how he distinguishes his perspective from the cult's, so that he can identify the boundaries between self and group which preserve personal freedom and prevent responsible commitment from becoming blind faith.

The outcome of such an intense conversation depends on a large number of factors within individual, family, counselors and circumstances. Because force is not used, the "situational" incentives to leave the cult are normally less strong than in forcible deprogrammings. Since the experience is not one of imprisonment but of respectful challenge, however, the posture of "holding fast in the face of persecution," which characterizes many cultists" attitudes during forcible deprogrammings, is also less strong or absent. Our principal concern is not to "force" a conclusion through an accumulation of information; rather, our focus is to assist the cultist to incorporate, beyond the information he receives, those qualities of decision-making that will enable him to "grow out" of the cult through his own personally-chosen decision.

4. **After the exit counseling session, counselors facilitate the former cultist's re-entry by assisting him and his family to assess the next steps in their lives together.** The former member needs to understand what has happened to him and to recover his personal direction. He needs to find the internal strengths and external supports that can help him realize his goals. The former member and family also need to learn how to utilize their new ways of relating such that future communication can be mutually satisfying. In this way the memory of this event can serve as a valuable resource for the whole family.

The substance of OPT exit counseling, then, is to combine specific information about individual, family and cult with more precise views of the nature and function of cultic control processes to accomplish three objectives:

- To facilitate and experience respectful and successful family communication to replace the disruption resulting from cult involvement.

- To provide the cultist with information and perspectives not meaningfully available in the cult milieu.

- To encourage the cultist to develop skills for more mature evaluation of life choices and commitment, and to assist the cultist to internalize and use those abilities in assessing his cult affiliation.

The choice to leave the cult immediately is one possible positive outcome of exit counseling. There is also the risk that the cultist might return to the group - a risk which accompanies any approach to exit counseling, coercive or noncoercive. However, the risk that a cultist will carry back to the cult severely antagonistic feelings toward his family is significantly reduced when respectful and honest communication in a free setting has occurred after a preparatory period of rebuilding mutuality and respect.

One important aspect of this form of exit counseling is its emphasis on the active role of the family in recovering a relationship with the cult member. Working hard to re-connect a strong and positive bond between themselves and the cultist is not only a practical, ongoing way for a family to express care for the cultist. It also tends to lead to smoother and quicker readjustment after exit from a cult, since leaving this way focuses more on growth in decision-making, developing skills in communication, and restoring family relationships.

The field of exit counseling is new and developing. As the complex factors involved in the induction and maintenance of social control are increasingly understood, the methods of intervention continue to be refined. Though our approach is certainly not an "automatic formula" for every situation, we look forward to continued knowledge and skill in providing assistance to the casualties of cult disruption.

* * *

Exit Counseling: Working to Undo the Shackles of Cult Mind Control

Steve Hassan, M.Ed.
Revised copyright, September 1984

This paper is designed to assist you in understanding my approach and how it differs from what other exit-counselors and deprogrammers have to offer. I bring to this paper ten years of experience: two and a half years as a member of the Moon cult; and more than eight years of studying, researching, lecturing as well as helping hundreds of people to leave totalistic cults. I have developed a new approach to exit-counseling and will present a brief overview of its fundamental elements. A much more extensive handbook is available from me. (See *Resource* section, Part 10) If you are interested in a consultation or workshop, it would be extremely useful for you to obtain my four page information form. Information is an extremely important component of effective counseling. The higher the quality of information you can supply me, the more specific and concrete my suggestions will be for your own particular situation.

Why is there a need for deprogramming or exit counseling at all? The answer lies within the practices of individual cult groups and within the concern of the relatives of cult members. Not every cult group is destructive to members and dangerous to society. However, when they employ deceit, trickery, and systematic mind-control to recruit and indoctrinate followers then there is good reason for relatives to be concerned. Such destructive cult groups violate people's integrity through the use of mind control.

Mind control technology involves a wide array of techniques which include hypnosis, behavior modification, information control, sleep and privacy deprivation, as well as intense manipulation of emotions including fear and guilt. It is important to understand that these techniques are subtly employed at first. The person has the sense of being in "control." Usually it is without coercion that the person gets manipulated step by step through the process that begins to change or "reform" his sense of personal identity. The individual comes to feel that what is occurring is of great personal benefit and for that matter of value to the rest of humanity. Consequently little resistance is offered. After a period of days, weeks, and months the new recruit gradually but systematically is taught how to think, feel and act in accordance with the great "Leader" and his "Doctrine." The new recruit's behavior is "shaped" by a combination of positive reinforcement and punishment. The person's identity and self-esteem becomes dependent on his devotion and obedience to cult leaders.

That person has become a "convert." He may or may not know the Leader personally or know much of what goes on at the upper levels of the group. He knows only what he is told - what he needs to know - any other information is unimportant or dangerous. If he is like most members of destructive cults, he learns to live a spartan, disciplined, and obedient life. His behavior is monitored and controlled, information (both incoming and outgoing) is controlled, and ultimately his thoughts are controlled. He is taught to be suspicious of anything that tries to undermine his commitment to the group. He learns to use "thought-stopping" techniques as a primary tool for maintaining "faith." Any negative thought that undermines the integrity of the cult leader, challenges the validity of the cult doctrine, or exposes flaws in the organization is automatically interrupted and stopped. This is accomplished mechanically using techniques such as chanting, meditating, speaking in tongues, praying or even singing to stop thoughts. The cult member is trained to use these techniques believing that they will help him to grow and be healthy. However, they serve only to constrict his ability to think.

The more fully this person is programmed, the more difficult it is for him to be able to mature and develop. Such a person has been indoctrinated into a totalistic belief system so thoroughly that it supersedes (but does not erase) many of his prior values, beliefs, and behavior patterns. He is unable to consider objectively the validity of so-called "negative" information or reason with people critical of the cult. He cannot exercise decisions independent of the cult's values and dictates. The focus of control has shifted from within the individual to the cult leader, doctrine and organization. In such a case, deprogramming or exit counseling is the process that family members rely on to help undo the mind-control of their loved one.

My Approach: Initially, following my deprogramming out of the Moonies, I participated in a number of forced "deprogrammings." None to my knowledge were kidnapings from a street corner, but were rather detainments - the cult member came home to visit, and restricted from leaving or contacting the cult for several days. A few were legal, conservatorship cases, where I acted as an agent of the Court. I never liked the forced method, although as a former cult member, I understood its necessity. At that time, (1976) there was no "other" way.

It has now been about five years since my last forceful deprogramming. I have experienced the emotional devastation of situations where the cult member escaped, went back to the cult and either "disappeared" or brought law suits against family and professionals. The emotional and psychological stress of counseling under those conditions; the ethical problems I had justifying the use of these tactics; the enormous expense to the family; as well as the legal considerations contributed to my desire to develop a workable non-coercive approach.

My experience has demonstrated to me that with a proper approach and the right combination of factors, a person can be brought out smoothly from the totalistic mindset into a more healthy and integrated identity. Such a person comes out of the cult with enhanced self-esteem, a greater sense of personal control and autonomy as well as a thorough understanding of the cult phenomenon and mind control technology.

At the core of my approach are several beliefs and assumptions that influence my work. I start with the belief that *my clients are unique individuals*; that despite cult programming they each have their own personal way of experiencing "reality." It is because people are different that I must bend and adapt my approach to each individual client rather than expect it to be the other way around. Second, I believe that *people will always choose those options which they believe are best for them*. Of course, cult programming convinces them to believe that whatever is best for the group is best for them. Knowing how to sidestep cult programming is critical here. Third, *I believe in the power of the unconscious mind to influence the conscious mind.* Even though a cult member is thoroughly indoctrinated, a vast storehouse of unconscious resources exist. These include not only the years of pre-cult experience, but also the doubts and questions about "cult reality" that result from cult membership. Even though these doubts are suppressed from consciousness, they can and eventually do exert influence on the cult member's behavior. The right kind of guidance can speed up this process and help the cult member become aware of the negative aspects of cult involvement.

My approach involves a number of steps or stages that build on one another and ultimately combine to insure a successful intervention and rehabilitation. The first step in the process is to collect and organize information that can give me some sense of who the cult member is as a person. Using the preliminary evaluation form which provides some of the background data I need, I can begin talking with family members and friends in order to accurately assess the individual's strengths, weaknesses, and personality style. Once I have reviewed all available sources of information, I can begin to develop and discuss strategies for setting up an intervention.

The next step is to conduct a preliminary training session, either privately with the family, or in a group "workshop" situation. The training session teaches the necessary communication skills that help friends and family members to: enhance rapport and trust; gather additional information about the cult member's ongoing experience; and begin planting positive "suggestions" for effecting change. This training is an essential component to the approach and is not available from other exit counselors.

Through the training, family members learn to develop new, more effective ways of communicating and responding to the cult member. For example, a significant component to effective communication with cult members is to learn how to avoid triggering the "thought-stopping" process. Too many families have learned the hard way that the confrontative approach does not work well. Often, direct criticisms force the cult member to turn off not only the "negative" information but also their feelings of warmth and trust. Family members must learn how to maximize their influence by cultivating rapport and by avoiding judgmental statements. This can be done by adopting an inquisitive, yet concerned stance.

I have found the group "workshop" an excellent setting to work on strategies that can help individuals learn new patterns for communication. Since the emphasis of the program is on the process of effective communication, it is possible for families affected by different cults to participate together, thus making the training more effective and cost efficient. The communication patterns taught in the workshop include a whole set of linguistic and behavioral alternatives that can be used to make a powerful impact on the cult member. By presenting information in special ways, critical messages can be conveyed without "thought-stopping" or alienation. The cult member will feel respected and loved and will be more willing to share feelings and thoughts. When parents and friends are able to develop a relationship with the cult member based on mutual respect, trust, and love; this greatly facilitates the exiting process. Under these conditions, the cult member can be more easily motivated to speak with exit counselors.

After the preliminary training is completed, families often desire additional opportunities for feedback which can take place over the phone or whenever possible, face to face. In this way, I can work closely with the family offering suggestions and responding immediately to any new developments. It takes time to learn how to think and act strategically, but with practice, progress is inevitable. Some families send me copies of letters they receive and plan to send. Other families even tape record phone conversations as part of their ongoing record. Some families organize study and support sessions with others that have taken the training. Intensive, follow-up trainings can be offered to interested people in a centralized location. The better equipped families are, the easier it will be to help the cult member.

After the initial training, some time is put aside to "tune in" to the cult member. Each member goes through cycles of ups and downs during the cult involvement. When there is good communication, it is relatively easy to determine what phase he or she is in. The more we know about the cult member, the easier it will be to time the intervention. The probability of success is greatly enhanced when the intervention is timed according to the cult member's mental state. Naturally, if they are in a "low" point in their involvement, they will be more open to new perspectives and consequently to new life choices.

At this point, I would like to discuss how the non-coercive intervention differs from a forced deprogramming. First of all, family relationships and efforts are instrumental to its success. Second, the intervention is timed to the cult member rather than at the family's convenience. Third, it requires finesse, rather than force, and depends heavily on high-quality information, access to significant people who have a good relationship with the cult member, and the right professionals.

The **advantages** of a non-coercive intervention are:

- It is not traumatic and stressful, consequently it is psychologically healthier for the cult member.

- It is not illegal, so there is no concern about lawsuits or other legal hassles.

- It is far less expensive than forceful deprogramming.

- There is room for many attempts without negative repercussions on the family, since the individual need not fear kidnap deprogramming.

The **disadvantages** of a non-coercive intervention are:

- It takes effort from family members (and friends) to develop their communication skills and build their relationship with the cult member.

- It requires patience, since it may take weeks, sometimes months to wait for the "right" moment to gain access to the cult member. Indeed, in the non-coercive approach the greatest difficulty is securing prolonged access to the cult member.

The next step entails determining how the intervention will take place. Based on the "intelligence" gathered, an appropriate strategy must be developed. Ultimately, an intervention will fall into either the overt or covert category. While it is always preferable to be straightforward and honest with the member, cult programming may prohibit any voluntary meeting. Typically, members are taught to fear and flee from any ex-members, especially professionals.

This section covers the two basic types of non-coercive interventions: the *overt* and *covert*. Each has its strengths and its limitations. However, the goal of both methods is the same, to encourage and motivate the cult member to investigate and research alternative sources of information in order to expand perspective, create options, and to enhance personal decision making. **The following descriptions are given only to offer a general understanding of the non-coercive approach.**

The Overt Intervention

The overt intervention represents the "heart" of the non-coercive approach. It is by far the most successful method. It requires a great deal of preparation, which includes patience, flexibility, determination and teamwork. It is usually set up by developing mutual trust, respect and a willingness to accommodate. Through a process of negotiation, the cult member agrees to meet and talk about the cult and his involvement for some prearranged time period.

There are numerous ways to set up a overt intervention. One strategy is to ask the cult member to demonstrate that he is a member of the group by his own free and informed choice (the challenge). Another approach uses an emotional appeal to allay the fears of family members (do it as a favor for us). When neither of these seem sufficient, there are a number of ways to create leverage. For instance, family members can negotiate with the cult member to attend cult lectures, if the cult member will agree to speak with ex-members and professionals for an equivalent amount of time (we'll go half way, if you'll do the same). Parents can offer a variety of benign forms of bribery in order to get the cult member to agree to spend a few days listening and talking about other points of view (inducement). Family members can make an effort to befriend their child's cult leader and negotiate with him/her directly - offering to pay the group the equivalent of their child's lost days of fundraising (going to the boss). Sometimes, parents have successfully gotten access to their child by threatening the cult leader with media pressure (blackmail), but this could easily backfire. Remember, whoever is closest to the cult member usually has the most influence. That should be the person to make the appeal. Remember, it is critical to time the request to when the cult member is most likely to respond favorably. Whenever planning an overt approach, careful evaluation and preparation must take place in order to ensure success.

The Covert Intervention

The covert intervention is used only when there is no chance of setting up an overt intervention. Its success depends upon finding a non-threatening way to get access for several days to the cult member during one of the "down" phases. Since the cult member does not know the exit-counselor's motives, the relationship must evolve as naturally as possible, touching on crucial areas of importance subtly and indirectly. Since the exit-counselor has background information on the cult member, he can develop topics of discussion that he knows will be of interest.

A covert intervention can take place in a number of ways. If the cult member is home visiting for a week, then it is relatively easy to introduce the professional as a "friend" of a brother or sister, a family counselor, a researcher, etc.. If the cult member doesn't come to visit relatives, or is very suspicious, then another option is available. The exit-counselor can go to where the member is stationed and can try to arrange to meet him/her and strike up a relationship (usually the professional acts like a potential convert). The cult member need never know that this "new person" is a professional hired by the family. This is one of the distinct advantages of the "covert" approach. If for some reason, the timing is not right, or there is not enough access to be successful, then there is little or no backlash at the family.

The covert intervention can follow one of three courses: it can fail; it can succeed; or it can partially succeed.

If it fails outright, the cult member can find out and become angry. This rarely happens, but when it does, it is because of an information "leak" or because the cult member recognized the exit-counselor. If this occurs, the family can explain it to the cult member that they didn't want it to be covert, but they had no choice. The cult member had repeatedly rejected their proposal of an "open" meeting and the family did not want to use kidnaping or force.

It can succeed - the cult member decides to leave the group immediately. When this occurs, the exit-counselor decides whether or not to tell the ex-member the whole story. My preference is always to tell all, except where it will have destructive consequences. Some people have great pride and need to feel that they did it all on their own. Others have such enmity for their parents that they would reject help just because they knew it was coming from them. So, I find myself at times struggling with my sense of ethics, trying to do the best thing for my clients. It is particularly hard for me to use a deceptive technique like the one many cults use to recruit, even though it is temporary and used for the purpose of helping people to regain autonomy. At this point, I acknowledge my conflict and choose to use this approach only when absolutely necessary. My choice is based on the lesser of the evils - I would rather misrepresent myself than to encourage the use of forced interventions or to do "nothing."

It can be particularly successful - the cult member is exposed to information and ideas, but continues with the group. This can occur due to a number of variables: the timing was not ideal; there wasn't enough time to interact; the location interfered with the process; the member wasn't alone; personalities didn't mesh well; exit-counselor error or lack of knowledge; or the cult member decides to stay for a variety of good reasons. Of course there are other factors that can contribute to the member's continued involvement in the group. Nevertheless, the effort was made to impart some information, offer substantial frames of reference, and encourage the member to reevaluate the commitment. Hopefully, with the passage of time, the member will have other opportunities to interact with others that will reinforce the work that was done. It is not uncommon for people to leave the group months or years after an intervention.

The method I use in actually working with the cult member is highly specialized and is beyond the scope of this paper. However, I will describe some aspects which may be of interest. By using my knowledge of cult indoctrination patterns, the individual's belief system and my communication skills, I carefully pace the cult member step-by-step paying close attention to their verbal and non-verbal responses. Of utmost importance is first to develop a high degree of rapport and trust. Initially, I do not even discuss cults or mind control directly. I have found it useful to tell my clients stories involving metaphors that are indirectly suggestive of the problem. By talking about how people get "stuck" in situations that are no longer beneficial to them, I can address the area of change with little resistance. Common subjects include broken love relationships, battered wife syndrome, exploitation within a large corporation, etc. Many times I even ask my clients how they would suggest making a change if they were in such a situation. Whenever I work with a client, I make sure to give the feeling that he or she is in control. I am "merely" a facilitator. By relying on the individual's own values and beliefs to guide me, I help to open the doorway to growth and change. When my client discovers the connection between the metaphors and their personal experiences, the effect is particularly powerful.

Regardless of which type of intervention is made, it is important to remember that the purpose of a non-coercive intervention is to help cult members to reevaluate their cult commitment--not to force them to leave. Interfering in their lives is necessary only because there is a need to offer them additional resources and alternatives so they can make real and informed choices. There should be no confusion about this point. Cults claim that parents interfere with their child's involvement because they want to control their lives. I accept only those clients who wish me to assist the individual to break free of cult mind control so that he/she can have the highest degree of personal autonomy. I believe that great care should be taken to respect the client's integrity as a human being.

Typically, the intervention will last from three to five days. However, each case is unique. Sometimes I will work an intervention all by myself, particularly when financial resources are low. When working with other cult groups, I usually insist that an ex-member of that group work with me. With long term members, it is often advisable to form a team of ex-members.

During the intervention, an assessment is made regarding rehabilitation. I prefer to use the word resocialization. The weeks that follow an intervention are extremely important, until the individual regains his/her own mental equilibrium. I encourage my clients to acknowledge the positive experiences they had while in the group, and to integrate them wherever possible into their lives. I also seek to enhance their self image and sense of self worth by emphasizing their personal resources and strengths. Meeting with ex-members, psychologists, vocational counselors, theologians is highly recommended for the ex-cult member depending on his/her own needs and interests.

Two types of follow-up are available: 1) a formal "rehab" center; or 2) a "vacation/ tour" approach. Over the years I have come to favor the latter, except in those cases where I feel the individual will do better in a more stable, structured environment. Depending on available resources, a one to two week tour can be set up to stop in and visit appropriate individuals. For some former members, the resocialization process is relatively smooth. For others, particularly long term members, the process can take months or even years. It is extremely important to monitor and assess the progress of the ex-member during the first year. Some have actually returned to the group because of problems or issues that went unresolved.

*I will now review the steps involved in the **non-coercive approach:*** 1) filling out evaluation form and assessing the situation; 2) preliminary communications training; 3) follow-up to training to "tune-in" on cult member; 4) strategizing to plan an intervention; 5) making the intervention; 6) resocialization; 7) long term follow-up.

Of course, the non-coercive approach works easiest when families come to me as soon as they discover their child's cult involvement. They have a "freer hand" in dealing with their child as well as with the cult leaders. Once a family has aggressively opposed the group, they limit their flexibility to influence the cult member. For those families who have unsuccessfully attempted a forced deprogramming, the rescue effort becomes more difficult, but not impossible. I believe there is always a way to proceed.

Extricating a loved one from a destructive cult can be an ordeal. Therefore, it is particularly important to adopt a constructive mental attitude. I urge family members to operate on the assumption that the cult member is going to leave the cult. It will either be sooner or later, smoothly or with more difficulty. The family must concentrate their energy on doing those things within their control to resolve the situation as quickly and as smoothly as possible. No one can do more.

The non-coercive approach to cult exit counseling offers a promising alternative to deprogramming. For many families, it offers a viable approach to helping loved ones return to a state of mind in which personal growth, autonomy, creativity, and healthy emotional relationships are encouraged.

I hope that I have successfully communicated some of the basic points about the non-coercive approach in this brief paper. Effective communication training for family and friends is the first important step to a successful intervention. Next, by using information collected about the cult member's past and current experiences in the cult, a strategy can be developed to make the intervention. Knowing when to initiate the intervention is very important. In addition, knowing how to set up a suitable meeting context and location for the cult member and exit counselor is crucial. By understanding cult programming and utilizing methods to counteract the "thought-stopping" technique, the exit counselor seeks to engage and motivate the cult-member into a state of mind which permits careful examination and reflection. The exit-counselor uses a variety of communication skills which encourage the cult member's subconscious mind to surface. It is at this point that the subconscious mind is encouraged to express buried thoughts and feelings crucial to the exiting process. By reviewing all relevant information, offering emotional support as well as a variety of resources, the cult member is helped to make a
successful transition into society.

* * *

PART 6:

STAYING OUT

PART 6: CONTENTS

PART 6: *STAYING OUT*

When beliefs are shaken - - -
- - - it's difficult to start over.

Barbara Bruno Lancaster
Former Cult Member

Extricating a person from a cult does not end with a successful walk-away, deprogramming, or exit counseling. Rather, departure is the beginning of the process that has come to be known as rehabilitation. Some parents of cult-involved children may believe that a good counselor would teach their child whatever he or she needs to know to go back into the real world. We wish that this were true, but most deprogrammers and exit counselors limit their role to making the cult member understand the forces that acted on them and to see the destructive factors in cult involvement. In other words, a counselor may be able to get someone out, but not necessarily to keep him or her out.

What is Rehabilitation?

Does it work better away from the family and friends of the former member or within the home? **Paul Engel**, a former cult member, provides our initial definition of rehabilitation:

Rehabilitation means "to restore to a normal or optimum state of health, constructive activity, etc. by medical treatment and physical or psychological therapy." In this context, rehabilitation can involve all three modalities, although the emphasis rests in the psychological realm. Involvement in a destructive cult carries special considerations in regards to any form of therapy.

* * *

Ideally, rehabilitation has several aspects. First of all, it is a period for dealing with "floating" (slipping back into a cult-altered state of consciousness). Second, the professional counselor explains to the individual how he or she was manipulated. Finally, the counselor helps the person integrate the group experience into present and future plans.

Part of the former cult member's rehabilitation may involve coming to terms with pre-existing family problems. This is often easier to do in a neutral environment, such as a clinic, rather than in the home. After the person feels stronger, he or she may wish to return to his or her family.

During this transition period, it is important for the family to be patient, and to realize that rehabilitation takes time. If their expectations are too high or they expect change too soon, they can jeopardize the family member's progress.

We have found a growing awareness of the need for rehabilitation of former members, but this awareness does not seem to have been translated into action. Considering the number of people becoming involved with cults and the ever-increasing number of people leaving them.

Cults & Kids

* * *

Is there a Need for Rehabilation?

Deprogrammers/exit counselors usually do not provide social skills and job training, for successful re-entry into society. It is their job to help break the cult's grip on the person's mind after they are separated from the cult environment. What happens then must involve rehabilitation.

Although one might think that a former cult member would want to put as much distance as possible between himself or herself and the cult, this is not always the case. Emotional ties with the cult's leaders, its ideology, and companions still in the cult are very strong. Even when the former member knows that it is in his or her best interest to sever those connections, he or she may find this difficult. Anyone who has attempted to give up a destructive but somehow alluring habit or relationship can understand the ambivalence that a former cult member may feel at the prospect of breaking all ties with his former source of emotional support.

This excerpt from *Challenge of the Cults* explores the problems facing the recently departed cult member, and how friends and family can help:

No matter how they leave cults -- on their own, after a voluntary reevaluation, through a conservatorship, or by a kidnaping -- former cultists nearly always have intense difficulties reentering more conventional society. Having been taught to fear and despise the world outside the cult, former members need help in establishing a new and healthier way of looking at their personalities and their lives. They need vindication and reinforcement for their decision to leave the cult and the opportunity to experience warmth, community, and acceptance.

This is the kind of help that parents and friends can rarely provide without assistance. Some kind of more formal rehabilitation program is needed. Minimally, his might mean treatment by an understanding and well-informed therapist. Even more desirable are therapy groups where a number of former cult members can get together to share their experiences and reinforce one another in the effort to establish new lives for themselves. Especially helpful for young people who have just left the cults are several live-in rehabilitation centers that have been established in various parts of the country in the past few years.

Challenge of the Cults

* * *

Some more specific reasons why we can anticipate a difficult adjustment for former members coming back into general society are suggested in *Cults, Quacks, & Nonprofessional Psychotherapies*:

Many young adults joined cults at a time when they were in states of mild to moderate depression; were struggling with issues concerning school, marriage, and sexuality; or were in conflict with their families. Often, they felt concerned about an insufficient sense of meaning or purpose to their daily lives. Cult life, by contrast, provided a totalistic system, similar in thought reform (Lifton, 1961), that used all their energies, provided constant companionships, and made all the decisions for them. Consequently, they emerged from the cult experience as passive, acquiescing persons in need of support while learning to function independently again.

L.J. West & M. T. Singer

* * *

This excerpt from *Cults & Kids* offers a compassionate view of some other reasons why former cult members need supportive rehabilitation:

These people have a lot of guilt over some of the practices in fundraising, over the fact that they recruited a lot of people who are still back in the cult," says (Margaret) Singer. "I've interviewed people who have left two or three small children back in the cult and are feeling very confused about whether they should go back and try to get them out. They also feel very guilty about having censored the mail and phone calls, and having diverted friends and family of cult members in the past."

Overwhelming moods of depression and loneliness also often arise. Former members realize and regret the fact that they are out of step both in the job and social worlds. Some feel abused by their cult experience. Because most cults restrict all physical contact and pairing, many former members also have intimacy and sexual-growth difficulties. And leaving a cult means leaving behind loved ones--comrades who shared a special experience with you. Former members must quickly find new friends in a world that they have been led to believe is hostile.

Cults & Kids

* * *

Are there specific signs, physical or mental, that would indicate a former member is having trouble making an adjustment? This excerpt from *Destructive Cult Conversion* suggests signs to watch for:

Observations of recent cult-leavers reveal in each many of the following characteristics. Bear in mind, however, that changes engendered by conversion in any individual can only be judged with certainty if they are measured against the preconversion personality. In order to understand a person's conversion, therefore, it is absolutely necessary to gain as complete a personal history as possible.

Recent cult-leavers look depressed much of the time. Posture is frequently stooped, conversational gesturing sparse, speech slow, and responses to external stimuli - a shout, even a question - lag behind normal expectations. There is often a fixed, intense focus in the eyes which reflected as well in a certain rigidity of facial expression and body posture. This attitude is clearest when there is a shift in the subject or mode of conversation, when the interlocutor, for example, makes a humorous remark in an otherwise serious conversation. The former member's response suggests that he is non-plussed, that he has suspended overt reaction while slowly evaluating the new information.

Many cult-leavers are pale, especially those who have belonged to groups which enforce poor diets. Acne is also observed among those whom one would expect to have already passed beyond this typically adolescent complaint. There is an apparent indifference to physical appearance - dress and grooming - particularly among former members of cults which remove converts from most contacts with the wide community.

There is commonly an uncritical passivity to life as it flows around the former member. He has great difficulty making decisions, even about such matters as what clothes to wear each day, or what food to eat.

In addition, his response to stress varies greatly. When pressed by unpleasant ideas, or the need to make difficult decisions, he takes refuge in chanting or other rituals learned in the cult. Yet he may also at times respond to stressful interpersonal relationships with wild verbal and even physical abuse. Indeed, his social interaction, reflecting the variability of stress responses, is punctuated by behavior which reflects little discrimination and low tolerance for frustration: he or she leaps toward romantic involvement, for example, but just as quickly withdraws when the response is not nearly so fervent. Despite this generally labile reaction to post-cult experiences, many former members are consistently, or at least for a time, hypomanic immediately after leaving the group, seemingly intoxicated by the process of rediscovery and reconnection with old memories and associations.

Clark, Langone, Schecter, Daly

* * *

In larger cities, former members have formed self-help groups for rehabilitation. Other former members are joined by mental health professionals in working on their re-entry. Still others, using cult clinics (like the Los Angeles Jewish Family Service Clinic mentioned previously), are involved in group therapy with the families of current cult members; this assists them in better understanding their own experience. Finally, there is single-family therapy, in which the family of the former member joins him or her in working through problems which might have made them more vulnerable to cult recruitment. During therapy, family relationships may readjust to allow the former member to go on with his or her life. Group or family therapy might be undertaken to supplement time spent in a residential rehabilitation center away from home.

What Happens During Rehabilitation?

Although expensive, with but few centers available, the away-from-home center appears to be the most effective form of rehabilitation. Here is a description of the Norfolk Enrichment Center's process for rehabilitation of former cult members. This center is no longer open. It is presented as an example only; its practices may be different from other centers. This article was written by **Carla Pfeiffer**, former Director of the Center.

Rehabilitation is a self testing and study time for reflection and re-entry into the real world rather than the isolated, idealistic, simplistic world of the cults. The individual can begin to examine in depth his experiences and begin to put these into perspective in order to plan for future endeavors. He/she intellectually understands the situation from the four-day session [of deprogramming], but now needs time to process this change physically and emotionally. More changes will be seen during rehabilitation than during deprogramming. The length of rehabilitation depends upon the length of involvement within the group and their physical state of health. I will not take on case responsibilities without a commitment to a six week stay, which I have found to be the minimal adequate for average needs.

What occurs is a rapid progression through adolescent stages. The client is accustomed to a rigidly structured schedule maintained by guilt and fear of some mystical retribution for not being "perfect" for God. This dependency and lack of practice in making conscious decisions necessitates milieu counseling in a protected environment away from close friends and family. An hour or two a week in someone's office doesn't fill the tremendous need to have someone knowledgeable near for the many moment to moment situations and floating which occurs early in the rehabilitation. The family at this time is not very patient with an adult child who shows adolescent moodiness. I, of course, in small steps at first, encourage responsibility toward independence and mature growth. One must be extremely careful to avoid the tendency that the former cult member has to set the therapist up as the new leader and substitute another dependency system. The client must make all his/her own decisions in a supportive atmosphere that is in no way restrictive and is very patient and forgiving of silly mistakes. Doors are open and phones are free to access as are all types of study material and tapes in the library.

I have not found any interference by the cults of my home or the rehabilitation situation. At this point, the client has been deprogrammed and is voluntarily remaining for further help. Therefore, the cults do not want other members to contact these clients for fear of further defections. The client is also educated as to his/her vulnerability to loaded language and group contact because the usual tendency is to rescue a best friend or make contact to regain belongings too early in rehabilitation.

A former member rides a roller coaster of emotions during rehabilitation. He/she is dealing with a tremendous loss of friendships, group reinforcements and a heavy "life" commitment to a spiritual cause. Besides a grief and mourning period, anger, fears, and guilts must be worked through and understood before he/she can move ahead to recognize his/her own values and needs and to discover new goals. Spiritual concerns are obviously in great turmoil at this time and the ministerial association is ready to assist any personal exploration in this area. Heavy bible study and church attendance for the first three months is discouraged because many religious symbols which are used in a deviant way by the cults, now trigger floating moments or a change in conscious thought levels. I have often heard the statement that former cult members become cynical and abandon all religious commitment. I have not found this to be true with my clients. They do show a suspicion for organized groups - a healthy discrimination at this point; but they express a deeper spiritual commitment to God and most, after a period of time, feel comfortable returning to participate in their past denominational affiliations.

For a time the individual is highly critical and judgmental of others. To help with all these discussed areas of concern, a great deal of socializing is encouraged during the rehabilitation process. That is; shopping, sports, dancing, restaurants, movies, etc. in the midst of public interaction to test and regain his/her social skills that have been so badly disrupted by the cult group's standards and manipulations. Contact with other former members by phone and in person is another essential step to gain self-confidence by seeing others succeed and sharing common experiences. I try to include each client during this time in a deprogramming session. The client now sees the family's critical and difficult decisions to rescue, reviews anew the materials from a non-defensive position, and by reaching out to help another client, he/she begins to let go and move ahead emotionally and cease nurturing his/her own emotional wounds. Another activity that supports rapid growth is the sharing of experiences with the public in a preventive effort. I often take former members to speaking engagements and educational seminars that may occur during their stay. Generally news media interviews are delayed until the client is ready to leave, and is at the client's personal discretion, since I feel this interview during rehabilitation is a probing invasion of personal privacy and it often brings up issues the client has not yet processed in depth.

Carla Pfeiffer

* * *

Although rehabilitation is an important sequel to leaving a cult, the end of formal "rehabilitation" does not mark the end of the cult member's difficulties in readjusting to society. The cult experience continue to be a strong memory. Successful integration into society may be achieved through rehabilitation but we are convinced that a continuing support network is needed for those former members who may need further encouragement in readjustment. For example, the Cult Awareness Network sponsors FOCUS, a national support network for former cult members. Additionally, there is often a social stigma attached to former members which makes an already difficult transition even more painful.

So few professionals know anything about what happens to these people (former members). So many psychiatrists, psychologists, and social workers feel that cults are a passing fad. But they're so much more sophisticated and organized than that. Secondly, there's a tendency for professionals to say there's pathology - some kind of abnormal condition - in the youth. Also, professionals tend to say that there's psychopathology in the parents, and that if the parents weren't peculiar people the children would never join cults. There's this blaming of the victim and the victim's parents. We see this same blaming-the-victim done in rape cases.

Dr. Margaret Thaler Singer

* * *

No efforts have been made at all by society to accommodate people who have left cults. This failure must be corrected. Former cult members have told us that they might have left the cult sooner, had there been anywhere they could go for shelter, food, clothing. Women with children have an especially difficult time leaving a cult. Single persons can make it easier. A center, such as for battered wives, would be a real help. Single persons need help, too, for they leave with no money, clothing, or friends. Unfortunately a void still exists in providing both material and psychological assistance to those who want to leave or have recently left destructive cults. The clinics cannot serve all those in need, nor are they available in every part of the country. Anyone who wishes to combat destructive cults would do well to try to start a rehabilitation center or a support network for former cult members in their own community.

Henrietta Crampton

* * *

Many, including government officials, clergy, mental health professionals, and families of former members, are unaware of the commitment required to return a person back into mainstream society after a long exposure to a destructive cult. We encourage the reader to share this information within their own communities and to act on it -- asking mental health clinics to explore the problems of former cult members, participating in founding a clinic or rehabilitation center for former members, or in other ways they think will help those leaving cults.

* * *

Study Guide

For the Group:

1. Discuss how you might create an effective environment for rehabilitation of an former cult member. How does your environment compare with those discussed in this chapter?

2. Discuss how you think interaction of former members living together might be effective rehabilitation. Do you think there is any harm to this living situation?

3. Discuss when one can say that rehabilitation has succeeded? How long should it take?

4. Discuss differences you see between the problems of a former member in "normal" society and those faced by others trying to make it? What are they?

Supporting Articles

Any discussion of rehabilitation must include parents of former members. It is as important for the parents to understand their children's experiences (even adult children) as it is for the children to understand them. For this reason we have included an article by Chris Carlson, a former member of the Unification Church, entitled, *For Parents: What Now! ?*

Group Work with Former Cultists, by Lorna and William Goldberg, deals with specific forms of rehabilitative therapy.

For Parents: What Now! ?

Chris Carlson

Your son or daughter has just been through a deprogramming, has spent time at a rehabilitation center or has walked out of a cult. What do you do? This is a summary of cult influenced tendencies and post-cult characteristics that can occur regularly in an former member's life for as long as two years after leaving a cult. Of immediate interest here will be the first few months of this period. Not all will apply to your particular case. Of those that do, most will heal with time and care.

Your daughter or son's transition away from cult life can be difficult. This has been written to help you ease your difficulty while building effective communication and strengthening family ties. This is not to suggest that you take on the role of counselor or therapist, but that your awareness can greatly help the process of readjustment.

1. Your daughter or son is not inadequate.

Joining a cult does not indicate fault, flaw or lack of character. The best qualities in him/her were looked for and drawn on by the cult.

The attempt by members was to live a giving and loving life. Don't treat her/him as if it was an act of weakness or evil. Your offspring was a victim of his or her own idealism and desire for change in conjunction with the cult's indoctrination process. It is important to realize also that weaknesses, fears, insecurities and guilt potential are brought to the surface and nurtured by cults to foster dependence and the dissolution of the individual will. Your daughter or son will be trying to recover from this kind of gross manipulation.

2. Your son or daughter is not sick.

Early observations of former cult members by professionals caused some guesses about occurrence of schizophrenia. There is a cult personality working at odds with the normal personality. For a time this cult-induced persona/altered personality may be visible. Again, time usually takes care of this. Talking to former members, researching, understanding mind control and stepping back into a normal life, even slowly, have proven the best remedies. There are those that might need additional professional psychological or psychiatric care. These people, however, usually needed such care before they became involved with a cult.

Patience and support are the best of what you have to offer.

3. Floating.

Occasional states of confusion or disorientation may occur. The term floating usually refers to a reactivation of the cult indoctrination. Confusion may come from either the difficulties of getting readjusted or floating. These spells are usually minor, being taken care of by a shorter conversation or switching attention to something else. Most former members go through them; there's no need to be afraid of discussing these with your offspring. This state of mind usually doesn't indicate an impending return to cult life, but it can. Consult with the rehabilitation staff as well, for they know your case.

4. Former cult members may have trouble with decisions.

On a subconscious level, cult members have taken refuge from some of the troubling, big decisions in their personal lives. The cult has been making most decisions for them. For most, getting back into the swing of decision-making takes practice. For some it's just plain difficult at first. The ambiguities of everyday life may loom ominously. Be aware of progress. It may take longer than you think it should.

5.   Due to the possible extent of the rebuilding job . . .

. . . your daughter or son's decisions about future plans, values, etc. may seem hazy and slow in coming. Your patience will be helpful here. Former members need to be patient with themselves too. Helping him/her make concrete, step-by-step decisions at this point would be best.

6.   Sometimes an former member will just feel lost.

Without the cult structure, flurry and support there is an empty space. It takes a while to fill it. They might not know what to do with themselves for a while. Some go through depressions that seem to have no specific cause. Be watchful too of new crutches that may be developing. Another contributing factor is the discovery of having been misused and deceived. The pain often leaves a sense of void and vulnerability. Then again, some are just so relieved to be out that they can't wait to get going.

7.   Social relationships.

A former member may be limited, perhaps due to shyness, in making friends at first. Ordinary social conversation may be difficult. Your son or daughter has just been burned, so he/she may have some trouble with trusting for a while. Talking about much besides cult issues may be difficult. Talking about cult issues may be difficult. It may not be necessary to discuss any particular subject. Just be aware of possibilities.

8.   Self esteem.

Self esteem will usually be down due to the degradation and sublimation of the individual within cult lifestyles. At first, a sense of rootlessness and vacantness may also be the source.

9.   Values and beliefs.

These will probably be fragile and unestablished. Go gently, and don't impose your own. It takes some time for an ex-member to get a sense of her or his own values, perceptions and beliefs. The cult has had an extreme influence over these, primarily by replacing them with its own system. The replacement procedure used necessitates tearing down the individual's previous value/belief structure to shove in the new one. Add to this some time as a member, then, possibly via deprogramming, the realization of having been conned, indoctrinated and exploited; your son or daughter has been through the proverbial mill. For parents with particularly strong religious convictions – be careful. Cults use religion as an insidious tool. Pushing your brand too soon could be a detriment. Let your son or daughter decide, in time.

10. Compensation (and over-compensation).

Some want to start making up for lost time, so they party. Some will be even more cautious than before.

Beware of anti-cult fanaticism. It can be too consuming and a crutch, but many former members decide to speak out publicly or even help others to escape cults and do so in a healthy fashion. Variety of activities, especially ones unrelated to having been in a cult are a helpful part of the mix. Many ex-members need to rest awhile, and not be involved in too much planned activity.

11. Totalist, *all-or-nothing* tendencies may show up.

They've lived in a state of mind where good and evil have been determined in storybook simplicity, too black and white. Encourage thoughtful consideration and evaluation at this point.

12. They will probably be more sensitive to emotions, their own and yours.

They will probably have many intense feelings. The clarity and fervor of cult involvement fosters this. Their defenses tend to be down. They can be hurt more easily. They also tend to be more sensitive to others because of this. It's a vulnerable period. Your daughter or son may want to stay home a lot – maybe not.

13. Relationships with those of the opposite sex . . .

. . . or just the subject may be difficult, even traumatic, for an ex-member. Cults smash sex and intimacy, claiming moral certitudes, but in essence using these as tools for control. Since most cults treat sexual desire as one of the ultimate taboos, there tends to be an unhealthy residue of guilt which an former member carries. While it's often difficult for parents to discuss sex, especially with their adult children, it could be useful now. Re-establishing sexual values can be a very fragile matter.

14. Friends.

Past friends may not have matured in the same way as the former member but have gone ahead with their lives, leaving the ex-member behind. Both going into a cult and coming out of one traumatizes yet teaches. The situation can mature one surprisingly. Friends might not understand the nature of the ex-member's cult experience. Some will be dying of curiosity; some won't care much. Friends can play an important part in feeling like yourself again.

15. Keep open the possibility of calling or seeing other former members.

Sharing the experience is very important. Having someone who understands is very important.

16. Calling friends still involved with a cult.

This is probably too much for a long time. Talk about it with your child. Encourage safety first. Writing letters is a good option.

17. Don't be afraid . . .

. . . of your daughter or son finding positive aspects about having been in a cult. Many positive and fun things can happen while being a member. They also made many friends there. Keep it in perspective. It's better to understand the experience in its entirety, without having to rationalize positive aspects into negative ones. Such a measure is too much like cult practice.

18. Feeling wanted and accepted by one's family is a real boon.

Gentle reassurance can ease the sting of the feelings of emptiness. It's important to relate to your daughter or son as an adult with valid concerns, thoughts and feelings. Communication is crucial. Try to understand each other. Effort on both parts is important. Talk about the family. Share yourself, your thoughts, hopes and disappointments. They need to know you're human too. **Listen;** *really hear.*

19. You have suffered because of your daughter or son's involvement in the cult.

Perhaps you have gone to a great deal of trouble and expense to effect a rescue. It's important that you hold no resentment towards your daughter or son due to your difficulties. It wasn't done to get at you, even if it feels that way. If necessary, find another vent for these resentments. The future may afford you a chance to discuss them with your offspring.

Every parent probably feels somehow to blame for what happened. *It is not your fault.* The task of helping a ex- member get re-established will take love, patience, sensitivity and understanding It will be worth the effort.

It was almost two years before I felt the last significant cult effects wane. But this didn't prevent beauty, fulfillment and love from touching my life.

I have written this to acquaint you with some of the problems peculiar to post-cult readjustment. The information is based on my own experience coming out of the Unification Church, my work with 36 former members and their families, and the understanding love of my parents to whom I am eternally grateful for their actions in rescuing me from the hold of the Unification Church movement.

* * *

Group Work with Former Cultists

Lorna Goldberg and William Goldberg
Social Work, March, 1982

The authors co-lead a therapeutic group for former members of religious cults. In this article they describe the purposes and structure of this group, delineate three stages of the "Post Mind Control" syndrome, and suggest inventive techniques appropriate to each of these stages.

The techniques of sensory bombardment, sleep deprivation, and manipulation are used by many cults as a means of inducing a "forced conversion." (1) From their work with ex-cultists, the authors have found all these techniques operating in cults. However, it is not the purpose of this article to explain the methods used to induce suggestibility. Instead, this article focuses on a treatment method that the authors have used in helping former cultists.

Writers who have acknowledged the cultic state to be one of induced pathology, or mind control, generally point to the impotence of mental health professionals when confronted by this state. Schwartz and Isser, referring to the state of mind control as an "involuntary conversion," reported that:

> ... neither conventional traditional techniques nor platitudes appear to be appropriate for helping cult recruits or their families weather the storms that involuntary conversions arouse. (2)

Clark of the Harvard Medical School commented that:

> ... (mental health professionals) are relatively helpless to restore thinking processes (for cult victims) because under the current interpretation of the laws, we cannot maintain physical control long enough to bring about the confrontation therapies which might be effective in re-establishing the original personality style in the way it was done with the Korean War prisoners. (3)

The authors (hereafter referred to as *group leaders*) have also found that their professional skills could only be of limited help during the acute phase of mind control and during the phase of reality-inducing therapy (or "deprogramming"). They can offer helpful intervention, however, during the "Post Mind Control" phase, when the victim is attempting to put his or her cult experiences into perspective. The small support group described in this article, which was formed in River Edge, New Jersey, a suburb ten miles from New York City, proved to be an excellent medium for helping deprogrammed individuals to accomplish this end.

This group serves as a mechanism for bridging the gap between cult life and the outside world. It is now entering its fifth year of regular meetings. The group provides the ex-cultists an opportunity to discuss their cult involvement in a nonjudgmental, supportive atmosphere. Cult life has rarely been shared by friends and family members. Ex-cultists, therefore, find themselves alone when attempting to come to grips with their experiences in the cult, including cult seduction, entrance into a state of altered consciousness, life in the "totalistic" atmosphere (that is, action, thought, and experience must relate to the "mission"), the decision to leave the cult, and the struggle to resume self-determination. Through the support group's process, the ex-cultists recognize that their circumstances are not unique and that a reference group can smooth the difficult transition from cult life to life in the outside world. The reference group encourages emotional growth and independence in contrast to the regression and repression reinforced in the cult.

The entire group meets monthly, although smaller, less formal groups meet as the need arises. Meetings last for two and one-half to three hours and have consisted of as few as six individuals and as many as twenty-five. The typical pattern is for group members to attend two or three meetings immediately after the decision to leave the cult and to attend subsequent meetings occasionally. Although the cults use the group process to increase dependence in their members, one of the purposes of the support group is to encourage a sense of autonomy. Therefore, members are free to attend as many or few group meetings as they desire. A core of members who live in the New York metropolitan area attend almost every meeting. Approximately two hundred individuals, aged 17-36, representing fourteen different cults, have become involved in the group.

The meetings begin with a restatement of the group contract, which specifies that the group is limited to former cult members and that its purpose is to enable members to talk about their experiences as ex-cultists. It is not the purpose of this group to take political, social or educational stands regarding cults. Within the context of the meetings, such discussions are considered resistance to the sharing of feelings. Another important aspect of the contract with the group is the assessment of each group member to insure that he or she has indeed decided to leave the cult. Enforcement of this policy is necessary for several reasons. One of the purposes of the group is for the ex-cultists to be given the opportunity to share their feelings. Before this rule was instituted, when the group leaders accepted word-of-mouth referrals, the meetings would occasionally be attended by an individual who had not yet recognized the manipulation to which he or she had been subjected, that is, who still interpreted the entry into a state of altered consciousness as "Divine Intervention" rather than as a predictable response to group pressure, environmental bombardment, and heightened suggestibility. This new member would interrupt the group's discussion of the after effects of these phenomena and argue that his or her cult did not use these forms of manipulation or that the cult used them only in the service of the Lord. After this assertion, the other group members would shift their focus to a discussion of the new member's cult in an attempt to clarify the process of manipulation. Although this discussion would be enlightening to the new member and although the provocative statements were often made in an attempt to solicit these arguments, this shifting of focus would prevent the other group members from grappling with their own problems and concerns.

Furthermore, the presence of an individual who still exhibited the symptoms of mind control aroused the anxiety of the other group members. In particular, those individuals still in the first stage of the Post Mind Control syndrome would become excessively anxious because of their own fears of slipping back into the state of altered consciousness.

Finally, the presence of a nondeprogrammed individual in the group inhibited others who had left that cult from expressing their anxieties or fears. Cults and cultists often do not feel themselves bound by rules of confidentiality when measured against their "mission." Because the process of inducing mind control includes a sophisticated exploitation of an individual's emotional needs, to permit someone who may return to the cult to have knowledge of one's vulnerabilities could be self-destructive. For all these reasons, the group leaders have found it best to assure the group that they have assessed all fellow group members.

Ex-cultists will often try to get in touch with others who have decided to leave. They will suggest that the individuals call the group leaders for an assessment interview. Most deprogrammings are conducted by several former cultists, and there is a good chance that at least one member of the deprogramming team has been a member of the support group or is aware of the group. Most referrals, therefore, are from other group members or deprogrammers. The group leaders have also, on occasion, received referrals from colleagues who have heard of their work in this area.

Assessment Interview

In the assessment interview, the main goal is to measure the degree of the individual's freedom from mind control. Some of the symptoms in individuals who are under mind control include a stiff, wooden response to emotionally charged situations; a general lack of ability to think in reality-oriented terms, that is, every thought, decision, and action has a cosmic significance; an overwhelming sense of guilt when entertaining thoughts considered "negative" by the cult; and a need to use the "thought terminating cliche" when confronted with any information that does not fit into a simplistic black-and-white view of reality. (4)

Specifically, the group leaders ask interviewees how the cult appealed to them, why they stayed in the cult, and what prompted their decision to leave. They are concerned about individuals who show no evidence of inner struggle, who describe the deprogramming in a matter-of-fact manner (for example, "the deprogrammer told me I had been deceived. What he said made sense to me so I decided to leave."), or who see the cult, during this assessment stage, as completely bad. The decision to abandon a group with which one has established an absolute identification is not made so easily. There is usually a sense of loss and confusion coupled with a restorative desire to learn about the state of mind control and its initiation. Furthermore, an individual who "snaps," or shifts, from total love to total hate might be exhibiting a characteristic of mind control. (5)

To assess the ability of interviewees to deal with objective, concrete reality, the group leaders ask them about their plans for the future. A relatively symptom-free response would be similar to that of Fran L. who had left college to join a cult:

"I'm not sure exactly what I want to do now. I know that I want to help people in some way but I don't know how. I'll probably return to school full time. Maybe I'll take a couple of courses at the local college next semester. Then I'll make up my mind."

Individuals who respond to the preceding question in global, grandiose terms and who imply that they have infinite abilities and have boundless faith in their skills continue to exhibit a symptom of mind control, as the following example shows:

Joseph L., who was briefly involved with a cult modeled after Eastern religions, spoke of his intention to "explore other avenues of higher consciousness" and named several mass fad therapies that he intended to try out. He said, "I know there's an answer, and I will devote the rest of my life to finding it."

As a means of assessing the degree of the interviewee's guilt on leaving the cult, the group leaders ask the interviewee what his or her response would be to meeting a member of the cult on the street. An answer similar to, "I would be ashamed" or "I would rush up to him to tell him that I'm still a good person even though I've left," indicates a continuation of cultic thought reform. The interviewee continues to permit the cult to define standards of proper and improper conduct. An answer similar to, "I feel sorry for him" or "I would want to rush up to him to talk him into leaving," indicates that the interviewee has abandoned the cultic reference points.

Finally, it is important to mention that not every individual involved with a cult display symptoms that stem only from mind control. People who exhibit severe emotional pathology may yearn for the cult's rigid controls as a means of providing structure for their lives. These individuals, for the most part, do not remain in the cult because of the state of mind control but because they require a strict behavioral pattern that they can follow. Therefore, the adoption of the cult life as their framework was a restitutive attempt. These individuals are not accepted into the group; instead, individual psychotherapy is recommended as the treatment of choice. Their prognosis for remaining out of the cult is fair. However, the cults themselves often expel their deviant (and financially unproductive) members:

Stewart B., a 21-year old man with a cyclical manic depressive disorder, was expelled from his cult. One of this cult's practices is the receipt of messages from God that come in the form of visions. Stewart received a vision that told him that he was destined to marry the cult leader's daughter. He was expelled after breaking into her bedroom late one night. Although he has spoken with several deprogrammers, Stewart is troubled by recurrent obsessive thoughts about the cult. He cannot determine whether his vision was inspired by God or Satan. There is a small group of people who can leave the cult on their own, that is, without participating in a deprogramming process after they leave the cult. After having accepted the cult life for several years, they find that the cultic atmosphere no longer meets their needs. These individuals usually have attained leadership status and have, in effect, become the controllers. Therefore, they are able to use their minds and are able to see what they label as the hypocrisy of the cult. In the group leaders' experience, those people who struggle to regain their precult thought processes without undergoing deprogramming are more prone to feelings of extreme guilt and confusion after leaving their cult. Because they were leaders, they did not experience the humiliation of passivity and degradation as severely as other ex-cultists, and they tended not to loathe the experience as much as others. They, therefore, take longer to disavow the experience. (6)   The irony, then, is that although these individuals are healthy enough to grow out of the cult's control, it takes them longer than those who have undergone deprogramming to integrate the cult experience with their life in the outside world.

Recovery Process

The recovery process is viewed as a "Post Mind Control" syndrome. The group leaders have found that members of the group pass through three stages after their deprogramming and that they manifest specific behavioral characteristics within each stage. As such, each stage requires a different treatment focus.

Stage 1:   Initial Post-deprogramming.

This stage commences with the completion of deprogramming and usually lasts from six to eight weeks. Although the ex-cult members begin to sever their emotional bonds to their cults during this stage, residues of the imposed personality remain stamped on them. When they entered the cult, they were forced to abandon old emotional ties (to their family), and their personality took on a new cast as the cult leader became the identified "parent." Their physical demeanor often bespeaks their cult. For example, individuals who were in cults that focus on subservience to the spiritual leader keep their heads bowed and speak in a quiet, meek manner. Women who were in cults that emphasize sexuality as a lure for new members are seductive. And those who were in cults that emphasize contact with spirits through constant meditation appear to be "other worldly."

Almost all the ex-cultists appear to be much younger than their chronological age and display an asexual innocence. They act childlike although they may be well into their twenties. Indeed, during their time in the cult women often stop menstruating and men's beards grow more slowly. During the initial postdeprogramming stage the ex-cultists regain their secondary sexual characteristics.

During this stage, group members focus on the effect that their life in the cult has had on their cognitive abilities. Those who remained in cults for many years and did not achieve a leadership position experienced what initially appears to be a diminished ability in the areas of perception, decision making, discrimination, judgment, memory, and speech. The ex-cult member's cognitive abilities have been repressed because the cults encourage and reinforce passivity, conformity to the cult, and following by rote. The following case demonstrates this point:

Edward C., a graduate from an Ivy League university, was a member of a cult for two years. After leaving the cult, he was unable to read a newspaper for several months. His inability to focus his mind provoked anxiety, which made him withdraw by falling asleep whenever he tried to read.

Speech during this first stage is monotonous, colorless, and halting. Emotionally charged words have taken on new meaning or have fallen away completely. Because the cult forces its members to follow passively the will of their leaders, ex-cult members often have difficulty making decisions for themselves, as the following example demonstrates:

Sara P., a 26-year-old woman who had lived for six months in a communal cult, described her initial inability to make decisions. When she went to a restaurant with her family and her deprogrammer, she stared at the menu for several minutes and asked each person around the table what they thought she should order. When they did not give her direction, she began to cry.

Cults adversely affect their members' ability to judge situations. Most of the cults teach that life is controlled by other-worldly forces, thus further encouraging passivity. The memory of cultists fades, particularly with respect to their "physical" families. Cultists often acquire new names and new birthdays to parallel their new identities and learn a cliche ridden language.

In group meetings the fears of ex-cult members, especially the fear of returning to a trancelike state, are discussed. This condition, called "floating" appears to be a conditioned response. In the cults, the nerves of members were constantly on edge because of the need to insure that their perceptions did not conflict with the cult's doctrine. They were often in a state of altered consciousness that was similar to a trance. By hearing a key word, a phrase, or a song, the ex-cultists may suddenly reenter the state of altered consciousness. Clark reported that:

"It is regularly observed for some time after the deprogramming affected individuals are very vulnerable. For about a year and especially during the first few weeks to two months they feel themselves aware of or close to two different mental worlds. Their strong impulses to return to the cult are controlled by logical reasoning processes and the great fear of someone taking control of their minds from the outside once again. During this time a former convert can quickly be recaptured either by a fleeting impulse or by entering a trance state through a key word or piece of music or by chanting or by a team from the cult." (7)

Singer observed that floating can be helped by speaking simply, clearly, and directly to the individual. This method of communication stands in contrast to the cults' use of global and abstract language. By focusing on concrete here-and-now realities, the ex-cultist can be helped to stop the sense of depersonalization that takes place during the floating episode. (8)

Former cultists who have left cults that imbued everyday objects with symbolic overtones are particularly prone to floating. The degree of floating also appears to be connected with the ego strength of the individual. Those people who feel themselves powerless and controlled by outside forces are more likely to float than those who feel strong enough to resist pressure to return to the cult environment.

Guilt plays a major role in the initial reentry stage. In the cult, members are generally taught that the outside world is an evil whirlpool seeking to suck them into the sins of worldly pleasure. The only place that they are safe is within the confines of the cult. They are often told "horror stories" of the terrible things that befall people who leave the cult:

In a group meeting, Bobbie U. who was a member of a cult for three years, told of hearing stories about Sam J when he left the cult. She turned to Sam (who was her deprogrammer and who was attending the meeting) and said, "I was told that you were a debaucher and that you were taking pills and alcohol. I was told that you were sleeping in flophouses and had completely abandoned God." During this stage, former cultists often feel overwhelmed by guilt without always understanding why they feel guilty. At times, their behavior is a manifestation of guilt. For example,

Fran L, who was a member of a cult for a one-year period, would wake up in the middle of the night for several weeks after her deprogramming and feel the need to scrub the kitchen floor on her hands and knees. She could not explain why she felt it necessary to perform this act.

Other individuals fear punishment for leaving the cult. For example, they fear that the airplane they will ride in will crash or that their parents will be hit by cars. Nightmares are not unusual during the first few months after leaving the cult.

The ex-cult members are also filled with self-doubt during the first stage. What they thought was the "most correct" decision in their lives (that is, the decision to join the cult) proved to be a tragic mistake. They fear what will happen as they make other life decisions, sometimes projecting their fears onto others:

Betty J., who was a member of a cult for one year, described her fears about her parents. "I'm glad they decided to deprogram me; but I'm afraid that now they won't let me make any decisions on my own, that they will watch over me like they did when I was in high school instead of treating me like an adult."

Another overwhelming feeling during the initial stage is that of loneliness. In the cult, one is constantly surrounded by others, rarely left alone, and is thus overstimulated. Every minute is accounted for and every day is structured. Each move the individual makes has a significance that is given by God, and the day-to-day lives of all cultists are suffused with the knowledge that they are personally serving the Messiah (or the living God or the perfect person). Upon leaving the cult, time is neither totally structured nor monitored. The state of not being invaded and not requiring a merging with the cult can be lonely. Because the ex-cultist's need for dependence is no longer fulfilled, the focus of the support group is to encourage new relationships in which intimacy can occur but in which the integrity and sense of self of the individual can be preserved. Those ex-cultists who find being alone most troublesome have often discovered through psychotherapy that part of the cult's appeal stemmed from a desire to escape from a sense of loneliness that developed in early childhood.

A grief reaction follows the loss of a way of life and of a leader who promised total fulfillment. Former cultists often describe feelings of disappointment and sadness because their dreams of a perfect world have been broken. While in the cult, they felt as if they were omnipotent as a result of their merging with an omnipotent leader. The support group helps them to understand that their sadness is a natural reaction to the loss of this sense of omnipotence. The group encourages its members to gain positive feelings from their own accomplishments rather than from their subjugation to a powerful other.

Through the group, members are helped to see their periods of feeling empty, lost, doubtful, and sad as normal and acceptable rather than as evidence of their "fallen nature." This acceptance of a wide range of feelings stands in contrast to the cults' demand that their members must constantly feel good as evidence of their having achieved a superior state of spirituality.

During the search for a perspective that is different from that of the cult, the former cultists often appear to be submissive and compliant. They respectfully focus on the words of a speaker. This behavior parallels their submissiveness in the cult. An example of such behavior occurred in one of the first meetings, when almost all the group consisted of people who had just left cults. As the group leaders sat down to begin the meeting, several of the members pulled out pads and pencils as if they were about to hear a lecture. They hung on to every word. This behavior made the group leaders feel their tremendous power in relation to the former cultists. The group leaders shared their feelings with the ex-cultists, who, in turn, were able to relate their behavior to their experiences with cult leaders. They told the ex-cultists that they were unable to give them "answers" but would encourage them to find their own way, relying on their own resources. Finding one's own way means disagreeing with other views expressed in the group. The group leaders actively encourage group members to feel free to express differences of opinion. This freedom contrasts sharply with the conformity paramount in cult groups.

As mentioned earlier, individuals who do not participate in the deprogramming process after leaving their cults generally have more difficulty placing their experience into perspective than those who undergo deprogramming. In the former, behavior characteristic of the first stage can last for several years.

Stage 2: Re-emergence.

This stage usually begins one to two months after the deprogramming progress and lasts for approximately six months to two years. It is characterized by reemergence of the precult personality. Within six months, most ex-cult members no longer appear to be depleted individuals, that is, their speech, personality, and physical demeanor become more appropriate for their age.

As the ex-cultists regain their self-esteem and a sense of their abilities, aggressiveness is externalized and released against those who failed to fulfill their promise of a perfect world. Those who, three months earlier, has described the cult leader as sincere but misguided now attack him or her as a monster. During the second stage, there is often a crusade against the cults, a flurry of activity that may include activity as a deprogrammer or making public speaking appearances condemning cults.

The group leaders react to this anger by reminding the group member that nothing is all good or all bad, in contrast to the duality portrayed by cults. They have found it helpful to focus on the positive elements of cult life during this stage. For example, they point out that group members learned they could push their bodies to the limit and survive long working hours, that they could influence others in their fund-raising efforts, and that they could live through the wrenching experiences of cult life and yet emerge. Seeing the world in shades of gray helps cut into the polarization that cults reinforce. (Some ex-cult members describe a tendency to use defensive splitting prior to their involvement with the cult. This defense, in fact, often led to their easy acceptance of the cult's view of the world.) One of the major goals during the second stage, then, is to raise the ex-cultists feelings of self-esteem by helping them to see that life in the cult was not a total waste.

During this period, ex-cult members also describe the testing out of previous "pleasures" that were seen as negative or selfish by the cult. Guilt about having left the cult dissipates as the hold of the cult diminishes:

Alice F., an actress who had ended her involvement with a cult seven weeks earlier, joined a health spa to shed the twenty pounds that she had gained while involved with the cult. She felt tense while in the cult because she had been told that her concern about her figure was Satanic vanity. After leaving the cult, she began to wear make-up again and decided to let her hair grow. It had been cut short while she was in the cult.

Another area of concern is related to feelings, about intimacy and authentic relationships with others. The cult encouraged the display of love for the leader but discouraged other emotional attachments. If one became sexually aroused by another person in the cult, feelings of shame would emerge. After leaving their cult, group members often found it difficult to enter into an intimate, fulfilling relationship without feeling ashamed and selfish. Former cultists, in describing their feelings, often learn that their anxiety about sex, which is implicit in intimate relationships, was a factor that led them to the "safety" of a religious cult. As the ex-cult members emerge from the submissive, passive states that were evident in the first stage, they sometimes describe conflicts with their parents arising from the overprotective behavior of their parents.

As the former cultists test out their independence during the second stage, their parents, fearing their reentry into the cult, may react in an overprotective fashion. Typically, parents of ex-cultists are concerned about signs indicating that their children may be thinking about rejoining the cult. It is possible that growing up in an overly protective environment rendered the young adults vulnerable to a naive acceptance of the cult's promise of a perfect world. Furthermore, by joining the cult, dependent young adults were able to escape from their families' anxiety about their initial steps toward independence. Theories of individual vulnerability, however, must also consider the state of induced pathology and mind control that the cults manage to achieve.

During the second stage, the ex-cult members shift their focus from integrating their experiences in their own minds to deciding how to deal with others. Group members often describe their extended families as treating them as if they were made of porcelain. At family functions, relatives will gingerly approach the ex-cultists and nervously talk about "safe" subjects, avoiding any mention of the past few years or months. The group leaders usually advise the ex-cultists to bring up the subject of their life in the cult as a means of clearing the air (for example, "I guess you're wondering about my years in the cult and my deprogramming. Why don't you ask me whatever is on your mind"?). There is usually a sigh of relief and a flood of questions from the relatives. This kind of dialogue is almost always necessary before the former cultists can resume their relationships with their families.

Another problem that confronts ex-cultists during this period is that of dealing with "missing" years on job applications. Here, again, the group leaders recommend that the former cultists focus on the skills that they learned in the cult. While involved with cults, some of the group members ran restaurants, taught children, printed newspapers, baked cookies and bread, built houses, or cooked for large numbers of people. All these are marketable skills. If nothing else, most former cultists have learned that they can work at a given task for fourteen hours a day, seven days a week.

Stage 3: Integration.

This stage usually begins six months to two years after leaving the cult. At this point, the former cultists have integrated their cult experience into their lives and no longer require the group's help. They no longer primarily identify themselves as ex-cultists and have become involved in relationships that do not revolve around anticult activities, as the following example demonstrates:

Fred B., who had been a member of a bizarre "scientific" cult for three years and who had been deprogrammed ten months earlier, announced to the group that he was seriously dating a young woman who had not been involved in a cult. "Before I met M., I never thought I could be serious about a girl who hadn't been in a cult. I felt that she wouldn't be able to understand me. M. and I find other things to talk about, though."

During the third stage, the former cultists are able to become involved in future-oriented goals rather than in attempts to understand their cult involvement. Most of them have either reentered school or are working in more traditional jobs than deprogramming. Individual psychotherapy may be indicated as a tool to help them focus on the factors in their personalities that made them vulnerable to the cult's manipulations. The former cultists who had completely cut themselves off from society or who had been involved in one of the more bizarre cults have the greatest difficulty reentering life outside the cults. Those who continued to use their ego strengths, often by rising to a position of authority within the cult, are the most successful in integrating the cultic experiences with their lives in the outside world. Thus, paradoxical as it may seem, individuals who have been involved in cults for relatively long periods of time and who have been deprogrammed sometimes have the fewest problems regaining their ability to function outside the cult.

Summary

The support group proved to be an excellent medium for helping former cultists readjust to society. The group provides its members with an opportunity to discuss their cultic involvement with others who have similar experiences and, by reinforcing healthy self-assertion and interpersonal relationships, supports them in their effort to overcome the aftereffects of cultic involvement. The group also provides a network of people who can offer advice and experience to those individuals who are having difficulty.

This article has delineated three stages of the Post Mind Control syndrome through which former cultists pass. The first stage is usually marked by blandness, self-doubt, confusion, and depression. During this stage, the group can be helpful by supporting the individual's decision to leave and by helping the individual recognize the lingering aspects of cultic thinking. The second stage is marked by the reemergence of the precult personality. The former cultist often feels a need to undo the cultic experience and embarks on a crusade against the cult. The group helps during this period by accepting different points of view. It also calls attention to the entirety of the cult experience. That is, despite the many negative aspects of cult life, most individuals made some gains and learned some skills. The final stage is that of integration. Former cultists have now moved on with their lives and are able to see the cult experience as a temporary diversion from their life's work. The group's usefulness to the former cultist has, at this point, waned, and individual psychotherapy is the treatment of choice for those who still experience the aftereffects of cultic involvement.

Notes & References:

(1) For a discussion of these techniques, see Christopher Edwards, *Crazy for God* (Englewood Cliffs, NJ: Prentice-Hall, 1979); Carroll Stoner and JoAnne Parke. *All God's Children* (Radnor, PA: Chilton Book Co., 1977); and Ronald Enroth. *Youth, Brainwashing and the Extremist Cults* (Grand Rapids, MI: Zondervan Publishing House, 1977).

(2) Lita Linger Schwartz and Natalie Isser, *Psychohistorical Perspective of Involuntary Conversion*, Adolescence. 14 (Summer 1979). pp. 351-359.

(3) John Clark, *Destructive Cults: Defined and Held Accountable*, (Mimeographed by the author, 1976), p. 10.

(4) For a discussion of the "thought terminating cliche," see Robert Jay Lifton, *Thought Reform and the Psychology of Totalism* (New York: W. W. Norton & Co., 1963), p. 429.

(5) Flo Conway and Jim Siegelman, *Snapping: America's Epidemic of Sudden Personality Change* (New York: J.B. Lippincott Co., 1978).

(6) The authors are grateful to Emily Schachter, Associate Director of Children's Services, Rockland County Community Mental Health Center, Pomona, New York, for this insight.

(7) Clark, op. cit., p. 11.

(8) Margaret Singer, "Coming Out of the Cults," *Psychology Today*, 12 (January 1979), p. 79.

PART 7:

LOOKING BACK

PART 7: CONTENTS

PART 7 - *LOOKING BACK*

When you meet the friendliest people you have ever known, who introduce you to the most loving group of people you've ever encountered, and you find the leader to be the most inspired, caring, compassionate, and understanding person you've ever met, and then you learn that the cause of the group is something you never dared hope could be accomplished, and all of this sounds too good to be true -- it probably is too good to be true! Don't give up your education, your hopes and ambitions, to follow a rainbow.

-- **Jeanne Mills,**
former member of the People's Temple and
subsequent victim of assassination.

With the fervor from negative aspects of cult involvement, it is sometimes easy to forget that no issue, even cults, is "black and white." It may be necessary for the parent of a cult member to see cults as *all bad* in order to justify the decision to extricate a child from such a group. However, this attitude is counter productive, because it limits one's perception of what the cult is and why the person may have become involved. We need to look at the experiences of those who have passed through cults to find out why they stayed in.

We blame much of the cult member's desire to stay in the cult on the indoctrination process, but that is not the only reason. Many times people, following a quest for spiritual satisfaction, have found themselves caught in a cult. People on the outside may disparage both the quest and the involvement, but such *seekers* often emerge from cults telling of authentic (by their standards) religious and spiritual experiences which came to them while they were involved.

We wish to emphasize that the Commission on Cults and Missionaries is not opposed to religious and spiritual quests or experiences; we support them as essential parts of human existence.

With this in mind, we have several former cult members looking back on their experiences just prior to, during, and following their time in the cults. Their responses point out reasons for staying, what they gained from participating, and perhaps can teach us something about the shortcomings of our own institutions.

Barbara Bruno Lancaster, Former Cult Member

In 1972, I joined a study group. In 1984, I woke up to find that I had willingly given away my life -- for 12 years -- under an illusion that I was making myself a better person and the world a better place to live in. This wasn't a dream, I was in a cult.

That sounds pretty drastic. How could anyone let themselves get hooked into such a situation? I was then 27 (hardly a child). Now I must take responsibility for *not having taken responsibility.* I was a thinker, an artist, a reader who envied the people in history who were lucky enough to live in times where there were opportunities to become part of a movement that made a contribution to humanity. I wanted to understand "what makes us tick," but found no answers in modern psychology. Perhaps there was an elusive ancient knowledge that I might discover today. I feared a wasted life, and doubted my ability to live self-directedly.

In 1972, I wished to study a psychology called *The 4th Way,* which is based on the early 20th century writings of George Gurdjieff and Peter Ouspensky. This philosophy proposes an esoteric system of achieving a permanent higher level of consciousness and stresses the need to find a "real" 4th Way school led by a consciously-developed teacher. After finding a bookmark from a group (I will call it the "SOS"), I attended a series of prospective student meetings and came into contact with people who certainly *acted* esoteric. They were speaking knowledgeably on a subject of great interest to me. I was asked to try a few of the school exercises in behavior modification, and felt awkward and stupid around the students. I couldn't believe that they wanted me to join! I made the first in a series of monthly donations, and then was directed to a silent, seemingly ineffectual man in the corner, whom they referred to as "The Teacher."

Within a few weeks, I had moved from my home in Hawaii and was living with other students in a house in Carmel, California. For six months I had little contact with anyone outside of the group. The Teacher and his inner circle of leaders took over the house to work on a book and hold meetings. My activities centered on a constant exposure to his words and to carrying out the directions of his leaders. There were mental exercises to be followed in all waking hours, i.e., words that we were to eliminate from our speech; not using contractions; not crossing our legs and physically moving in a manner that indicated intentionality (we looked like robots). When one could begin to adjust to an exercise, it would be changed. I now spoke only in the special "work language" of the school. For five years I followed a word exercise that forbade the use of the word "I." One was to refer to themselves only in the 3rd person. (Try ordering a meal without using "I.") We were used to hearing each other speak, but our special language added to the discomfort of outside communication.

The aim was a heightened state of awareness in which one could regard oneself objectively as a *machine-like being*. Man existed in a state of walking sleep and needed constant shocks in order to awaken to his real potential. My words, reactions, physical appearance, and basic character were always open for discussion by the others. My behavior and attitudes were constantly observed and classified as indications of a "good" student or a 'bad" student. This was always done as suggestions for my own good. I was not supposed to express negativity.

This environment was not all unpleasant. There was a strong feeling of community, a sense of purpose, of spiritual fulfillment, and a *new state of awareness* of the world that was exhilarating. There were times when I felt that I was losing control of my mind. This was taken care of by taking me for a walk where another student would softly remind me that this was simply a stage in my development, and that confusion itself was really a high state. There was a kindness and humility among the lower ranks of students that made me feel accepted. I was approaching all of this as a one-year experiment in self-knowledge.

Three months after joining this "study group", a special meeting was called and it was announced that a woman who had left the school had committed suicide. This was seen as an example of what happens when students do not value the knowledge they have been exposed to. The school had become a lifetime endeavor! (Only for those who were strong enough to succeed.)

We were *now* told that there were invisible higher level beings, called "C Influence" that were around us constantly and would provide shocks to remind us of their presence. When something pleasant, or unpleasant, occurred it was said to be C Influence, providing shocks to awaken me from my lowly state. C Influence spoke directly through the Teacher, and to question this was considered a manifestation of a low level of being. *We had been chosen* to become the enlightened people who would found a new civilization after a soon-to-come nuclear holocaust. **Please remember, this was said in an insulated environment.** I began to think that I was constantly being watched and that even my thoughts were subject to judgement by these "higher forces." Lifton refers to this as the "psychology of the pawn."

When my savings ran out, I began working again in ordinary life and found that there was a profound distance between myself and my co-workers who were not part of the school. I was quiet and just did my work. My "real" life was elsewhere, and I was thoroughly committed to it.

Although the school control never succeeded in becoming absolute, my ability to measure reality and to maintain personal atonomy was greatly diminished. In George Orwell's *1984*, he saw this regulating restraint as being accomplished by means of the 2-way telescreen. But a mechanical device is not necessary when one is sufficiently surrounded by "human" apparatus.

The world became divided into black & white. Ideas, feelings, and actions consistent with school policy were praised. Inconsistencies were explained as a waste of my precious time and an incorrect valuation of the opportunities that had been extended to me. Policy was changed over the years, but an unwavering demand was placed upon me to strive permanently for a perfection which did not exist. I became guilty and depressed. *I was no longer working for something --I was fighting against myself.* Guilt always followed a self-observation, and my repressed negativity could be expressed through complaints about my attitudes. I wanted to "confess" my awareness of a personal failing before someone else could point it out it out. The more I admitted to weakness, the easier it was to judge others.

I was the enemy! I began to think that I just wasn't capable of knowing myself. Other people's opinion of me was "real." The school became a living being and I was just a cell in it. *The group was more important than me.*

I became a "master of justification." Former cult members all say that they had doubts throughout their involvement. My misgivings became a closely guarded secret, unbearable to admit, even to myself. I developed subtle ways of rebelling, but outwardly I towed the party line. This core of doubt looked for an open door, and I lived in fear of finding it. *It was Catch-22.*

I sided with the liberal-wing of the school, who felt that they could bring about a more humanizing element, and perhaps ensure their own survival. Yet, too often, I took no action against injustice, deceit, and outright bullying by the Teacher's appointed leaders, whose power he supported. I watched children being given away when the Teacher decided they were unecessary distractions. Relationships and marriages were broken at his suggestion. The rich were courted and fleeced. The 10% of gross salary for monthly donations rose with an ever-rising list of required special donations. It was almost impossible (both financially, and as proof of commitment) to live outside of a communal situation. Within a "teaching house" there was little or no room for deviation or personal expression. We were an intellectual and cultural group, but the form this took was always at the whim of the Teacher's taste. He wanted us to become an 18th century culture (imagine a woman's place in such a society), and a large part of funds went to his antique purchases (the finest works went to his home).

Eventually the group had centers in most major cities in the U.S., Europe, and Mexico. The Teacher got the school a State Charter as a Church. He established a winery on the school property in Northern California as a non-profit corporation. We were expected to spend weekends and vacations working at the headquarters. Those with especially high levels of "valuation for the work" lived and worked there full-time. There was no housing provided. People lived crowded together in houses outside the grounds, or in trailers, or slept under a table and kept their belongings in their car trunk. But on Saturday night, they wore tuxedos and gowns to the concert hall, where prestigious musicians would play to an audience who would overwhelm them with applause at the appropriate moments.

In the "SOS" an attitude of *them-versus-us* **prevailed.** The outside world was dead. Apparently, people who knew too much about the secret activities of the Teacher had been given direct tasks not to tell the others. You were asked to leave if you broke a task. If you left the school you were ostracized.

I was happily married to another student, whom I trusted with some of my doubts. We had a little mixed-breed dog who was very precious to us. I came close to a nervous breakdown in 1980 when the Teacher declared that we could only have pedigreed animals. I began to realize how much control the Teacher had over anything I cared about. I saw only two choices: become quietly insane (as others had), or commit suicide. I could not imagine having the strength to leave the school. My husband Ronald suffered greatly in his fear that I was losing my commitment. He began defending me to people who were offering him advice about changing my behavior. We became part of a developing underground of discontent where small confidences were shared. In time, an ethical member of the Board of Directors discovered criminal actions and called for public censure of the Teacher. This information was strong enough to penetrate through to what was left of my self-respect, and I could not offer a single justification. Even then, I thought that things could now change for the better. A meeting was called, by a representative of the Teacher, to discuss the situation. I brought up my concerns: Students were not free to seek help from mental professionals; many were becoming alcoholics, and we were, generally, living in a state of fear. I was told that *these problems were my imagination and the fear was only within me.* **I snapped!**

I left the group – after 12 years. I felt helpless. I had no friends and was deeply in debt. I couldn't explain the lost years. To the outside world a cult experience itself indicates a flawed mentality. I grieved for those left behind, imprisoned by their learned ability to accept the unacceptable. Ronald, myself, and a few others felt marooned on a strange shore, cringing, clinging, and finally, setting out to discover our new world.

Within a few months, we became part of a former cult members group at the Cult Clinic in Los Angeles. The Clinic was a flame burning in my dark night. I will always be grateful for their understanding. What has been most helpful is hearing that ex-members share the same experience even though the form of each group is different. *What cults believe is not important* (it may be truth or nonsense). The key indication of danger lies in an insulated organization that lacks a system of checks and balances.

I choose to believe that the positive things I retain from my experience are a credit to the sincere relationships I once shared, to my abiding faith in the goodness of God and nature, and to my own intelligence and self-respect.

However, I did not gain this from the "SOS," but rather, in spite of it.

Most ex-cult members do not speak out. Many never realize they were in a cult. They just leave one day, and eventually look for something else to replace it. My activities in cult awareness -- reading, writing, lecturing, and creating publications -- are looked upon as extreme by some of the people who left the school with me.

The most common reaction to my story is: "Well, that could never happen to me!" I've met with a lot of former members and they are not stupid. Most are highly intelligent. The newer groups are especially appealing to the well-educated. Recruitment is directed to the best, the brightest, and the most idealistic of persons. **Every cult member is a recruiter whose sincerity is infectious.** *Please note:* Because cult members can only associate with people inside the group, they will see outsiders purely as potential recruits or losers. I did not feel I "recruited" my mother and my life-long friend when they joined the "SOS" at my encouragement -- I wanted to "help" them down the one true path.

Mind control exists -- it produces an inability to act from one's own integrity. Brainwashing is spiritual rape. **Remember:** No one ever thinks they are joining a cult.

Barbara Bruno Lancaster

* * *

Ellen Berlfein
Former Six-Year Member of the Unification Church

I always imagined life would be good once I could live out in the country and not have to be concerned with what I thought was the disgusting city life. I would often have romantic fantasies of an idyllic life.

Upon graduating high school I immediately moved up to a small town on the coast of Washington. I chose to go to a college there which would allow me to live out my hoped-for dreams. Through classes such as beekeeping, organic gardening and bird watching I got to taste what "getting back to the land" was like. I remember one day, I was bicycling around the lake where I lived, exploring the country roads. Everything was as I'd hoped for, except for the feeling inside that this beautiful country life just didn't fulfill me. I began to desperately search within for "what has meaning, what has value?" How could I help to make the world a better place and realize my own creative potential? **I want to dedicate my life to something, but what's worth being dedicated to?**

After spending two years at this school, I left to find something new. I spent some time at several craft schools, developing skills in weaving, pottery and woodworking, but still I was restlessly looking for more. I decided to go back to college, this time in Santa Rosa, California. It was a choice primarily out of default. I spent the first day of school anonymously making my way through the crowds and at the end of the day, while waiting to make a phone call, the girl waiting next to me started up a conversation.

"At last, someone sees that I'm alive," I thought to myself. She explained that she lived on a 600-acre farm in Mendocino with a small group of friends who called themselves, "Creative Community Project." As one of their community projects, they were providing a free dinner which would take place the coming Friday in a nearby park, and I was welcome to join them. I liked Diana, this young woman, right away. Her soft, warm and sincere manner reminded me of myself. Although I only conditionally accepted her dinner offer, the Creative Community Project already sounded like the fulfillment of my dreams.

Friday night arrived after a week of frustrations and disillusionments and with nowhere else to go for dinner, I ended up joining 20 or 30 people gathered in the park. As I approached their campfire, I heard them all singing camp songs, songs for peace, and songs for finding your dream. My heart swelled. They adorned me with compliments and smiles. Some of the smiles were too big and the insincerity bothered me, but the kindness and concern couldn't help but touch me somewhere inside. After dinner, the leader told a short philosophical story. Realizing that this group of people was not only concerned with daily life, but also pursuing deeper questions, enticed me all the more. **The Unification Church, and religion in general, was not even mentioned.**

I was invited to come to a special seminar on their farm in Boonville that weekend. They assured me that I'd have time to get my homework done, so I said I would come. As we drove through the dark night for several hours, I felt I was being carried away into another time, another dimension. We arrived at the farm, where the women were led to a small trailer where one needed a magnifying glass in order to find room to roll out a sleeping bag. I awoke early the next morning, to find myself in the midst of 200 others.

The rest of the weekend was an intense whirlwind of activities and emotions (I certainly never remembered my homework). We were divided into groups of ten, each group with a leader. The day began with individuals in my group (members of the community setting the tone) sharing about their lives prior to joining the Family (as they referred to the Unification Church). Their stories all reflected their search for meaning, love, and happiness in life. After many disillusioning paths, each member of the Family was certain that here they had finally found the perfect road. Their stories sounded similar to my own, and their conviction to the Family couldn't help but captivate me.

After the first group meeting, everyone gathered together to hear a lecture. The weekend continued with lectures and group meetings until Sunday night. The family members were usually ecstatic with joy, or overcome with tears after each of the lectures. It made you feel like only a stone-hearted person wouldn't react with that same intensity of emotion. These animated presentations basically declared that by overcoming our evil selfish thought and actions, we could create a unified, happy, healthy, God-centered world. The Family was pioneering this road, which meant that all members would have to sacrifice themselves more, in order to make it easy for all those that would follow.

I'd lived in beautiful places with lots of people before, but no other environment encapsulated so many of the qualities I thought I was looking for. On the farm everyone totally invested themselves in the community goal, whether that goal be farm maintenance, cooking, or listening to a lecture. Everywhere else that I lived, either the community divided into factions or people were lazy and irresponsible. Rarely had I seen people actively commit themselves to helping the whole group accomplish a goal.

Although country living had always attracted me, I felt the seclusion would be neglecting my social responsibility. After a weekend on the farm, it appeared that the Family had a noble purpose behind their country life. They claimed that Boonville was created as a model community, which would some day inspire the whole world. So by joining the Family, I would not only get the country life, cooperative living, and satisfied social conscience, but **every action of my life would have the ultimate meaning – I'd be saving the world and attaining my own perfection.**

I stayed in Boonville for about a month. I think I can say I'd never been happier … feeling every dream had finally come true (I'd often pinch myself to make sure it wasn't a dream). Probably if I'd been able to leave after that month I could have gained a totally positive experience, avoiding the deprivations that were to come. But possibly because my initial experience was so intensely moving, it became a powerful tool to more tightly tie me into the Family. During later years, in times of doubt or frustration, I would reflect back on my first month in order to assure myself that this path must be the (true) way.

After the initial month on the farm, I moved to one of the centers in San Francisco; discovering that the daily life of a Unification Church member has little resemblance to the delicious days I experienced as a new recruit. For six years I continued on, trying to live off the hopes which had first inspired me to join. I repressed the doubts and fears, desperate to maintain some reason for staying alive. Throughout the time I was a Unification Church member, I kept up contact with my family, although it became less and less as the years moved on. Our relationship, or lack thereof, was a nagging torment to me. I couldn't stand the pain of being reminded how much it hurt each of us to be out of touch with each other. I wished my family would cut me off so I wouldn't have to think about them anymore. But they wouldn't give up and finally after years of investigations, vacillation, grave concern, they decided to kidnap me. They hired a group of men to scout me out, grab me, and deprogram me.

Although it was probably the only way to get me out, the experience was a devastating trauma. I was outraged at my parents, terrified of the deprogrammers, and boiling with confusion. It felt like the only reason I'd found to live for was being viciously destroyed. I spent several months going through deprogramming and rehabilitation. Eventually, I regained my ability to logically understand the mind manipulations I'd undergone during my years in the Church. I could rationally say I was glad to be out and free, but, emotionally it didn't feel that way. After three months at a rehab center I returned to my parents' house in Los Angeles.

Once back home the torturous pain I was feeling often seemed worse than the grueling, repressive lifestyle in the cult. Other ex-cult members would refer to their "rescue" from the cult, but it still seemed like a "kidnap" to me. It took a couple more months before I felt capable of going back out and doing something in "reality." I was very fortunate to have such a supportive (emotionally and financially) family. The healing process seemed to take forever. Eventually I got a job, then started attending college again.

In a lot of ways, I felt I was back to where I'd been six years earlier, before I joined the Church. But, then again, I know I gained precious qualities from my multitude of adventures while in the Church. Although rebuilding my life was difficult, I often experienced overwhelming relief that my mind and body were no longer in the grips of the Unification Church. Now, nearly two years after my kidnaping (it is still difficult to call it rescue), I finally can whole-heartedly bless the day that I left the Church.

Ellen Berlfein

* * *

Don Haigler
Former Member of the Church of Scientology.

I was a member of the "Church of Scientology" for a little over six years. When I joined, I had recently graduated from high school and was attending my first year of college. I later dropped out to do more Scientology courses.

My sister introduced me to it and it was something she had just started. She told me she was taking a communications course, which is like a self improvement course. She would tell me nothing more about it, that I should come in to hear a lecture. She gave my mother a copy of Dianetics, Evolution of a Science, which is a small introductory book, and is part of the Scientology organization. My mother, not really knowing what it was or having read the book, gave it to me to read. She trusted my sister.

I read the book and thought L. Ron Hubbard was a very interesting and entertaining writer. So after some more persistence from my sister I decided to go listen to a lecture. The lecture was interesting. He talked about communication and how it affects relationships and those around you. After the lecture, I talked with the Executive Director who urged me to take the Communication Course which was $40. My parents came in for a lecture the next day and they were impressed enough to pay for the course for me and my brother.

The Communications Course consisted of seven drills called T. R.'s or Training Routines. In all seven drills we were seated in a chair facing another "student," with knees almost touching. The first drill was called "TR-O with eyes closed". We were instructed to sit with eyes closed and remove everything from your mind except for what was going on in "present time" which they shortened to "P.T.". We did this for two and a half hour sessions a night for almost two weeks.

When we could erase everything from our minds and be in P.T., then we passed the drill. The next drill was "TR-O with eyes open", which was exactly the same as the first except we had our eyes open. In this drill we were supposed to "confront" each other and was probably the one which affected me most, because all kinds of things went through my mind when doing this drill. My eyes started to water, ache, and excessive blinking. This meant I wasn't doing the drill right, and I was to concentrate on present time. After a week of doing this drill for two and a half hours straight, something happened in my mind and went bang! At the time, I thought it was something wonderful and great and I was now in P.T. and not stuck in the past. I had successfully won a small battle against my Reactive Mind. The Reactive Mind we were told was the part of the mind which held all of the bad experiences of our lives. Scientology was the way out, with Scientology auditing we could erase our Reactive Mind and become "well and happy human beings". When a person has successfully erased his Reactive Mind (through a lot of Audit) he was called a "clear", which was considered nothing less than superhuman state of being. Far superior to any people on earth at this time, but one had to "get up the bridge" by buying a lot of auditing to get to this stage and higher states of being beyond that. The bridge was a chart invented by L. Ron Hubbard who, he said, carefully researched it for over 30 years of his life. It was a step by step procedure of what auditing and courses we were to take. One who had reached the top of the bridge was looked at as an utterly superhuman being.

Each course and auditing was more expensive than the one before, which bothered me at first. But I was told that it was because each stage was more complex and had more of Ron's fantastic "tech" (technology).

TR-1, the next drill, was called the "Dear Alice Drill". We were to recite passages (phrases) from the book "Alice in Wonderland" to the coach who would flunk you if you moved, flinched or looked or sounded in any way "unnatural". It was up to the coach to decide what was "natural."

TR-2 involved the Alice book also, but the coach recited phrases and the student was to acknowledge him by saying "OK", "fine", "good", "alright", or "thank you". No other responses were permitted, and they had to sound "natural."

TR-3 we were to ask one of two questions, "Do birds fly?"or "Do fish swim?" to the coach. The so-called object was to get the question answered no matter what the coach might say or do. The coach could say or do anything, but the student was to calmly repeat the question until the coach finally answered it. You passed when you could look and sound natural and not get upset and get your question answered.

TR-4, which is the last drill, in the communications course, involved all previous drills put together, with a little twist. The student is to use the questions in TR-3, and then "handle" any of the coaches "originations". For example, I would ask "Do birds fly?". The coach might say "I've got a headache". My response would be to try to be understanding, but get back to the question, and get it answered. I passed when I could "confront" the coach and look and sound "natural" and get my question answered. By this time we were complete robots, but thought we were being natural and more efficient in communicating. Throughout the course, we are constantly being battered with L. Ron Hubbard's policies to read and on how to do each drill exactly or else the drill wouldn't work. In the higher courses, it meant certain "ethics actions" if one strayed from the policies.

This more or less summarizes how I got started in Scientology, but for each Scientologist it is a little different, although the communication course is something that is pushed to do as early training. How I finally left Scientology is a little more complex, but I'll try to keep it short, but sweet.

My parents started getting suspicious of Scientology after just a few months. They felt we were spending too much time at the "Mission", and had noticed some personality changes in all three of us (my sister, brother, and I). By this time I didn't want to hear anything negative about Scientology. In Scientology, any bad news (like newspapers and T.V.) or negative talk is called "entheta", a coined word by L. Ron Hubbard, and you weren't supposed to listen to it. It was bad, but more centered on bad news about Scientology. Anything bad that was heard or read in the news about Scientology was lies, and trying to stop Scientology from saving the world.

I joined the staff at the mission after a few months. My job was handing out leaflets on the streets to come and take a free personality test at the mission. We didn't solicit money on the streets, that would have made us look no better than the cults in the streets. We didn't even consider ourselves to be in a cult, because we were the superhumans saving the planet, and even the people in the other cults eventually had to be saved. I did this for about a year and a half for very little pay. We were paid a certain percentage of the gross income which was always small. The most I was paid in one week was $80.00, the least $9.00. Some "recruiters" came from "Flag", as it was called for the "Flag Land Base" in Clearwater, Florida, the world wide headquarters of Scientology. It was run by

"Sea Org" (Sea Organization) members who signed a billion year staff contract, who vow to work for L. Ron Hubbard to "clear the planet and the universe", no matter how long it takes. I decided to go and flew down the next day. They paid for the flight. I didn't even call my parents to let them know until I was already in Clearwater. The starting pay for "Sea Org Members" was $8.75 a week, and after some training would go up to $25.00 a week which was the highest you could get. When I suddenly left for Clearwater my parents started getting worried, but didn't know what to do. Then my parents met a woman who counseled people out of Scientology. She was not and is not a "deprogrammer" (who sometimes use extreme methods). She was also once a member of Scientology and had a lot of evidence and documents on how the upper structure of Scientology really operated. It was called the G.O. or Guardians Office. Their purpose was "to make the environment safe for Scientology to expand". She, the counselor, also had data on L. Ron Hubbard's shady past. At first, my parents tried phone calls to me. They got nowhere with that; so they drove from Virginia in person to see and talk to me. It created quite a stir in Clearwater because Scientology is not well liked there. We were met with an onslaught of reporters and T.V. crews and a bunch of town officials, and we were in the headlines for about two weeks. During this time my grandfather got seriously ill. At first I thought this was another ploy on their part to snatch me away. I found out my mistake a little too late, after my grandfather died. I was allowed to leave to go to his funeral, but had to stay in a hotel, and not with my parents. I went back to Clearwater after the funeral, and my parents went back home to Virginia. When I got back, I was told I was being transferred to California to work and live in the complex in Los Angeles. I didn't really want to go, but I had no choice.

I was in Los Angeles two years, and had become more and more disillusioned with Scientology. During this time, my parents had kept in constant contact with me, which helped a lot. They reminded me I could still come home and go through school, so I decided to come back for a visit. I crossed the country with a friend of mine, and stopped off at Cleveland, Ohio where his parents live. He decided to stay a while; so I took a bus the rest of the way to my parents. I was still a little leery of them, and didn't fully trust them. I also felt a lot of loss of Scientology, but not fully disillusioned by any means. They made one last attempt to get me to talk with this "counselor" and hear her side of Scientology. To their surprise, and mine too actually, I decided OK. She flew down from Canada with suitcases (literally) of material for me to look at. I read a lot of stuff and was shocked with what I read, of the illegal activities against their alleged "enemies" that had to be stopped. Anyone viewed as a threat to Scientology is an enemy to be destroyed. I read of one operation where they tried to destroy a cartoonist career because he made a joke about Scientology in a newspaper.

The "counselor" stayed with us about a week, then went back to Canada. A couple of months later we went to see her and her family who had been victimized by Scientology. I talked with all of them and heard their stories which were interesting to say the least. We stayed about a week and went to see a prominent Boston lawyer who's had experience with Scientology. After talking to him, that was it. I didn't want to have anything more to do with Scientology. When we got back home, I enrolled in college to major in Administration of Justice and have completed one year.

Getting back into the "wogworld" as Scientologists call it, wasn't easy at first. I experienced a lot of depression and loneliness because former friends in Scientology were no longer friends. It was like starting life over again, but I am doing very well now and have a full time job and a 3.0 GPA at school.

Don Haigler

* * *

The Moonie Life: And How One Left It

Doug Lenz
U.S. News and World Report, July 5, 1982

Each year, thousands of young people are drawn to about 3,000 religious cults in the U.S., some of them highly controversial because of alleged mind-control practices.

Last year, Doug Lenz, now a 25-year-old graduate student at the University of Massachusetts at Amherst, left one of the biggest of these groups, Sun Myung Moon's Unification Church. Below, he describes that experience.

When you join the Unification Church, you put your personality in a deep freeze. That's why, when I left the Moonies after spending 22 months in the cult, I felt as if I were still 22 years old and just out of college -- the way I was when I joined.

I was ripe material for the Moonies because I had all the traits they look for in a convert --idealistic, innocent, indecisive and seeking an identity. I was brought up by people who worry about more than their own lives. My mother volunteers in a hospital; my father is a world-renowned chemist. I had just graduated from the University of New Hampshire and was planning to go to the University of Texas for a graduate degree. I like working with people, and I went into engineering to serve humanity.

Appeal to altruism. Out of curiosity, I went to a dinner given by a Moonie front group, the Creative Community Project. The people there said they were building a new age through their social programs by giving people food, clothing and a moral standard. The Unification Church leaders told me they would meet my basic needs so I could be free to serve the world. That appealed to my altruistic nature.

I accepted all this because I was naive. I was a middle-class kid without street smarts growing up in suburbia. When you're that innocent, the alarm bells don't go off in your head, and you just accept the Moonies as sincere. You don't think they are lying to you.

The Moonies seemed to have absolute answers to all the questions I was asking about my own identity, about life and the supernatural. Their responses are too simple for real life, but how are young people lacking experience supposed to know?

So there I was on Fisherman's Wharf in San Francisco, talking and listening to Mose Durst, who is now president of the Unification Church in America. I can remember actually being struck by his eyes--so clear and friendly. I didn't think this man would lead me into a brainwashing situation. I didn't even realize then that he was with a religious group.

When Durst invited me to come to an open-house dinner where he was going to give a lecture--all you can eat for $1--I jumped at the chance. After the dinner, Durst mentioned a special weekend seminar. I thought it would be like a retreat and I agreed to go.

At the retreat, I was struck by the ideas they were talking about: How there are fundamental things wrong in society--violence, the use of drugs and premarital sex. They kept saying that they were pioneers, revolutionaries. That appealed to me.

When the weekend was over, I was told that there was more to be gained if I stayed a full week. Graduate school was still three weeks off; my parents were away in Germany; it was a new environment and the people were nice. So I spent three weeks and it seemed like a total high. All we did was go to lectures and discussions.

Then I had what are called "snapping" experiences. In one, I seemed to see myself standing outside my body. Another was a feeling of ecstasy that filled my body. It was described to me as what it is to be totally in love with God every moment. After six weeks, the Moonies had me under their absolute control.

In Los Angeles and San Francisco, I got into the rigors of Moonie life, sleeping only 4 hours a night and working hard for Moonie businesses. I worked in a warehouse, washed dishes in a restaurant, cleaned carpets, sold pictures and flowers on streets.

Cheap Labor. In September, 1980, I went to Canada and helped start a successful art gallery and pictures-selling business in Calgary, working seven days a week. I was a slave laborer, working illegally without a license or a work visa. Clothes came from a thrift shop, and unless I kept badgering, I couldn't get my bronchitis examined or my teeth checked. Yet while I was a Moonie, I would estimate that I took in at least $70,000, tax-free, and most of it clear profit. It all went to the church.

Sometimes I had doubts, but if it got to the point where I'd question the Moonie principles, I would stop. I knew it would be evil to question. I was always made aware that someone might try to deprogram me.

On April 14 of last year, I was hurrying to what I thought was an appointment with someone in Calgary who wanted to buy some art. Two guys grabbed me, and I thought it was a mugging--until I heard my father's voice. "It's O.K., Doug," he said. "We just want to talk."

After two weeks of counseling in Canada and more at a rehabilitation center in the U.S.--all I can say is that it's in one of the middle-Atlantic states--I was an ex-Moonie. The process is known as deprogramming, but the Moonies call it "faith breaking."

Looking back, the experience was probably more traumatic for my parents and friends than for me. My parents went through hell. When the cult finally denied us the right to see each other and then one of my Moonie leaders was killed in a car crash, that was too much for comfort for my parents. That's when they decided to deprogram me.

Despite everything, I try not to think that I blew two years of my life. When you've had your personality taken apart and put back together, you've got to learn something. I'd like to think that I've developed a much healthier skepticism. Still, it's possible that something like what happened to me two years ago could happen again.

Doug Lenz

* * *

These reminiscences of cult life show that former members often have mixed feelings about their cult involvement. They may be glad to be out, but still recall pleasant aspects of cult life, sense of communal involvement, purpose, and so forth. Remember that former members, have invested years in cult involvement, and that they may have had powerful spiritual and religious experiences, even though these experiences were later outweighed by the negative aspects of cult life. We must recognize that they are rebuilding their lives. It might be helpful to encourage them to see what they learned from their experience, integrate it into their current life, and move on.

Study Guide

For the Group:

1. The selections from former members in this chapter are only a small part of a growing number of biographies of former members. Look through the reference listings in Part 10 and select several auto-biographies to read and discuss in the group.

2. Do the selections in this chapter agree in tone and content? Is the picture painted by these authors of their experiences in cults totally bleak? Do any of them talk about positive experiences they had in the cult? Why do you think that is?

3. Consult your local librarian to find out if there are books describing the positive aspects of cult involvement? If you find any, contrast them with the books which are primarily counter-cult. Discuss which of the books has more credibility and why.

For the Individual:

1. Read over the material in this chapter. Try to visualize the author of each of the pieces. Can you understand that person? Would you call that person, prior to his or her cult experience, normal and well-balanced? Could you see yourself falling into the same kind of situations that they fell into? If you can't, take the test, entitled, *I Could Never Get Involved*, in Part 2.

2. Do you feel you have been given tools necessary to avoid entrapment in a destructive cult from this book? Would the former members in this chapter have been as likely to go through a cult experience if they had these tools?

Supporting Article

Coming Out of the Cults

Margaret Thaler Singer
Psychology Today , January, 1979

Clinical research has identified specific cult-related emotional problems with which ex-members must cope during their reentry into society. Among them: indecisiveness, uncritical passivity - and fear of the cult itself.

The recent upsurge of cults in the United States began in the late 60s and became a highly visible social phenomenon by the mid-70s. Many thousands of young adults - some say two to three million - have had varying contacts with such groups, frequently leaving home, school, job, spouses and children to follow one or another of the most variegated array of gurus, messiahs, and Pied Pipers to appear in a single generation. By now, a number of adherents have left such groups, for a variety of reasons. And as they try to reestablish their lives in the mainstream of society, they are having a number of special -- and I believe cult-related -- psychological problems that say a good deal about what the experience in some of these groups can be like.

The term "cult" is always one of individual judgment. It has been variously applied to groups involved in beliefs and practices just off the beat of traditional religions; to groups making exploratory excursions into non-Western philosophical practices; and to groups involving intense relationships between followers and a powerful idea or leader. The people I have studied, however, come from groups in the last, narrow band of the spectrum: groups such as the Children of God, the Unification Church of the Reverend Sun Myung Moon, the Krishna Consciousness movement, the Divine Light Mission, and the Church of Scientology. I have not had occasion to meet with members of the People's Temple founded by the late Reverend Jim Jones, who practiced what he preached about being prepared to commit murder and suicide, if necessary, in defense of the faith.

Over the past two years, about 100 persons have taken part in discussion groups that I have organized with my fellow psychologist, Jesse Miller of the University of California, Berkeley. The young people who have taken part are generally from middle- and upper-middle-class families, average 23 years of age, and usually have two or more years of college. Though a few followed some of the smaller evangelical leaders or commune movements, most belonged to a half-dozen of the largest, most highly structured, and best known of the groups.

Our sessions are devoted to discussion and education: we neither engage in the intense badgering reportedly carried on by some much-publicized "deprogrammers," nor do we provide group psychotherapy. We expected to learn from the participants in the groups, and to relieve some of their distress by offering a setting for mutual support. We also hoped to help by explaining something of what we know about the processes the members had been exposed to, and particularly what is known of the mechanisms for behavior change that seem to have affected the capacity of ex-cultists to adjust to life after cultism. My own background includes the study of coercive persuasion, the techniques of so-called "brain-washing"; Dr. Miller is interested in trance-induction methods.

It might be argued that the various cult groups bear resemblances to certain fervent sectors of long-established and respected religious traditions, as well as to utopian communities of the past. Clearly, the groups are far from uniform, and what goes on in one may or may not go on in another. Still, when in the course of research on young adults and their families over the last four years, I interviewed nearly 300 people who were in or who had come out of such cults. I was struck by similarities in their accounts. For example, the groups' recruitment and indoctrination procedures seemed to involve highly sophisticated techniques for inducing behavioral change.

I also came to understand the need of many former cult members for help in adjusting to life on the outside. According to their own reports, many participants joined these religious cults during periods of depression and confusion, when they had a sense that life was meaningless. The cult had promised--and for many had provided--a solution to the distress of the developmental crises that are frequent at this age. Cults supply ready-made friendships and ready-made decisions about careers, dating, sex, and marriage, and they outline a clear "meaning of life." In return, they may demand total obedience to cult commands.

The cults these people belonged to maintain intense allegiance through the arguments of their ideology, and through social and psychological pressures and practices that, intentionally or not, amount to conditioning techniques that constrict attention, limit personal relationships, and devalue reasoning. Adherents and ex-members describe constant exhortation and training to arrive at exalted spiritual states, altered consciousness, and automatic submission to directives; there are long hours of prayer, chanting, or meditation (in one Zen sect, 21 hours on 21 consecutive days several times a year), and lengthy repetitive lectures day and night.

The exclusion of family and other outside contacts, rigid moral judgments of the unconverted outside world, and restriction of sexual behavior are all geared to increasing followers' commitment to the goals of the group and in some cases to its powerful leader. Some former cult members were happy during their membership, gratified to submerge their troubled selves into a selfless whole. Converted to the ideals of the group, they welcomed the indoctrination procedures that bound them closer to it and gradually eliminated any conflicting ties or information.

Gradually, however, some of the members of our groups grew disillusioned with cult life, found themselves incapable of submitting to the cult's demands, or grew bitter about discrepancies they perceived between cult words and practices. Several of these people had left on their own or with the help of family or friends who had gotten word of their restlessness and picked them up at their request from locations outside cult headquarters. Some 75 percent of the people attending our discussion groups, however, had left the cults not entirely on their own volition but through legal conservatorships, a temporary power of supervision that courts in California and several other states grant to the family of an adult. The grounds for granting such power are in flux, but under such orders, a person can be temporarily removed from a cult. Some cults resist strenuously, sometimes moving members out of state; other acquiesce.

Many members of our groups tell us they were grateful for the intervention and had been hoping for rescue. These people say that they had felt themselves powerless to carry out their desire to leave because of psychological and social pressures from companions and officials inside. They often speak of a combination of guilt over defecting and fear of the cult's retaliation--excommunication--if they tried. In addition, they were uncertain over how they would manage in the outside world that they had for so long held in contempt.

Most of our group members had seen deprogrammers as they left their sects, as part of their families' effort to reorient them. But none in our groups cited experiences of the counterbrainwashing sort that some accounts of deprogramming have described and that the cults had warned them to be ready for. (Several ex-members of one group reported they had been instructed in a method for slashing their wrists safely, to evade pressure by "satanic" deprogrammers--an instruction that alerted them to the possibility that the cult's declarations of love might have some not-so-loving aspects.)

Instead, our group members said they met young former cultists like themselves, who described their own disaffection, provided political and economic information they had been unaware of about cult activities, and described the behavioral effects to be expected from the practices they had undergone. Meanwhile, elective or not, the days away from the cult atmosphere gave the former members a chance to think, rest, and see friends—and to collect perspective on their feelings. Some persons return to cult life after the period at home, but many more elect to try to remake life on the outside.

Leaving any restricted community can pose problems -- leaving the Army for civilian life is hard, too, of course. In addition, it is often argued that people who join cults are troubled to begin with, and that the problems we see in post-cult treatment are only those they postponed by conversion and adherence. But some residues that some of these cults leave in many former members seem special: slippage into dissociated states, severe incapacity to make decisions, and related extreme suggestibility derive, I believe, from the effects of specific behavior-conditioning practices on some especially susceptible persons.

Most former cultists we have seen struggle at one time or another with some or all of the following difficulties and problems. Not all the former cultists have all of these problems, nor do most have them in severe and extended form. But almost all my informants report that it takes them anywhere from six to 18 months to get their lives functioning again at a level commensurate with their histories and talents.

Depression

With their 24-hour regime of ritual, work, worship, and community, the cults provide members with tasks and purpose. When members leave, a sense of meaninglessness often reappears. They must also deal with family and personal issues left unresolved at the time of conversion.

But former members have a variety of new losses to contend with. Ex-cultists in our groups often speak of their regret for the lost years during which they wandered off the main paths of everyday life; they regret being out of step and behind their peers in career and life pursuits. They feel a loss of innocence and self-esteem if they come to believe that they were used, or that they wrongly surrendered their autonomy.

Loneliness

Leaving a cult also means leaving many friends, a brotherhood with common interests, and the intimacy of sharing a very significant experience. It means having to look for new friends in an uncomprehending or suspicious world.

Many of our informants had been struggling with issues of sexuality, dating, and marriage before they joined the cult, and most cults reduce such struggles by restricting sexual contacts and pairings, ostensibly to keep the members targeted on doing the "work of the master." Even marriages, if permitted, are subject to cult rules. Having sexuality highly controlled made friendships especially safe for certain people: rules that permit only brotherly and sisterly love can take a heavy burden off a conflicted young adult.

On leaving the cult, some people respond by trying to make up for lost time in binges of dating, drinking, and sexual adventures. These often produce overwhelming guilt and shame when former members contrast the cult's prohibitions to their new freedom. Said Valerie, a 26-year-old former teacher, "When I first came out, I went with any guy that seemed interested in me--bikers, bums--I was even dating a drug-dealer until I crashed his car on the freeway. I was never like that before."

Others simply panic and avoid dating altogether. One man remarked, "I had been pretty active sexually before I joined. Now it's as if I'd never had those experiences, because I'm more inhibited than I was in junior high. I feel sexually guilty if I even think of asking a girl out. They really impressed me that sex was wrong." In at least one case, the rules restricting sexuality seem to have contributed to highly charged interpersonal manipulations. Ruth said she was often chastised by Mary, a prestigious cult member, for "showing lustful thoughts toward the brothers." Mary would have me lie on my face on the floor. She would lie on top of me and massage me to drive Satan out. Soon, she'd begin accusing me of being a lesbian." Needless to say, anyone who had been through experiences of the sort described would be likely to have sexual conflicts to work out.

A very few who were in orgiastic cults had undergone enforced sexuality rather than celibacy. Describing the cult leader, one woman said, "He used orgies to break down our inhibitions. If a person didn't feel comfortable in group sex, he said it indicated a psychological hang-up that had to be stripped away because it prevented us all from melding and unifying."

Indecisiveness

Some groups prescribed virtually every activity: what and when to eat, wear, and do during the day and night, showering, defecating procedures, and sleep positions. The loss of a way of life in which everything is planned often creates what some of our group members call a "future void" in which they must plan and execute all their tomorrows on their own. Said one, "Freedom is great, but it takes a lot of work." Certain individuals cannot put together any organized plan for taking care of themselves, whether problems involve a job, school, or social life. Some have to be urged to buy alarm clocks and notebooks in order to get up, get going, and plan their days. One woman, who had been unable to keep a job or even care for her apartment since leaving the cult, said, "I come in and can't decide whether to clean the place, make the bed, cook, sleep, or what. I just can't decide about anything and I sleep instead. I don't even know what to cook. The group used to reward me with candy and sugar when I was good. Now I'm ruining my teeth by just eating candy bars and cake." Except for some aspects of the difficulty with making decisions, these problems do not seem to stem especially from the techniques of behavior modification that some cults apply to their members. But the next two items are another matter.

Slipping into Altered States

From the time prospective recruits are invited to the cult's domicile -- "the ashram," "our place in the country," "the retreat," "the family," "the center" -- and after initiation, as well, they are caught up in a round of long, repetitive lectures couched in hypnotic metaphors and exalted ideas, hours of chanting while half-awake, attention-focusing songs and games, and meditating. Several groups send their members to bed wearing headsets that pipe sermons into their ears as they sleep, after hours of listening to tapes of the leader's exhortations while awake. These are all practices that tend to produce states of altered consciousness, exaltation, and suggestibility.

When they leave the cult, many members find that a variety of conditions -- stress and conflict, a depressive low, certain significant words or ideas --can trigger a return to the trancelike state they knew in cult days. They report that they fall into the familiar, unshakable lethargy, and seem to hear bits of exhortations from cult speakers. These episodes of "floating" --like the flashbacks of drug-users -- are most frequent immediately after leaving the group, but in certain persons they still occur weeks or months later.

Ira had acquired a master's degree in business administration before he joined his cult, emerging after two years of nightly headsets and daily tapes, he is working in a factory "until I get my head together. "He thought he was going crazy: "Weeks after I left, I would suddenly feel spacy and hear the cult leader saying, "You'll always come back. You are one with us. You can never separate." I'd forget where I was, that I'm out now; I'd feel his presence and hear his voice. I got so frightened once that I slapped my face to make it stop."

Jack, a former graduate student in physiology who had been in a cult for several years, reported, "I went back to my university to see my dissertation adviser. As we talked, he wrote ideas on the board. suddenly he gave me the chalk and said, "Outline some of your ideas." He wanted me briefly to present my plans. I walked over and drew a circle around the professor's words. It was like a child doing it. I heard his words as a literal command: I drew a line around the outside of the ideas written on the board. I was suddenly embarrassed when I saw what I had done. I had spaced out, and I keep doing little things like that."

During our group discussions, unless we keep some focus, we often see members float off; they have difficulty concentrating and expressing practical needs concretely. Prolonged recitals using abstract cult jargon can set off a kind of contagion of this detached, "spacy" condition among certain participants. They say these episodes duplicate the conditions they fell into at meditations or lectures during cult days, and disturb them terribly when they occur now. They worry that they are going mad, and that they may never be able to control the floating. But it can be controlled by avoiding the vague, cosmic terms encouraged in cult talk and sticking to concrete topics and precise language spoken directly to a listener.

In one session, Rosemary was describing a floating incident from the day before. "In the office yesterday, I couldn't keep centered . . . I couldn't keep a positive belief system going," she said.

"Now, look, Rosemary," I said. "Tell us concretely exactly what it was that happened, and what you were feeling." With effort, she told us she had been using the Xerox machine when the paper jammed; she didn't know how to fix it, felt inadequate, was ashamed to go and ask. Instead, she stood silent and dissociated before the machine. Under pressure now, she found ways to tell the story. In cult days, she had been encouraged to generalize to vague categories of feeling, to be imprecise, to translate personal responses into code.

People affected by floating are immensely relieved to learn that others have experienced these same flashbacks, that they can be controlled, and that the condition eventually diminishes. Those who still float for a long time -- it can go on for two years -- are generally the same ones to have reported severe depression, extreme indecisiveness, and other signs of pathology before entering the cult.

Blurring of Mental Activity

Most cult veterans are neither grossly incompetent nor blatantly disturbed. Nevertheless, they report--and their families confirm--subtle cognitive inefficiencies and changes that take some time to pass. Ex-cultists often have trouble putting into words the inefficiencies they want to describe. Jack, the physiology graduate, said, "It's more that after a while outside, something comes back. One day I realized my thinking had gradually expanded. I could see everything in more complex ways. The group had slowly, a step at a time, cut me off from anything but the simplest right-wrong notions. They keep you from thinking and reasoning about all the contingencies by always telling you, "Don't doubt, don't be negative." And after a while you hardly think about anything except in yes-no, right-wrong, simpleminded ways." Many ex-cultists, like Ira, the factory worker, or Jack, now working as a hospital orderly, have to take simple jobs until they regain former levels of competence.

Uncritical Passivity

Many former cultists report they accept almost everything they hear, as if their pre-cult skills for evaluating and criticizing were in relative abeyance. They cannot listen and judge: they listen, believe, and obey. Simple remarks of friends, dates, co-workers, and roommates are taken as commands, even though the person does not feel like doing the bidding, or even abhors it. One woman had gotten up in the middle of the night to respond to the telephoned command of a near stranger: "I borrowed my dad's car to drive about 65 miles out into the country and help this guy I had just met once in a coffeehouse to transport some stolen merchandise, because he spoke in such a strong and authoritative way to me on the phone. I can't believe how much I still obey people."

When this behavior comes up in our group sessions, we discuss the various cults' injunctions against questioning doctrine or directives, and the effects of living for months or years in situations that encourage acquiescence. Ex-members of some of the more authoritarian cults describe constant urging to "surrender your mind ... accept ... melt ... flow with it ... Don't question now, later you will understand." Reluctance or objections are reprimanded: "Don't be negative, don't be resistant, surrender."

Joan had been the nemesis of many college teachers before she joined a cult. "I was into the radical feminist group at school; I was a political radical; I was trying to overthrow the system. In three months, they recycled me and I was obeying everybody. I still have that tendency to obey anybody who says "Gimme, fetch me, go for...." Ginny was described by her family as having been "strong-willed. It was impossible to make her do anything she didn't want to do." Now she complains, "Any guy who asks me anything, I feel compelled to say yes; I feel I should sacrifice for them; that's how I did for four years in the group."

Fear of the Cult

Most of the groups work hard to prevent defections: some ex-members cite warnings of heavenly damnation for themselves, their ancestors, and their children. Since many cult veterans retain some residual belief in the cult doctrines, this alone can be a horrifying burden.

When members do leave, efforts to get them back reportedly range from moderate harassment to incidents involving the use of force. Many former members and their families secure unlisted phone numbers; some move away from known addresses; some even take assumed names in distant places.

At the root of former members, fear is often the memory of old humiliations administered for stepping out of line. Kathy, who had been in a group for over five years, said, "Some of the older members might still be able to get to me and crush my spirit like they did when I became depressed and couldn't go out and fund-raise or recruit. I had been unable to eat or sleep; I was weak and ineffectual. They called me in and the leader screamed at me, "You're too rebellious. I'm going to break your spirit. You are too strong-willed." And they made me crawl at their feet. I still freak out when I think about how close they drove me to suicide that day; for a long time afterward, all I could do was help with cooking. I can hardly remember the details, it was a nightmare."

It appears that most cult groups soon turn their energies to recruiting new members rather than prolonging efforts to reattract defectors. Still, even after the initial fear of retaliation has passed, former members worry about how to handle the inevitable chance street meetings with old colleagues, expecting them to try to stir up feelings of guilt over leaving and condemn their present life.

Fear may be most acute for former members who have left a spouse or children behind in the cults that recruited couples and families. Any effort to make contact risks breaking the link completely. Often painful legal actions ensue over child custody or conservatorship between former and continuing adherents. Even reporters who have gone into a cult as bogus recruits to get a story, staying only a few days, have felt a terrible compassion for the real recruits who stay behind. One, Dana Gosney, formerly of the Redwood City Tribune, wrote that it took him three and a half hours to extract himself from the group once he announced he wanted to leave. He was denied permission to go, he was pleaded with, he was told the phone did not work so he could not contact a ride. Eventually, he says, "Two steps beyond the gate, I experienced the sensation of falling and reached out to steady myself. My stomach, after churning for several hours, forced its contents from my mouth. Then I began to weep uncontrollably. I was crying for those I had left behind."

The Fishbowl Effect

A special problem for cult veterans is the constant watchfulness of family and friends, who are on the alert for any signs that the difficulties of real life will send the person back. Mild dissociation, deep preoccupations, temporary altered states of consciousness, and any positive talk about cult days can cause alarm in a former member's family. Often the former member senses it, but neither side knows how to open up discussion.

New acquaintances and old friends can also trigger an former cultist's feelings that people are staring, wondering why he joined such a group. In our discussion, ex-members share ways they have managed to deal with these situations. The best advice seems to be to try focusing on the current conversation until the sense of living under scrutiny gradually fades.

As I suggested above, returnees often want to talk to people about positive aspects of the cult experience. Yet they commonly feel that others refuse to hear anything but the negative aspects, even in our groups. Apart from the pleasure of commitment and the simplicity of life in the old regime, they generally want to discuss a few warm friendships, or even romances, and the sense that group living taught them to connect more openly and warmly to other people than they could before their cult days. As one man exclaimed, "How can I get across the greatest thing--that I no longer fear rejection the way I used to? While I was in the Church, and selling on the street, I was rejected by thousands of people I approached, and I learned to take it. Before I went in, I was terrified that anyone would reject me in any way!"

Conditioned by the cults' condemnation of the beliefs and conduct of outsiders, ex-members tend to remain hypocritical of much of the ordinary behavior of humans. This makes reentry still harder. When parents, friends, or therapists try to convince them to be less rigid in their attitudes, they tend to see such as evidence of casual moral relativism.

The Agonies of Explaining

Why one joined is difficult to tell anyone who is unfamiliar with cults. One has to describe the subtleties and power of the recruitment procedures, and how one was persuaded and indoctrinated. Most difficult of all is to try to explain why a person is unable simply to walk away from a cult, for that entails being able to give a long and sophisticated explanation of social and psychological coercion, influence, and control procedures.

"People just can't understand what the group puts into your mind," one ex-cultist said. "How they play on your guilts and needs. Psychological pressure is much heavier than a locked door. You can bust a locked door down in terror or anger, but chains that are mental are real hard to break. The heaviest thing I've ever done is leaving the group, breaking those real heavy bonds on my mind."

Guilt

According to our informants, significant parts of cult activity are based on deception, particularly fund-raising and recruitment. The dishonesty is rationalized as being for the greater good of the cult or the person recruited. One girl said she had censored mail from and to new recruits, kept phone calls from them, lied to their parents saying she didn't know where they were when they phoned or appeared, and deceived donors on the street when she was fund-raising. "There is something inside me that wants to survive more than anything, that wants to live, wants to give, wants to be honest," she noted. "And I wasn't honest when I was in the group. How could they have gotten me to believe it was right to do that? I never really thought it was right, but they kept saying it was okay because there was so little time left to save the world." As they take up their personal consciences again, many ex-members feel great remorse over the lies they have told, and they frequently worry over how to right the wrongs they did.

Perplexities about Altruism

Many of these people want to find ways to put their altruism and energy back to work without becoming a pawn in another manipulative group. Some fear they have become "groupies" who are defenseless against getting entangled in a controlling organization. Yet, they also feel a need for affiliations. They wonder how they can properly select among the myriad contending organizations--social, religious, philanthropic, service-oriented, psychological--and remain their own boss. The group consensus on this tends to advise caution about joining any new "uplift" group, and to suggest instead purely social, work, or school-related activities.

Money

An additional issue is the cult members' curious experience with money: many cult members raise more per day fund-raising on the streets than they will ever be able to earn a day on any job. Most cults assign members daily quotas to fill of $100 to $150. Especially skillful and dedicated solicitors say they can bring in as much as $1,500 day after day. In one of our groups, one person claimed to have raised $30,000 in a month selling flowers, and others to have raised $69,000 in nine months, one testified in court to raising a quarter of a million dollars selling flowers and candy and begging over a three-year period.

Elite No More

"They get you to believing that they alone know how to save the world," recalled one member. "You think you are in the vanguard of history. You have been called out of the anonymous masses to assist the messiah. As the chosen, you are above the law. They have arrived at the humbling and exalting conclusion that they are more valuable to God, to history, and to the future than other people are." Clearly one of the more poignant comedowns of post-group life is the end of feeling a chosen person, a member of an elite.

It appears from our work that if they hope to help, therapists -- and friends and family -- need to have at least some knowledge of the content of a particular cult's program in order to grasp what the ex-member is trying to describe. A capacity to explain certain behavioral reconstruction techniques is also important. One ex-member saw a therapist for two sessions but left because the therapist "reacted as if I were making it up, or crazy, he couldn't tell which. But I was just telling it like it was in The Family."

Many therapists try to bypass the content of the experience in order to focus on long-term personality attributes. But unless he or she knows something of the events of the experience that prey on the former cultist's mind, we believe, the therapist is unable to open up discussions or even understand what is happening. Looking at the experience in general ways, he may think the young person has undergone a spontaneous religious conversion and may fail to be aware of the sophisticated, high-pressure recruitment tactics and intense influence procedures the cults use to attract and keep members. He may mistakenly see all the ex-cultist's behavior as manifestations of long-standing psychopathology.

Many ex-cult members fear they will never recover their full functioning. Learning from the group that most of those affected eventually come to feel fully competent and independent is most encouraging for them. Their experiences might well be taken into account by people considering allying themselves with such groups in the future.

Dr. Margaret Thaler Singer

* * *

PART 8:

LEGAL ISSUES

PART 8: CONTENTS

PART 8: *LEGAL ISSUES*

My children are legally, totally mine.
Now they can lead a normal life.

Bob Miller, Former Cult Member
After being granted sole custody of his sons.

Of all the aspects of the cult phenomena, the legal issues have often been the most misunderstood. The Commission firmly believes in the First Amendment freedoms regarding religion. What has always been our concern is the numerous abuses of the legal system in the name of religion.

The Commission has held three legal seminars on cults and the law. The following two reports by the American Family Foundation highlight material covered in Seminars II and III. *Litigating the Cult-Related Child Custody Case* by Attorney Randy Frances Kandel, explores in depth the issues involved with the ever-increasing custody battles with cults. *The Legal Ramifications of Deprogramming/Exit Counseling*, by Attorney George B. Driesen further delves into the topics discussed in Part 5.

Cultism and the Law, September 1986

A Report of the National Legal Seminar, II

The special litigation problems faced by the victims of cultism, and their lawyers, was the subject in early May of the second in a unique series of national legal seminars sponsored by the Commission on Cults & Missionaries of the Jewish Federation Council of Greater Los Angeles. Although the participants -- attorneys experienced in cult-related litigation -- were candid about the ineffectiveness of certain legal approaches, they offered practical advice about more promising ways to gain redress for individuals and families harmed by unethically and illegally manipulative groups.

The Legal Activist

Pittsburgh attorney **Peter Georgiades** (Rothman, Gordon, Foreman & Groudine) keynoted the seminar by suggesting that a broad approach to curbing the abuses of cult groups would be to fund a legal activist lawyer who could work in the cult area much as public interest attorneys have done in other areas -- such as public smoking, environmental pollution, migrant labor conditions, and consumer products safety -- rather than exclusively by representing particular clients in particular cases.

Mr. Georgiades, who as a public interest lawyer himself gained significant victories for the effort to ban or curb smoking in airliners, stressed that the budgets of public interest groups do not have to be great in order to successfully assert existing legal rights and administrative remedies for problems ranging from the abuse of women and children and wage laws to deceptive business practices and all kinds of fraud. He also pointed out that in many cases it is appropriate to sue the state to compel it to enforce existing laws and regulations which outlaw certain cult practices.

Cult Vulnerabilities: Mr. Georgiades argued that cultic groups are especially vulnerable to such legal activism. Unlike environmental pollution, for example, where there may be strong countervailing interests against pollution control --like the economic costs of such control-- there appear to be no such countervailing concerns to inhibit restrictions against cultic exploitation of the elderly or children, or the various kinds of fraud in which cultic groups engage. Many statutory opportunities exist. But they cannot be adequately exploited, Mr. Georgiades said, by attorneys representing particular victims of cultism; the lawyer's primary interest is to help his often suffering client, and this frequently means subordinating the wider issue, and the tactics appropriate to dealing with it, to the client's need.

Mr. Georgiades held out hope, finally, for the development of a national legal activist group that might, he suggested, be called "C.U.L.T., Inc." (Citizens Union for the Liberation of Thought). But he felt that the legislative route to curbing cult abuses was precluded because the opposition was simply too wealthy and organized to attack on that level. Similarly, public education and consciousness raising seem to him largely unachievable given the limited funding available. But he agreed with other participants that actions brought under the civil Corrupt Practices and Racketeering Act (RICO) -- he himself has just brought such a case against a cultic group on behalf of a number of clients -- seem promising, so long as adequate documentation is available.

Don't Fear Torts

Attorney **Lawrence Levy**, Sherman Oaks, California, who with his colleague, Lyle Middleton, recently won a multi-million dollar judgement for client Gregory Mull against the Church Universal and Triumphant and its leader, Elizabeth Clare Prophet, urged seminar participants not to be afraid of the basic tort in prosecuting cult-related cases. Responding to a C.U.T. suit against Mr. Mull for money Mr. Mull allegedly owed C.U.T., Mr. Levy cross-complained for fraud, extortion, intentional infliction of emotional distress, breach of fiduciary relationship -- a cause of action which C.U.T. called non-existent – violation of the priest-penitent relationship, involuntary servitude, assault, and *quantum meruit*. After hearing how C.U.T. and its leader manipulated, coerced, harassed, and breached agreements with Mr. Mull over the years of his membership, the jury found for him earlier this year on all but two counts and awarded him $1.5 million in compensatory and punitive damages.

Handling Cult-related Litigation

When you undertake a cult-related case, be prepared for "legal, psychological, sociological, and metaphysical warfare." This was the admonition of Oregon attorney **Garry McMurry** (of Rankin, McMurry, VavRosky & Doherty, Portland, OR), who has great experience in such litigation, most notably against the Church of Scientology. The aim should not be money, he said. You should get involved. Be aware that other lawyers have "been there" already. Make use of the legal network that exists, not only for advice, briefs, affidavits, model jury instructions, and the like, but for psychological support and camaraderie in an undertaking that is likely to make you controversial. Be aware that commitment to the client, who is usually fragile because of the cult experience, must be greater than in an ordinary case. Be sensitive to the fact that ex-members still feel that there was something good about the group. So don't attack and say that the entire episode was an evil scam. An don't attack low level cult members who may come to court. They often don't know the whole story about the cult themselves. There is usually idealism involved in cult membership, and your understanding and support will have therapeutic value for the client and provide psychic rewards to you. Keep a cheerful demeanor; humor infuriates cults.

It is also vital, Mr. McMurry said, to understand the opposing counsel. There are two kinds: one who is a member of the cult group or who has been its counsel for some time; the other is one who has been hired for a specific case and who does not appreciate the nature of cult-related litigation. Go to the latter and say that the case at hand is not likely to be an ordinary one, the kind with which he is familiar. His ethics will be tested by the cultic group. He may become alienated and even unable to function well. Tell him that you want to operate on the up and up; create a bond between two professionals. Also, tell your partners about what is involved in the case and about the emotional commitment, because the firm will be tested, too. A supportive colleague to handle some of the burden will be a great help. But don't get friends and spouses involved.

Patience advised: Mr. McMurry went on to caution colleagues to have patience. Look through all of the evidence available, because cultic groups can be sloppy and self-incriminating. Don't overplead, and plead carefully; then, cult motions and other delaying tactics will begin to work in your favor. Also, try to get the case assigned to a judge who will look at the brief early on, and not simply at the constitution and what is has to say about freedom of religion. He will see the First Amendment issues from the perspective of the cult victim. Get a special judge, if only for the pre-trial, and do not assume that he knows anything about First Amendment issues; they simply do not come up that often. Go back to *Ballard* and build a brief.

You are, Mr. McMurry said, involved in an educational process. Make clear that you do not care about the religious nature of the group in question. No garb will protect intentional tortious conduct. Start and finish with the tort. Religion has nothing to do with it. Do not try to show that the group is not a religion. The religious defense is something that the other side will bring up, and when they do, you must make them show that their conduct was aimed to further their religious beliefs.

It is imperative, Mr. McMurry said, that briefing and the drawing of instructions start early on. As these crystallize, use the appropriate language in your motions, appeals, and briefings so that the layperson will understand. This will enhance your jury instructions.

Expert Witnesses. Psychologists, Mr. McMurry noted, are usually unfamiliar with the issues, loath to testify, and sometimes not willing to learn from the literature in the field. Psychologists who are knowledgeable and willing to testify are overused and abused, and mainly appear in court to argue about coercive persuasion. But the best witnesses are really family members; and questions of fraud do not need expert psychological testimony. The use of experts like Dr. Margaret Singer would be husbanded for appropriate cases. Mr.

Georgiades remarked here that he used a state magician as an expert witness to show that a therapy group against which he litigated had intentionally and fraudulently manipulated alleged psychic phenomena. He advised lawyers to stop using the medical model to explain what cult groups do to recruits and concentrate on how they con people. Both Mr. McMurry and Mr. Georgiades agreed that jury trials, rather than decisions by judges alone, were preferable in cult-related cases.

Torts Will Not Solve The Problem

Herbert L. Rosedale (Parker, Chapin, Flattau & Klimpl, New York City) stated his belief that the possibility of tort awards in cult-related cases was not going to solve the cult problem; but he emphasized that there are many other areas without the promise of a large award -- for example, the divorce or custody case in which one spouse is in a cult -- where lawyers who have an understanding of cult-related litigation can be a great help to clients. Mr. Rosedale called for the creation of a body of lawyers who could assist in developing procedures and arguments in such areas, and who could educate social workers and judges in family court about cultism. This would prevent authorities from avoiding the difficult issues, e.g., what does it really mean when the cult-involved parent says he wants to take a child away to the group's camp for a week? Similarly, lawyers must consider how best to assist the elderly and disabled who often give large gifts to cults as a result of undue influence, or parents whose child is in the cultic group mainly for the actual and potential financial benefit of the group. Attorneys also have an important role to play in advising families on the implications of forced deprogramming and bringing to their attention its legal alternatives, such as custody and conservatorships. Attorney's can also advise professionals and laymen about what the latter cannot say about cults, whether in or out of court, thus allowing them to act and speak with less inhibition than they otherwise might.

Lawyers also have another not greatly renumerative role to play in the cult area, said Mr. Rosedale, and this is helping to rebuild lives in a very practical way. What, he asked, is to be done by an ex-cult member about getting a decent credit rating when a cult illegally ran up thousands of dollars in charges on his cards? Or about ex-members who got educational loans which they turned over to the cult for its use? The legal system can help these victims get back into the mainstream. Less tractible is the problem of how to account, in a job resume, for years in a cult. All of these areas need legal consideration. We may not eliminate cults, but by helping people one at a time we can make law responsive to new needs, and thus help formulate public policy toward cultism.

Cults will test your degree of commitment to the law and the legal system, Mr. Rosedale concluded. But do what you can, measure success one case at a time, and don't get intimidated.

Mr. Rosedale pointedly remarked -- and his view was shared by the other attorneys -- that a lawyer could do nothing worse than become involved in a forced deprogramming because the damage to his legal status would prevent him from being able to help anybody else in the future. Clients had to be told, he added, that involvement in such a deprogramming would expose them to serious tort liability, albeit Mr. Rosedale acknowledged that many parents were willing to take the consequences.

American Family Foundation

* * *

Cults and the Law

A Report of the National Legal Seminar, III

This seminar took place on October 29, 1987 at Pittsburgh's Westin William Penn Hotel. It was organized by Rachel Andres, Director of the Commission on Cults and Missionaries of the Community Relations Committee of the Jewish Federation Council of Los Angeles, and co-sponsored by the Cult Awareness Network.

I. Religious Freedom and the First Amendment: The Price We Need Not Pay

The First Amendment, according to attorney **Peter Georgiades**, does not protect any conduct carried out pursuant to a professed religious belief which is not sincerely held, nor does it absolutely protect conduct which is carried out pursuant to a religious belief which is in fact sincere. To those who argue that immunization of fraud committed in a religious setting is a "price of liberty," he says that is one price we did **not** pay when we, as a nation, adopted the Constitution.

Stressing that practice, not belief, must always be the issue in litigation, Mr. Georgiades noted that the key to the problem is to determine whether the action complained of is one which is or should be protected. Tax-avoidance churches are easily recognized by courts as unprotected, but cult-related slave labor, or indecent assault in the name of religious ritual, and a host of "garden-variety cons" with a religious gloss, are more difficult to deal with. Nonetheless, they are actionable.

Lawyers litigating against cults must first be prepared to deal with preliminary motions to dismiss on grounds of religious protection by showing, if it is the case, that the group is claiming the status of a religion only as a last-minute expedient. If the group passes the standard tests for a religion, it ought then to be asked how the actions for which it is being sued are part of the religion (and thus protected). Asking, "Is it part of your religion to engage in extra-marital sexual relations with your followers?" can put the group in a difficult position. If it answers "no," the court is likely to rule that the action is unprotected. If the defendant answers "yes," group followers will have access to that answer in public court records and may see the inconsistency between what they are being told in the group and what the court is being told. The cult will then move for a protective order so that it does not have to let its members see the truth; every effort should be made to see that this tactic does not work.

No lower court appears to have accepted the argument that everything a cult leader does is divine or part of the religion. This argument is always made, but two appellate courts have rejected it and one has indicated that it would reject the argument if presented. Mr. Georgiades added that lawyers could argue compellingly that if all causes of action were to be denied on preliminary motions, the plaintiff would have no means of redress, which courts are reluctant to let happen.

Arguments that the validity of a representation made to the plaintiff in a religious context cannot be questioned ought not to be allowed. There are *dicta*, and dozens of fraud cases, for example, showing that the government can intervene to prosecute fraudulent solicitation perpetrated under the cloak of religion. Mr. Georgiades next noted that civil actions testing the sincerity of religious beliefs are common.

When a plaintiff challenges the sincerity of a professed religious belief, he must be prepared to confront the precedent of U.S. v. Ballard. Here, the Supreme Court ruled that the jury could not determine the truth of the belief that the defendants were divinely inspired to collect money; but the Ninth Circuit, on remand, held that the conviction was proper because the jury found that the Ballards did not "truly believe" what they professed.

Defendants will argue that the sincerity of professed religious beliefs has only been tested in cases where the U.S. government was itself a party. According to Mr. Georgiades, however, that argument begs the question. The sole purpose of the religious clauses of the First Amendment is to restrain government action, so that it is natural that cases in which a sincerity test has been invoked would involve the government. A private civil action does, in fact, involve government action in that the court itself is a government agency. Further, certain governmental enforcement functions have been expressly delegated to private statutes such as the Fair Labor Standards Act (FLSA) and the Racketeer Influenced Corrupt Organizations Act (RICO).

Mr. Georgiades advised it should be maintained that there is no good faith belief, if that is the case, and that the acts complained of are secular. Pleadings should very specifically state the particular acts which are alleged to be wrongful; otherwise a great deal of money will be spent on preliminary motions. The defense should not be allowed to argue, for example, that beating is part of Yoga, and thus part of the "spirituality" of the religion.

Even if the group establishes itself as a religion, attorneys can still proceed against it, but only under specific circumstances. The question will be: is the action going to impose a burden on the practice of religion (which the defendant must show); and if it will, is that burden necessary in order to protect some greater societal interest? Society's interest in obeying laws to protect the health, safety, and welfare of the citizenry will frequently outweigh the need to protect a religious practice.

II. Psychological Damage Suits

Attorney **Gerald Ragland** said that lawyers bringing psychological damage cases should be very conventional in most instances, eschewing the word "cult" and the concept of "mind control" if they hope to convince the jury that the difficult issues at hand can really be adjudicated. Lawyers should refer, simply, to traditional psychological injury as described in DSM-III. "It is always best to take the position with the judge," he added, "that the plaintiff is presenting a traditional tort case, and not attempting to make new law."

Mr. Ragland pointed out that clients in these cases tend to be different from others in two important respects. First, they have psychological problems which prevent them from communicating adequately with their attorneys and make it difficult for them to handle trial stress. Attorneys must thus be psychologically supportive, although they must also know when to say, "see your doctor."

Second, clients who may have been involved in alternative lifestyles often want to make irrelevant litigation points. Here, the lawyer must educate the client - -who is usually intelligent--about the law, while the client, in turn, must educate the lawyer about the myriad details of his experience. Together, they can make a good case. The attorney's education by the client is invaluable preparation, especially for cross examination.

Mr. Ragland emphasized that attorneys must assume that judge and jury know little about the processes of social influence and control that explain what happened to the client. Being aware of how one reacted oneself upon hearing a client's story will help guide one's approach. Discuss with colleagues difficult issues (for example, the notion that a person's will is not as free as we think) to determine the best approach in court. Fit the case into a narrow legal liability theory, Mr. Ragland said, rather than try every theory imaginable hoping that one will work.

There are, Mr. Ragland continued, several important problems to keep in mind when pursuing this sort of case. Groups being sued tend to use discovery as a financial weapon, and they can usually outspend you. Also, your client can be badly intimidated during depositions because of his experience with the group. A good substitute for your own discovery is the frequently voluminous record of prior cases involving the group. Indeed, Mr. Ragland feels that in a recent trial he did as well without extensive discovery as he would have with it. An exception to this suggestion occurs when you are the first attorney to litigate against a new group. When the defendant group is unsophisticated about the litigation process, you will achieve the greatest rewards from discovery, and the resultant materials can be used again and again by other attorneys. Once the defendants become litigation wise, you will not achieve such good results through conventional discovery. In any event, one should resist protective orders. The defendants are usually trying to avoid the exchange of discovery product, without which subsequent cases could be fatally hamstrung.

Mr. Ragland concluded with two further points to keep in mind as you present your case. First, make your client's history with the group seem reasonable, as indeed it will seem to be when the psychological processes are explained. Second, be the first to tell the court about the inevitable "warts" that your client has, partly as a result of his experience with the group. Such disclosure will show the jury that you are a reliable source of the truth about a complex and puzzling phenomenon.

III. Fundamentalism and Free Exercise

Attorney **Eric Dannenmaier**, whose firm recently won a large judgment against Rev. Carl Stevens and the Bible Speaks in Massachusetts, advised lawyers to consider following his example by refusing in litigation to use the term "cult" to describe a group and to argue only that certain well-established laws had been broken, in his case statutes against secular fraud and undue influence. Such an approach is much more effective, he maintained, than discussing the correctness of religious beliefs or trying to develop new causes of action suggested by the cult phenomenon. Arguing thus, Mr. Dannenmaier was himself able to avoid involvement in First Amendment issues and to get on with establishing a set of facts showing that the plaintiff had been subjected to a calculated plan of manipulation and influence, indeed an illegal "pattern of conduct," which the defendant had previously brought to bear on others in order to gain money. Mr. Dannenmaier stressed the importance in such cases of expert witnesses who knew about undue influence in cultic situations and who could make it clear to the court that conduct, which may be the expression of belief, but not belief itself, was the key issue. The experts also helped him to understand his own case in a way that is not usually possible from a lawyer's perspective.

Mr. Dannenmaier had responded to the defense that his client gave the Rev. Stevens $6 million dollars out of faith, which action ought to be protected, by arguing that the gift was based not simply on the parishioner's belief, but on the Rev. Stevens's conduct. And as the Supreme Court has found, the presence of faith does not necessarily sanction such conduct. Manipulated faith, in any event, was inexcusable.

Mr. Dannenmaier concluded by urging attorneys to argue in future cases, as he did in this one and in the appellate brief, that holding a church above a law that would otherwise apply amounts to the same kind of prohibited "establishment" of religion as state support of a church.

IV. The Role of the Expert

Professor **Richard Ofshe** said that the job of the expert witness in cases related to commercial thought reform organizations was to make clear to initially uncomprehending attorneys that they are dealing with businesses that deploy complex systems of influence and social control. Armed with this knowledge and an understanding of the system, the attorney can then explain clearly and compellingly to the court why his client is a casualty of a program which promised some kind of personal development, but instead victimized the plaintiff through economic exploitation, physical and sexual assault, or psychological damage.

Professor Ofshe reviewed techniques employed by certain groups to arouse a target's emotions and create doubts about his self and his perceptions of reality so that he becomes "deployable" enough to get him to take and pay for developmental courses. There is an explanation, he said, for how people are made and kept deployable.

There are, however, problems inherent in making such cases in court. Causality is difficult to show because the processes are so complex, although this can be overcome by showing that others have been manipulated in similar ways by the group.

The expert is again helpful, Professor Ofshe went on, because he can interpret the subtly altered meanings of words learned in the group, thus making the client's experience more accessible and understandable to the court. And because he knows the system in question, the expert can elicit details of the client's experience that would otherwise remain unexplored. One woman, for example, never mentioned to attorneys that she had been coerced to have sex with her supervisor, "for her own good," because the self-blame instilled by the group had prevented her from doing so until questioned by someone who knew how the system worked. Probing thus for all the facts and presenting them systematically is tedious work, but necessary, and rewarding.

Professor Ofshe warned, finally, against total reliance on experts who did not know about the group in question, or who relied, for example, on evidence from the client's intrapsychic experience (as learned from therapy), which might never elicit facts about the group experience. Such experts had to be educated about the group and its processes.

V. A Judicial Perspective

Judge **Aubrey E. Robinson, Jr.**, Chief Judge of the U. S. District Court for the District of Columbia, said that while he had received many invitations to speak before legal groups, he had never until now received "written indications" that he should not attend or address such a gathering. These "indications" made him angry; he did not give up his freedom simply because he was a judge. The episode, he added, illustrates the length to which some are prepared to go to suppress discussion of a serious social problem.

Judge Robinson characterized the field of cult-related litigation today as an area of law evolving on all judicial levels and through a wide variety of case types.

Thus, there is as yet no body of law clearly defined and applicable to the phenomenon, although very fundamental issues are at stake. This means, said the judge, that involved jurists and lawyers, including himself, must move slowly and carefully. The worst thing that could happen, he added, was to put this area of law into the hands of people "looking for a rainbow" at the end of litigation, rather than into the care of attorneys who want to gain justice for clients and contribute to the development of legal theory.

Judge Robinson admonished lawyers and clients in cult-related litigation not to advance "causes" ill-advisedly. They should realize that most judges do not have the time or knowledge (yet) to deal with unfamiliar, difficult, and novel legal issues and approaches. Attorneys should sharply define their cases rather than take a shotgun approach that obscures the fundamental points and may drive a judge to put the case on a back burner. Lawyers must appreciate that there is a time to sue and a time not to sue, ways to sue and ways not to sue. They must, while networking among themselves, carefully consider how they can advance legal understanding of cult-related issues while advancing their own particular cases.

Judge Robinson concluded by saying that there was great value in seminars such as this one. Attorneys shared information and further developed their networks, while the legal profession, the bench, and the general public became more sensitized to the problems and issues which had stimulated the seminar.

American Family Foundation

* * *

Cultism and the Law, September 1988

Litigating the Cult-Related Child Custody Case

Randy Frances Kandel, J. D., Ph. D.
Mayerson Zorn Pérez & Kandel (New York City)

Successful litigation of child custody cases in which one parent is a member of a destructive cult requires strategies and techniques that focus the court's attention on the fact that the hierarchical totalitarian structure of the cult controls both parent and child. The cult leaders substantially usurp the parenting function; their dictates replace the decision-making usually exercised by custodial parents; and the parent/child interaction is embedded in and inseparable from cult practices and relationships.

Child custody litigation between a cult member parent and an independent parent can involve a broader judicial inquiry into the techniques of mind, lifestyle, and environmental control practiced by destructive cults than virtually any other type of cult-related litigation. In cases involving adults, the courts have been generally reluctant to recognize causes of action grounded in psychological manipulation (such as "coercive persuasion" or "mind control") because of the law's strong presumption that adults act autonomously and voluntarily. But no comparable presumption attaches to children when custody is at issue. To the contrary, the very purpose of child custody litigation is to decide on an environment (human and otherwise) which will be "in the best interests of the child." The court may evaluate the rules and relationships to which the child will be exposed common-sensically and qualitatively (if not judgmentally) precisely with regard to the formative effect they may have on the child's developing psyche.

The statutory recitation of the factors to be considered in determining child custody varies slightly from state to state, but it universally involves broad, sweeping inquiry into the relative "fitness" of the parents emotionally, financially, and otherwise. Testimony on the daily ritual and minutiae of cult life, including how and with whom the child spends time, the extent and nature of parental interaction, the methods of child discipline, the child's education, and the non-parental adults who will interact with the child, is relevant to the determination.

Sullivanian Beliefs and Practices

In the past several years, our firm and others have represented in child custody matters several former members of the so-called "psychotherapeutic community" known as the Sullivan Institute for Research in Psychoanalysis/Fourth Wall Repertory Company. This entity, located on New York City's Upper West Side, has approximately 250 members, most of whom are well-educated professionals in their late twenties to early forties.

The core of the Sullivanian theory is that the nuclear family and all strong dyadic relationships are psychologically destructive, and that parent/child bonds in particular are the root of all evil and the mainspring of psychological maladjustment.

Members must break off contact with parents and friends "outside" and learn to loathe them; avoid forming intense dyadic relationships; and maintain ongoing sexual relationships with other group members. Marriages, although permitted for reasons of convenience, financial and the like, are non-monogamous, non-co-residential, and frequently formed and dissolved at the dictates of the leadership.

The heart of the various profit and not-for-profit entities under which the Sullivanians operate is a "psychotherapeutic institute" to which the leaders and both licensed and lay therapists belong. All members are required to be in perpetual therapy with these therapists. According to former Sullivanians, the therapists control members' lives through manipulation of the transference phenomenon. Transference is the process by which the patient transfers onto the therapist many of the primary reactions, feelings, and thoughts that were once associated with other highly significant persons in the patient's life. Responsibly handled transference can be therapeutic, but it offers the therapist an opportunity to exercise great control over the patient. Unscrupulously handled transference can become a medium to foster cult allegiance and a means to the authoritarian domination of cult members.

Former Sullivanian therapists admit that therapeutic confidentiality is broken down in the group. Therapy sessions are a means for the leaders to extract information and exert control. The therapists themselves report the substance of therapy sessions to their own supervisors, the Sullivanian leaders.

Most Sullivanians, married or unmarried, live with other Sullivanians in sex-segregated apartments. Peer pressure, encouraged and directed by Sullivanian therapists, reinforces conformity to Sullivanian mores and dictates of the leaders.

Not surprisingly, Sullivanian child-raising practices manifest Sullivanian ideology. As described by former Sullivanians, the therapist's consent is needed to bear or raise a child. Sometimes it is decided, prior to birth or even conception, that the biological parent and the nurturing parent will be different people. From infancy the cult applies stringent measures to interfere with the development of loving bonds between mother and baby. Full-time babysitters or "committees" of cult members, under the authoritarian direction of the cult leader, are assigned to each child and act as guards and gossips to ward off any show of maternal affection. Others who are excessively demonstrative toward their children may have their babies taken from them for foster-parenting or adoption by other group members.

As the child grows up, a continuous round of adults other than the parent or full-time babysitter supervises the child for some brief period of time each day so that parents may be literally forced to "date" their own children.

Parents must discuss every aspect of their children's lives with their therapists, and the children themselves are frequently in therapy from an early age. Thus, every aspect of the children's lives — what they shall do, who their friends shall be, where they shall go to school, how they shall spend vacations — comes directly under the purview and control of the therapist/leaders.

Litigation Strategies and Tactics

In one of the custody proceedings which are the basis for this report, our firm represented a mother who had been forbidden contact with her infant daughter by the Sullivanian leadership. The mother took the child and left the Sullivanian community, at which point the father/husband petitioned for a writ of habeas corpus. In the other two proceedings, handled by other counsel not of our firm, fathers who are former Sullivanians sought custody of their children from their ex-wives who continue to live in the Sullivanian community. Based upon our experience and observations, we can suggest certain general guidelines for attorneys to consider in similar situations.

Emphasize the Destructive and
Dangerous Influence of the Cult on the Child.

Make the court aware at the outset that the adversary is the cult and that the cult is dangerous. In the case handled by my firm, this issue emerged immediately when we refused to disclose the address of the mother and child. We maintained that confidentiality was needed because of the risk of physically and psychologically dangerous reprisals from the Sullivanians.

Indeed, courts have held quite uniformly that the whereabouts of a spouse and children are protected by the attorney/client privilege where one spouse fears the other's violent propensities or where the marital situation appears to be potentially explosive. We argued that confidentiality was even more necessary in a case, like the one in question, where the wife/mother fears not merely an estranged husband, but the combined force of a cult group which operates through physical violence and psychological terrorism.

When we refused to reveal the mother's address, the court held several days of evidentiary hearings on the dangerous aspects of the Sullivanians — placing the destructiveness of the cult environment into issue prior to any concerns about individual parental fitness.

Former Sullivanians testified about physical and psychological control within the group. Former Sullivanian parents testified that they had been forced to surrender their children or required to send them to boarding school at ages as young as three years. Testimony was given by young adults who had been raised within the Sullivanians on the suffering they had experienced. (One Sullivanian-raised young adult had become a teenage alcoholic. Another had committed suicide.)

Although never formally concluded because our case was happily resolved, these hearings set the stage for all further proceedings. Most significantly through these hearings, a kind of "longitudinal evidence" was brought into the case by which the destructiveness of Sullivanian child-raising patterns was demonstrated through testimony of the psychological injuries suffered by other children raised in the group.

Focus on Control: The Cult Leader as the Real Parent

Bring the cult leaders into the case. Put them on the stand and let them expose themselves through their own testimony. If procedurally possible (for example, as respondents on a habeas corpus petition) join the cult leaders or significant members as parties in the case. Their "parenting" role is a genuine and material factor in determining custody.

In child custody litigation, the issue of relative parental "fitness" can be dispositive. A fit parent is a parent capable of making independent, mature, autonomous, and rational decisions about the raising of a child, and also capable of acting upon those decisions. Parents who must "clear everything" with their therapist or who must respond blindly to the dictates of the leadership do not meet this standard.

Fortunately, during the course of extended litigation the authoritarian control of the cult leaders will frequently make itself evident. For example, decisions to move all the cult children from one school to another or from one summer camp to another; or to permit or deny all cult children to engage in a certain activity or to play with other children, betray the absence of responsible, independent parenting. Bring all such examples of controlled group action to the court's attention.

The fact of leadership control is related to the issue of parents' rights as well as parental fitness. The right to decide how one's child shall be raised is not necessarily equivalent to the right to turn over to someone else decisions about how one's child shall be raised. While both parents may be assumed at the outset to have equal rights to their children, the same is not true of parental surrogates whom the cult may appoint.

In the Sullivanian cases particularly, the practices of appointing perpetual babysitters, rotating cult members in turn to care for the baby, and limiting the parents' own time with the child, were arguments against cult parents' having primary custody.

The amount of time and the amount of quality time which a parent is able to spend with a child are usually factors in deciding the ordinary custody case. Thus, the extraordinarily small amount of private quality time a cult parent spends with a child may be of particular significance.

Keep Multiple Cases Before the Same Judge

Few things can be more advantageous in cult-related custody litigation than to keep several cases involving the same cult before the same judge.

First, the repetition and expansion of contextual information which can thus be provided to the court makes a strong evidentiary statement on the quality and nature of a child's life in a cult. Besides, cults are exposed when the same patterns of oddities and abuse in child-raising matters and husband/wife relations occur again and again in multiple cases. From an evidentiary perspective, trying multiple cult cases before the same judge permits evidence on the often bizarre similarities in the lives of different cult children — revealing and proving as cult pattern and practice what might otherwise appear to be vagaries and idiosyncrasies of parental personalities. When various cult cases are assigned to a single judge, the court can gain a thorough understanding of the manipulations of the cult leadership which may be impossible to perceive by viewing any single case in isolation.

Second, assignment to the same judge makes possible cooperation and collaboration among the various non-cult parents and their attorneys. Working through such a "quasi-class action" structure allows non-cult parties to meet the power of the cult with their own power. All attorneys, and sometimes all parties, may attend judicial conferences. It enables non-cult parties to combine financial resources against the vastly greater financial power of the cult by sharing the costs of trial preparation, expert witness fees, and clerical costs. Use of the same judge, in addition, allows an intimate support network to form among the non-cult parties, which is essential to maintaining stamina, spirits, and morale in the face of cult forces' continuing psychological influence. Ex-cult members leave behind both an authoritarian structure which has dictated their lifestyles and decisions and all the friendships and emotional attachments they have known for years. They re-enter a world which is strange, threatening, lonely, and confusing without the supportive reintegrative network of other former cult members.

The assignment of three Sullivanian custody cases to the same judge proved to be a markedly effective tool. Fortunately, only a month before the commencement of the Sullivanian cases, a massive reorganization of litigation management took place in the New York State judicial system. Under the new organization, known as the IAS (Individual Assignment System), each case is assigned at the outset to one particular judge who thereafter hears all motions, matters, and evidentiary hearings, and conducts all conferences related to the case.

Initially, cases are randomly assigned to judges by computer. However, by attorney request or administrative decision, cases may be assigned to a particular judge before whom other related matters are pending. When first requesting judicial attention, an attorney is required to indicate such other, related pending cases.

The first two Sullivanian cases were assigned to the same judge without objection from the Sullivanians. Although the actions were not formally consolidated, the cases were combined for the purposes of the evidentiary hearings, and most judicial conferences were also informally combined.

When the third ex-Sullivanian parent requested assignment to the same judge, the issue was hotly although belatedly litigated by counsel for the Sullivanian parent. The independent parents won a substantial victory when the administrative law judge ruled that all Sullivanian cases were to be handled by the same judge. Finding such assignment to be of the very essence of the IAS system, the administrative judge stated that a major benefit of the IAS is the ability to eliminate duplication and waste of judicial resources by assigning cases arising from the same subject matter to the same judge. He found a sufficient legal and factual nexus among the cases to warrant assigning the Sullivanian custody cases to the same judge.

Consolidate Actions for Hearings and Trial

An even more powerful tactic is the actual consolidation of actions for hearing and trial. Such consolidation allows evidentiary emphasis to be placed dramatically on the acts and attitudes of the cult. Moreover, it enables clients to more easily bear the costs of protracted litigation by sharing them.

Winning a motion for consolidation of matrimonial actions is, in and of itself, a victory against the cult because it necessarily entails a judicial determination that the commonalities of cult life and childraising provide a sufficient common nexus of fact and law even in the intimate, unique, and variable area of relationships among nuclear family members.

In the Sullivanian cases, the issue of consolidation came up twice. The first time was at the very beginning of the litigation, during the hearings on the dangerousness of the cult. Consolidation was essentially de facto. While hearings were proceeding in regard to the confidentiality of the mother's address in the first action, a second former cult parent was attacked, allegedly by a member of the cult's security forces who was reputed to be a black belt in karate. As the two cases were proceeding in tandem before the same judge, the hearings, almost as a matter of course, came to apply to both cases.

The attempt at consolidation was less successful the second time. The two ex-Sullivanian fathers, who by that time were both represented by the same attorney and were living in a house they had rented together, made a formal motion to consolidate their trials.

In a published opinion, the New York State Supreme Court (Walter Shackman, J.) held: "[T]he Court finds a joint trial is inappropriate. In each case the Court is separately concerned with the psychological environment surrounding the children as a result of the interaction between their parents, each parent and child/children, and between the children and significant other adults and children with whom the children interact as well as the physical environment in which they reside. Combining these two cases would make the Court's task of evaluating the evidence pertaining to the individuals involved more difficult. While the Court is cognizant of the fact that a joint trial would reduce the fathers' cost of litigation, the Court does not believe it would result in a more economical use of judicial resources, for it deprives the parties of the individual attention each case warrants. Furthermore, a joint trial might create the impression that the court "should" or "would" decide the issues of custody and visitation similarly, without acknowledging that the Court is concerned with two separate family units. Having decided to have children together, these parents have implicitly committed themselves to an ongoing relationship to each other insofar as it relates to the best interests of their children. This relationship is now distinct from any communal relationship the parents once shared, and must necessarily grow to encompass the differing needs and preferences of maturing children. The Court finds a separate trial better fosters autonomous parenting and independent reflection upon parental guidance and the children's well-being."

Notably, this decision was reached despite the fact that the common questions of fact were unusually great. The children did not merely share a similar life with their mothers among the Sullivanians; they shared a similar life with their fathers as well. The fathers shared a house with a common living space and outdoor play space for the children, and frequently engaged in activities together when the children resided with them. Moreover, the judge was familiar with these arrangements and had presided over the entirety of the three cases.

The consolidation decision perhaps exemplifies the difficulties which may be encountered by an attorney who attempts in any sense to "litigate against the cult" rather than exposing the cult activities which may be detrimental to the best interests of the child.

Make Special Use of Expert Witnesses

In planning a trial strategy, attorneys should consider and select among the multiple possible uses of psychologists, psychiatrists, anthropologists, and sociologists as expert witnesses. Testimony by social and behavioral scientists who have done primary research on a cult, or clinicians who have treated former cult members and their families, can be invaluable in providing information on the patterns of child-raising within the cult.

If such experts testify in court, caution them to concentrate on facts about the social organization, culture, and interpersonal dynamics in the group and about the psychological consequences of these factors. Avoid the battle of theories that is subject to First Amendment protection and which creates a tangle of ideologies while raising issues of admissibility under the Frye test. As first enunciated in the case of Frye v. United States, 293 F. 1013 (CADC 1923), the rule holds that "in admitting expert testimony deduced from a well-recognized scientific principle or discovery, the thing from which the deduction is made must be sufficiently established to have gained general acceptance in the particular field in which it belongs." The test can be used to exclude expert testimony in the behavioral and social sciences where the nature of academic debate often makes it impossible to meet the "general acceptance" standard.

But do elicit sufficient ethnographic detail to assist the clinical experts in giving their testimony. Such experts may also be helpful out of court in providing ethnographic and theoretical information to clinical experts. The body of scientific literature has swelled to substantial proportions, and any attorney litigating cult cases is well advised to become familiar with some of this material whether or not its authors are to testify as expert witnesses.

The use of clinical experts must, almost necessarily, be more extensive than in a typical matrimonial action. The usual psychiatric or psychological evaluative consultation is done in the expert's office and typically consists of interviews with the parents and children and observations of parent/child interaction.

In a cult-related case this is simply not enough. The inquiry must not end with the question of whether the parent/child relationship is good or bad because much of the psychologically destructive quality of life in a cult comes from the mental and psychological control exercised by the cult leadership. The expert evaluation must include other issues such as: 1) who controls and directs the parent's functioning and decision-making; 2) who, other than the parent, disciplines and cares for the child; 3) how much time parents spend with their children and what is the nature of the interaction; 4) who, other than the parents, makes decisions about the child's upbringing and education, and what is the basis for these decisions.

Ideally, the expert witness should have a substantial opportunity to observe the parent/child interaction in ethnographic context (at home in the cult interacting with cult leaders and other cult members who are significant adults in the child's life). Alternatively, the expert should have the opportunity to testify about the effects of the cult's practices as developed through the testimony of others or through information provided by research-oriented experts and their scholarly works.

Enlist the Help and Support of Other Ex-Members

Individuals who had left the Sullivanians relatively recently formed a supportive, informal "re-entry" network of friends and associates who were in close and frequent contact with one another. The same is true for former members of many other groups.

The people in this network provided invaluable assistance to both the litigators and the litigants. They testified as witnesses. They provided volunteer clerical services (helping, in a small way, to minimize the inordinate financial discrepancies between the wealth of the cult and the budgets of the independent parties). And, perhaps most importantly, they provided emotional and practical support to the ex-member parent parties during the long ordeal of litigation which, for the litigants, meant slowly and painfully breaking with and publicly exposing a former total way of life. Non-party former cult members are a litigation resource not to be underestimated.

Randy Frances Kandel, Esq.

* * *

The Legal Ramifications of Deprogramming / Exit Counseling

George B. Driesen, Esquire

Deprogramming/exit counseling is a technique designed to free a cult member from the organization's totalitarian domination and to restore his or her capacity to think and act independently. In deprogramming/exit counseling, family members, friends, former cult members and, in many instances "professional deprogrammers" seek to undo the harmful effects of cult "processing" by showing the devotee the contradictions between cult's "religious" and existential claims and what the organization commands its members to do. The cult conversion/indoctrination process induces a disassociative, trance-like and extraordinary destructive dependency state. Typically, the organization's highly sophisticated, manipulative processes inculcate paranoia-like fears and hostility toward parents, family members and formerly intimate friends. At the same time, these processes induce startling changes in emotional tone and response, and often in physical appearance and functioning as well. Mental capacity may also be affected adversely. Last, but by no means least, the process works profound changes in life choices and fundamental values. Since the process is at once as mysterious as it is unexpected, family and friends come to feel that the devotee has been "kidnaped."

In addition, the deprogrammers try to inform the member of facts about the organization and its leaders that have not been disclosed or disclosed in such a form that the devotee simply fails to confront them. Deprogramming/exit counseling may be conducted at the request or with the consent of the devotee. But given the intense hostility and fear of the "outside world" that the conversion/indoctrination process induces, and the overwhelming demands the cult makes upon the indoctrinee, it is not unusual for members to shun all contact with family and friends, especially when, as is natural, they vehemently oppose the "conversion" and its effects. Given their desperation, family and friends may feel justified in "rescuing" the devotee without regard to consent.

It is then that the law may become involved - on one side or the other. Parents and friends may seek to gain access to the cult member by legal means. If the cult member is a minor, parents may seek to regain custody through the legal process. In general, the law confers upon parents a legal right to custody over the child and to control his education and upbringing - including religious training, if the parents wish to afford such training. When the devotee is a minor, therefore, parents may quite readily obtain access to the child by bringing an action in state court. The custody suit results in an order good against "the world," including the cult if it has actual control over the child. Even if the child is in another state, various statutes may enable the parent to enforce the out of state order and to obtain the assistance of law enforcement agencies in their effort.

If the devotee has reached the age of majority (usually between sixteen and eighteen, depending upon the state statutes), however, the legal situation is entirely different. In most states, the conventional means whereby one adult can obtain a legal right to a form of custody over another is through a conservatorship. Conservatorship statutes in most states authorize courts to compel adults to submit to medical treatment when an interested party can show that the person is suffering from a recognized medical condition and is unable to care for him or herself. If the requisite factual showing can be made, these statutes authorize courts to commit adults to hospitals or psychiatric institutions for care and treatment and may in some circumstances give custody over them and their property to a suitable third party.

Some cult members suffer from serious, life threatening illnesses such as diabetes. Others may be afflicted with psychosis or other serious mental illnesses. In addition, the American Psychiatric Association has recently added "cult indoctrinee syndrome" to its authoritative list of mental illnesses. If a competent physician has had an opportunity to observe the devotee and is prepared to testify to his or her opinion that the devotee is in fact suffering from one of these conditions, courts may order the cultist committed for observation and treatment.

But conservatorship orders pose serious legal and practical problems. First, an expert may not readily have an opportunity to observe the member, and that may create insurmountable proof problems. Second, cults claim religious status. Given the very broad legal definition of religion that has evolved over the last decade, legal writers and courts are quite ready to accord that status to organizations that properly may be characterized as "destructive cults". See *Malnak v. Yogi*, 592 F.2d 197, 200 (3d Cir. 1979) (Concurring opinion). Conservatorships based upon symptoms or harms grounded in cult membership may thus run afoul of the first amendment protections afforded to religious organizations, practices, membership and activities. E.g., *Katz v. Superior Court*, 73 Cal App.3d, 952, 141 Cal. Rep. 234 (1977). In particular circumstances, of course, evidence of serious physical or mental illness may be sufficient to override these very real concerns. But it is probably safe to say that in most instances, courts will be extremely reluctant to grant conservatorships over absent or objecting adults under existing law even for limited periods and under carefully supervised conditions.

Faced with such cruel circumstances, parents and others with a profound and wholly proper commitment to the welfare of a devotee may resort to extra-legal means to obtain access to those they love in order to restore their independence, and not infrequently their mental and physical health. Tragically, such efforts often involve kidnaping, assaults, and false imprisonment. Such tactics can embroil the parents, other family members, friends and former cult members who assist because they recognize the psychological and physical enslavement that cult membership often entails, in criminal prosecutions and civil actions (instigated by the devotee with the support, if not, control, of the cult).

Most of these proceedings arise under state law. But the Federal Civil Rights statutes may also be used by cult members if a deprogramming effort, utilizing the unlawful means described, fails. See *Ward v. Connor*, 657 F.2d 45 (4th Cir. 1981). But see *Carpenters, Local 610 v. Scott* 51 U.S. Law Week 5173 (Sup. Ct., decided July 5, 1983) (recent Supreme Court decision refusing to extend the Civil Rights Act to permit suit against labor union for violence against non-strikers). The theory of *Ward v. Connor* is that those who abducted a cult member in order to induce the confrontation described above engaged in a conspiracy to deprive him of civil rights established by the Constitution, in that case the right to travel between the States. To establish that cause of action, however, the plaintiffs had to show that defendants acted out of animus towards the devotee's religious affiliation, a "class based animus." Whether such a showing can be made to the satisfaction of a jury would depend on the facts, of course. That showing may not be difficult in many cases, however, since the motivation for the confrontation I have described is often rooted in the psychological and physical harm that accompanies cult conversion/indoctrination.

Law vs. The Cults

The discussion so far might lead one to conclude that most of the time the law favors the cults, not those who are injured by their depredations—that is not the case. Courts are beginning to recognize that some destructive cults utilize techniques that have been characterized as "persuasive coercion," a form of indoctrination that, if accompanied, as it often is, by fraud and deception undercuts the law's basic assumption that reasonable men and women should be left free to pursue whatever "life style" they prefer. See *Peterson v. Sorlien*, 299 n.w. 2d 123 (Sup. Ct. Minn. 1980), cert. denied , 450 U.S. 1031 (1981). Juries, too, are quite willing to find for the cults' opponents when the facts are made clear. And the federal government has moved forcefully against cult leaders who break the law.

Peterson v. Sorlien illustrates the greater sensitivity the courts have shown to the perplexing problem of "coercive persuasion," or "mind control." In that case the parents of a Way member tricked her into entering their car and drove her to an isolated locale where she was forced to talk to a "professional" deprogrammer and a group of young people. As a result of their efforts, and those of her parents, the plaintiffs emerged for a time from her trance-like state and willingly remained with her parents. Subsequently, after her boy friend, a Way member played a tape and songs over the telephone to her, she reverted to her former state and escaped to the cult.

She sued, and the jury, as juries may do in such cases, found for the parents, a minister who had assisted them, and the rest of the group who had participated in the deprogramming. Plaintiff appealed, claiming, among other things, that the jury finding should have been set aside and a finding in her favor entered by the lower court -- as it might have been had the lower court determined that the evidence required a verdict for plaintiff as a matter of law.

The appeals court sustained the jury's finding. It found that the dynamics of "coercive persuasion," as shown by the record, robbed devotees of ". . . the capacity for informed consent." Hence, when plaintiff's volitional capacity was restored, but she nevertheless remained with her parents for almost two weeks, plaintiff waived any claim that she might have had against the defendants for false imprisonment (which was the claim she sued upon). Consequently, the Minnesota Supreme Court refused to set aside the jury verdict.

The First Amendment does not ordinarily protect religious leaders and their followers from prosecution and conviction when they violate criminal laws. Reverend Moon was recently convicted of filing false income tax returns. His conviction was affirmed on appeal, although further proceedings may be had in the Supreme Court. And eleven leaders of the Church of Scientology have been convicted, based on documents seized from Church files, of conspiracy to obstruct justice, to burglarize government offices and to steal documents and of theft of government property. *United States v. Mary Sue Hubbard*, et al., No. 79-2447 (D.C. Cir. 1981). The Internal Revenue Service has recently moved to take away the tax exempt status of certain corporations through which the Church of Scientology carries on its activities on the ground that the Church engages in activities that violate the fundamental public policy of this nation. That case, like some others mentioned above, presents serious legal issues that divide both scholars and interested religious and civic groups, not unlike the recent Supreme Court decision affirming the denial of tax exemption to Bob Jones University for discriminating against blacks. These cases show that upon proper facts, cults may prove no more immune from the law than ordinary citizens and organizations.

In addition, numerous civil suits have been brought by former members alleging wrongs ranging from fraud and false imprisonment through outrageous conduct and alienation of affections. Such cases tax the resources of the litigants. In fraud cases, moreover, if the cult can prove that its claims were religious in nature, the truth of those claims may not be challenged and plaintiff must show that the statements made were not made in good faith. Verdicts against the cults may be large indeed. In the recent case of *Christofferson v. Church of Scientology*, 57 Ore. App. 203, 644 P.2d 577 (1982), cert. denied, 103 S. Ct. 1196, 1234 (1982), the jury awarded the plaintiff $2,176,000 for fraud and outrageous conduct, only to have the verdict set aside on appeal, partly for technical reasons. The case may be tried again---illustrating the fact that plaintiffs must be prepared for long and arduous battles if they are to reap any real rewards from such litigation.

It is impossible to summarize in the space and time provided the momentous legal battles that are being fought, or the often serious and troubling legal issues that constantly surface in both the criminal and civil proceedings that grow out of the novel and potentially dangerous conversion/indoctrination techniques that cults practice upon the unsuspecting. Indeed, the law, like serious researchers, is just beginning to grapple with these new phenomena. As society learns more about the problems cults pose, it seems probable that courts and scholars will have to develop new tools to properly protect cult victims while, at the same time, safeguarding freedom of choice and religion which lie at the heart of our democratic system. Easy assumptions that cults are simply new religions and are being persecuted on account of their novelty will no doubt give way to a subtler appreciation of the need to safeguard citizens from those who use religion as a cloak to prey upon the naive and unsophisticated. Just how the balance will be struck remains for the future to reveal.

George B. Driesen

* * *

Study Guide

For the Group:

1. Discuss First Amendment concerns. Do they play a role in most cult cases?

2. Role play a court room situation with one parent in a cult and the other on the outside trying to gain custody of their child? Have one person question the child about his/her preference.

For the Individual:

1. Do you think the laws regarding deprogramming are fair?

2. Imagine being caught between your parents, one in a cult and the other outside. How would you feel?

PART 9:

CLOSING COMMENTS

PART 9: *CLOSING COMMENTS*

The cult phenomenon will not end with the publication of this book. Nevertheless, if the book has increased your awareness of what destructive cults are and how they function, it will have made a contribution. The Commission does not want to bring about the demise of all cults or all small, new "religious" organizations. It only wishes to draw attention to those which use deceptive and totalitarian practices to aggrandize themselves at the expense of their members. To the extent that the groups or any individuals break the laws of the United States, they should be prosecuted. From a moral standpoint, we feel that the use of thought control methods of indoctrination is unjustifiable.

Anyone can be recruited into a cult, if that person is caught in a particular way and that person is at a particular point in life. The desires that lead people to join cults are desires that each of us has: to feel loved, to be included, to be part of a committed community working to improve the world, to have a sense of life's meaning, and to feel closer to God. The major difference between individuals in cults and those outside cults is the way those desires have been fulfilled. A person may have entered a cult with a profound commitment to bettering the world and improving oneself -- without realizing the potential dangers of the path chosen. We do not judge or blame those individuals for their involvement in these groups or their desires (be it secret or overt) to leave. Today's lifestyle options are numerous. The pressures that drive individuals to take refuge in religious cults will not abate, since they are a product of natural desires for social support and religious meaning.

The success of cults teaches us about the cults and about ourselves. This success must indicate that there is a significant problem to which they are offering a solution. The disproportionately high number of Jewish members in destructive cults is one symptom of the decline in Jewish identity. All quarters of the Jewish community can agree on the need to stop destructive cults from impinging further on our people.

Granted that the cults use deceptive practices to attract members, the fact remains that they strike a responsive chord in people when they speak of leading a religious life, a life of adherence to fundamental moral values, a life of commitment to community and service. These ideas are not alien to Judaism:

in fact, they are at its very core. How is it that Jews do not know that their own tradition offers them the very path they are seeking without asking them to give up their family, their possessions, and their free will?

What is our Commitment for the Future?

Judaism is one of the most spiritually and intellectually rich traditions on earth; its teachings form the basis of both Christianity and Islam; its laws profoundly influenced the formation of the legal system under which the entire free world lives today. Millions, perhaps billions, of people are affected by the teachings of the Torah. Yet so many of our own people are unaware of what their tradition offers them, or they no longer care. They seek community and religion elsewhere.

How can the Jewish community respond to the disproportionate number of Jews who enter these cults? Have we forfeited our right and our obligation to meet the spiritual and religious needs of our community? It is important to limit the proliferation of cults by continuing to educate the public about who the leaders truly are and about the real fate that awaits the individuals who are seduced by sugary promises of spiritual bliss. Even as we continue this educational effort, we must seriously ask ourselves: What we can offer the person in transition -- the religious seeker, the frightened young adult, the recently divorced and the older person who does not know whether he or she is needed or wanted by society?

The Commission feels it is immoral for other religions to assume the right to change the lives of members of our community because they disagree with our beliefs or because they feel *they* have the "divine truth." We believe in freedom of religion for all people, including our own community; therefore, we need to find a way to protect the principle of freedom of religion which we feel is being violated.

The Commission seeks to educate people in such a way that they will always be able to make an informed choice. The Cult Clinic through Jewish Family Service makes it possible for people who are experiencing the pain of cult activity to be helped, to reflect on the experience, and come to a conclusion on their own. A system of information gathering and dispersal is available so that people may become further educated. An active Speaker's Bureau avails itself to the community-at-large for educational awareness programs.

Afterword

We have learned a great deal, both about the contemporary Jewish community and about cults, in the course of preparing this book. We hope that you, our readers, have also found it valuable. The presence of destructive cults offers us both a problem and an opportunity. By delving into reasons for the proliferation of destructive cults and questioning why so many Jewish people have been drawn into them, we return to our own source: the Jewish people and the Jewish tradition. As a people, we have survived far more hostile challenges than those posed by destructive religious cults and we have thrived. In fact, challenges to the integrity of the Jewish community have always stimulated movement and growth for us as a people. By realizing that the needs which cult members want to have met can in fact be answered by Judaism -- whether we answer them by returning to our original tradition or by reinterpreting the tradition for modern times -- we find that we do in fact have the resources to meet the challenge of these destructive cults. Our task now is to continue using these resources and to let Jewish people today know that their own community is available to them, and that it *can* and *will* serve them.

***

PART 10:

RESOURCES /
REFERENCES

PART 10: CONTENTS

Resources

PART 10: *RESOURCES /REFERENCES*

Cult awareness is a two step process. The first step is to creating knowledge that can be used by the public to keep people from being drawn into destructive cults. But this knowledge is not enough. Creating an effective network to disseminate this knowledge is the second, and critical, part of the cult awareness process.

The following list is a "beginning" of cult awareness networking. A beginning, because it is incomplete. We urge you, the reader, to participate in improving this resource network by letting us know of other individuals and organizations which can provide information on this issue.

If you are looking for further information and/or assistance, start by contacting the network resource nearest to you. Also contact one of the national organizations for more current information. Don't stop there! Contact as many of the resources as possible. It is better to have too much information than not enough.

RESOURCES

American Organizations (National)

American Family Foundation (AFF)
P.O. Box 336
Weston, MA 02193
(617) 893-0930

Commission on Cults & Missionaries
Community Relations Committee
Jewish Federation Council
of Greater Los Angeles
6505 Wilshire Blvd., Suite 802
Los Angeles, CA 90048
(213) 852-1234, Ext. 2813

Cult Awareness Network (CAN)
2421 West Pratt Blvd., Suite 1173
Chicago, IL ,60645
(312) 267-7777

International Cult Education Program
(ICEP)
P.O. Box 1232, Gracie Station
New York, NY 10028
(212) 439-1550

FOCUS - Former Cult Members
2567 Columbus Avenue
Oceanside, NY 11572
(516) 764-4584

Task Force on Missionaries & Cults
Jewish Community Relations
Council of New York
111 West 40th St.
New York, NY 10018
(212) 860-8533

(continued)

Union of American Hebrew
Congregations (U.A.H.C.)
838 Fifth Avenue
New York, NY
(212) 249-0100

American Organizations (Local)

Arizona:
Rick Ross
221 East Camelback, #1
Phoenix, AZ 85012
(602) 264-0324

Rabbi Robert L. Kravitz
American Jewish Committee
2021 North 7th St.
Phoenix, AZ 85006
(602) 258-8354

Rabbi Joseph Wiezenbaum
Temple Emanuel
225 North Country Club Drive
Tucson, AZ 85716
(602) 327-4501

California:
Cult Awareness Network
1917 Hampton Lane
Glendale, CA 91201
(818) 845-4354

Cult Awareness Network
P. O. Box 4915
Mountain View, CA 94040
(415) 525-1162

Cult Clinic
Jewish Family Service
6505 Wilshire Blvd. 6th floor
Los Angeles, CA 90048
(213) 852-1234

Ronald Enroth
Westmont College
955 La Paz Road
Monticito, CA 93108
(805) 969-5051

Karen Meyer
FOCUS - Los Angeles
Former Cult Members
1409 Kuehner Drive, Suite 202
Simi Valley, CA 93063
(805) 522-8401

Dr. Marvin Galper
4024 Ibis Street, Suite A
San Diego, CA 92103
(619) 295-4450

Jews For Judaism
Rabbi BenTzion Kravitz
1045 South Robertson Suite 205
Los Angeles, CA 90035
(213) 854-3381

Spiritual Counterfeits Project
Christian Research Organization
P. O. Box 4308
Berkeley, CA 94704
(415) 540-0300
(415) 540-5767

Dr. Louis J. West
UCLA/N.P.I.
760 Westwood Plaza
Los Angeles, CA 90024
(213) 825-0085

Colorado:
Mark Roggeman
P. O. Box 36065
Denver, CO 80236
(303) 826-1692

Connecticut:
Cult Awareness Network
P.O. Box 1164
Madison, Connecticut 06443
(203) 467-2251

Florida:
Sandy Andron
Central Agency for Jewish Education
4200 Biscayne Blvd.
Miami, FL 33137
(302) 576-4030

Cult Awareness Network
P. O. Box 290173
Tampa, FL 33687
(813) 985-7936

Illinois:
Response Center
9304 N. Skokie Blvd.
Skokie, IL 6007
(312) 338-2292

Cult Awareness Network
P. O. Box 381
Crystal Lake, IL 60014
(312) 528-4401

Indiana:
Cult Awareness Network
719 Stratton Road
Fort Wayne, IN 46895
(219) 484-4434

Cult Awareness Network
P. O. Box 30398
Indianapolis, IN 46230
(317) 251-005

Cult Awareness Network
6111 Spring Mill Road
Indianapolis, IN 46208

Iowa:
Unbound, Inc.
P. O. Box 1963
Iowa City, IA 52244
(319) 337-3723

Kansas:
Cult Awareness Network
P. O. Box 384
Great Bend, KS 67530
(316) 793-7390

Louisiana:
Rabbi Barry Weinstein
Temble B'nai Israel
3354 Kleinert
Baton Rouge, LA 70806
(504) 343-0111

Maryland:
JCRC - Baltimore
5700 Park Heights
Baltimore, MD 21215
(301) 542-4900 X132

Cult Awareness Network
P. O. Box 5816
Bethesda, MD 20814
(301) 656-2447

Cult Awareness Network
P. O. Box 365
Riva, MD 21140
(301) 269-1709

Cult Awareness Network
P. O. Box 10065
Towson, MD 21204
(301) 669-1929

Jews For Judaism
6508 Park Heights Avenue, Suite T-1
Baltimore, Maryland 21215
(301) 764-7788

Hillel Zeitlin
Choicework Counseling Center
6118 Park Heights Avenue
Baltimore, MD 21215
(301) 358-7316

Massachusetts:
Sheila Decter
American Jewish Congress
1 Lincoln Plaza
Boston, MA 02111
(617) 330-9630

Cult Awareness Network
P. O. Box 472
Lincoln, MA 01773
(617) 259-1940

Steve Hassan
P. O. Box 686
Boston, MA 02258
(617) 964-6977

Dr. Michael Langone
American Family Foundation
295 Main Street
Boxford, MA 01921
(617) 893-0932 893-0930

Michigan:
Cult Awareness Network
P. O. Box 68016
Grand Rapids, MI 49516
(616) 245-6868

Minnesota:
Free Minds, Inc. /
Cult Awareness Network
P. O. Box 4216
Minneapolis, MN 55414
(612) 378-2528

Montana:
Cult Awareness Network
108 South F Street
Livingston, MT 59047
(406) 222-1853

Cindy Jacobs
Love Our Children
P. O. Box 4198
Omaha, NE 68104
(402) 331-8094

New Hampshire:
Rev. Roger Daly, Pastoral Counselor
P. O. Box 222
East Kingston, NH 03827
(603) 642-5335

New Jersey:
Bill & Lorna Goldberg
302 Van Saun Drive
River Edge, NJ 07661
(201) 488-8787

New Mexico:
Dr. Marylou Butler
Counseling Psychologist
2905 Vista Bonita
Santa Fe Springs, NM 87501
(505) 473-6447

New York:
Cult Awareness Network
P. O. Box 183
Boston, NY 14025
(716) 649-3561

Rabbi Yehuda Fine
Choices for the Jewish Family
1903 Avenue J Brooklyn, NY 11230
(212) 338-9611

Alan Schwartz
Anti-Defamation League
823 United Nations Plaza
New York, NY 10017
(212) 490-2525

Cult Awareness Network
2567 Columbus Ave.
Oceanside, NY 11572
(516) 764-4584

Cult Awareness Network
P. O. Box 18088
12 Corners
Rochester, NY 14618
(716) 244-7149

Cult Awareness Network
New York / New Jersey
67 Irving Place
New York, NY 10003
(212) 777-7137

Interfaith Coalition
of Concern About Cults
711 3rd. Avenue 12th Floor
New York, NY 10017
(212) 983-4977

Cult Clinic
Jewish Board of Family
and Children's Services
1651 Third Avenue
New York, NY 10028
(212) 860-8533

Rabbi James Rudin
American Jewish Committee
165 E. 56th Street
New York, NY 10022
(212) 751-4000

Ohio:
Cult Awareness Network
P. O. Box 21362
Columbus, OH 43221
(614) 451-7755

Oklahoma:
Cult Awareness Network
Route 5 Box 49 C
Enid, Oklahoma 73701
(405) 446-5406

Oregon:
Positive Action Center /
Cult Awareness Network
P. O. Box 20997
Portland, OR 97220
(503) 252-0997 252-0998

Pennsylvania:
Cult Awareness Network
P. O. Box 131
Allison Park, PA 15101
(412) 486-7117

Cult Awareness Network
P. O. Box 2129
Jenkintown, PA 19040
(215) 885-5442

Joe Flanagan
2211 Lantern Lane
Lafayette Hill, PA 19444
(215) 836-7963

CEFM / Cult Awareness Network
P. O. Box 5307
New Castle, PA 19105
(412) 654-9272

Professor Arthur Dole
Graduate School of Education
University of Pennsylvania
3700 Walnut Street
Philadelphia, PA 19104
(215) 898-6626

JCRC - Philadelphia
1520 Locust, 5th Floor
Philadelphia, PA 19102
(215) 545-8430

JFS - Philadelphia
1610 Spruce Street
Philadelphia, PA 19103
(215) 545-3290

Texas:
Cult Awareness Council/
Cult Awareness Network
Dallas/Ft. Worth Chapter
P. O. Box 610922
DFW Airport, Texas 75261-0922
(817) 498-0109 & (214) 855-0377

Virginia:
Jewish Family Services
Jewish Community Center
7300 Newport Avenue
Norfolk, Virginia 23505
(804) 489-3111

Cult Awareness Network
810 Dumville Avenue
Suffolk, Virginia 23434
(804) 539-0870

Wisconsin:
Cult Awareness Network
424 North 24th
La Crosse, WI 54601
(608) 782-3012

Cult Awareness Network
P. O. Box 266
McFarland, WI
53558 (608) 838-8090

Cult Awareness Network
P. O. Box 5255
Racine, WI   53405
(414) 554-0378

Canadian Organizations

Alberta:
Society Against Mind Abuse
(SOMA) / Cult Awareness Network
P.O. Box 5024
Postal Station E
Edmonton, Alberta T5B 4C1

Manitoba:
Manitoba Cult Awareness
Centre, Inc.
Box 31 Norwood Grove
Winnepeg, Manitoba R2H 3B8
(204) 474-1201

Ontario:
Cult Information Center
c/o Jewish Community Centre
151 Chapel Street
Ottawa, Ontario K1N 7Y2

Quebec:
Cult Project
3460 Stanley St.
Montreal, Quebec H3A 1R8
(514) 845-9171

Saskatchewan:
Sasketchewan Citizens Against
Mind Control, Inc. (SCAMC)
Box 74
Saskatoon, Saskatchewan S7K 3K1
(306) 966-8500

Toronto:
Council on Mind Abuse
P.O. Box 575, Station Z
Toronto, Canada M5N 2Z6
(416) 484-1112

International Organizations

Australia:
The Jewish Center
Box 34 (Melbourne)
Balaclaca, Victoria 3183
Australia
011-61-3-527-5069

Reverend Adrienne van Leen
CCG Ministries
(Concerned Christian Growth)
P.O. Box 6 North Perth
Western Australia 6006

Belgium:
ADIF, Hertogenweg #8
1980 Tervuren
Belgium
011-32-2-767-54-21

Denmark:
Dialog Center
Katrinebjergvej 46
DK-8200
Aarhusn, Denmark

England:
FAIR
BCM Box 3535
P.O. Box 12
London WCIN 3XX
United Kingdom
011-44-1539-3940

France:
Association Pur La Defense
De L'Individu Et La Famille
41 Rue de Gergovie
75014 Paris, France

(continued)

Germany:
Pastor Friedrich W. Haack
Evangelical Lutheran Church
Kirche In Bayaern Postfach 500-305
Bunzlauer Strasse 28
D-8000 Munchen 50
Federal Republic of Germany
011-49-89-141-2841

AGPF
E.V. Postfach 1131
Graurheindorfer
Strasse 5300 Bonn #1
Federal Republic of Germany
011-49-228-63-1547

Ireland:
The Irish Family Foundation
Box 1628
Ballsbridge Dublin 4 Ireland

Israel:
Concerned Parents Against Cults
Box 1806
Haifa 31018
Israel

Netherlands:
SOS Graasseweg 255G 52 13A J's
Hertogenbosch, Netherlands
011-31-8360-28773

New Zealand:
New Zealand Parents Group
P.O. Box 685
Aukland, New Zealand

Spain:
Pro. Juventud
Mariano Cubi, 111
Barcelona 21 - Spain
011-34-3-201-4886

Pro. Juventud
c/. Pez 27, 2 o1ZQ 4B
Madrid 10, Spain

Sweden:
Professor Abe Z. Strom
Nehr Mans Zag #2
S-223 60 Lund Sweden

* * *

REFERENCE MATERIALS

In addition to uncovering a great many individuals and organizations which could serve as resources for cult awareness, we found a large, and growing ever larger, collection of resource material in the form of books, pamphlets and periodicals. In most cases, the cult awareness resource network is developed around large communities, leaving families in smaller communities to fend for themselves. Although this book and the listings to follow are not in and of themselves a equal substitute for a live resource person they can be a most valuable asset in the information-gathering stage. We suggest you talk to one of the national organizations to get a more specific list of materials that might be appropriate to your needs.

As with the resource network listings, we hope the readers will cooperate with us in expanding our references to include any and all materials that deal with the cult phenomenon.

Appel, Willa *Cults in America: Programmed for Paradise*, 1983, Holt, Rinehart, and Winston

Boettcher, Robert B. *Gifts of Deceit*, 1980, Holt, Rinehart, and Winston, NY

Bugliosi, Vincent *Helter Skelter*, 1975, Bantam Books

Casey, H.M. *In the Name of Religion: Cult conversion and Judeo Christian Values*, 1982, American Family Foundation, MA

Clark, Jr., J.G., Langone, M.D., Schecter, R.E. and Daly, R.C.B. *Destructive Cult Conversion: Theory, Research and Treatment*, 1981, American Family Foundation, MA

Cohen, Daniel *The New Believers: Young Religion in America*, 1975, Evans, NY

Connor, Robert *Walled In: The True Story of a Cult*, 1979, Signet

Conway, Flo and Siegelman, Jim *Snapping: America's Epidemic of Sudden Personality Change*, 1978, Lippincott

Corydon, Bent and L. Ron Hubbard, Jr. *L.R. Hubbard, Messiah or Madman?*, 1987, Lyle Stuart, NJ

Daner, Francine Jeanne, *The American Children of Krishna: A Study of the Hare Krishna Movement*, 1976, Holt, Rinehart and Winston

Daum, Annette, ed. *Missionary and Cult Movements*, 1977, Union of American Hebrew Congregations, NY

Edwards, Christopher, *Crazy for God: The Nightmare of Cult Life*, 1979 Prentice Hall

Eisenberg, Gary, *Smashing the Idols: A Jewish Inquiry into the Cult Phenomenon*, 1988, Jason Aronson Publishers, NJ

Enroth, Ronald et al. *The Jesus People: Old time Religion in the Age of Aquarius*, 1972, Eerdmans, Mich.

Enroth, Ronald *Youth, Brainwashing, and the Extremist Cults*, 1977, Zondervan Publications

Enroth, Ronald *The Lure of the Cults*, 1979, Christian Herald Books, NY

Freed, Josh *Moonwebs: Journey into the Mind of a Cult*, 1980, Dorset Publishing, Canada

Halperin, David *Psychodynamic Perspectives on Religion, Sect and Cult*, 1983, John Wright, PSG Inc., Boston, London

Hassan, Steve *Combatting Cult Mind Control*, 1988, Inner Traditions International, VT

Jewish Community Relations Council, *The Challenge of the Cults*, 1981, Philadelphia, PA

Langford, Harris *Traps: A Probe of Those Strange New Cults*, Presbyterian Church of America, GA

Lifton, Robert *Thought Reform & The Psychology of Totalism*, 1963, Norton Press

Lofland, John *Doomsday Cult*, 1977, Irvington NY

MacCollam, Joel. A. *The Way of Victor Paul Wierwille*, 1978, Inter-Varsity Press, IL

MacCollam, Joel A. *Carnival of Souls*, 1978, Seabury Services, NY

Miller, Russell *Barefaced Messiah*, 1988, Henry Holt Publishing, NY

Mills, Jeanne *Six Years with God: Life Inside Rev. Jim Jones People's Temple*, 1979, A&W Publishers, NY

Patrick, Ted & Dulack, Tom *Let Our Children Go!*, 1976, E.P. Dutton & Co., NY

Petersen, William J. *Those Curious New Cults*, 1976, Keats Publishing, CT

Reiterman, Tim *Raven: The Untold Story of the Rev. Jim Jones and His People*, 1982, E.P. Dutton, Inc., NY

Rudin, James and Marcia *Prison or Paradise: The New Religious Cults*, 1980, Fortress

Sargent, W. *Battle for the Mind: A Psychology of Conversion and Brainwashing*, 1971, NY

Schein, Edgar H. *Coercive Persuasion*, 1971, W.W. Norton & Co., NY

Sparks, Beatrice, *Voices*, 1978, Times Books, NY

Sparks, Jack *The Mindbenders*, 1977, Thomas Nelson, Tenn.

Spiritual Counterfeits Journal, *Eckankar: A Hard Look at a New Religion*, 1980, CA

Stoner, Carroll & Parks, JoAnne *All God's Children*, 1978, Chilton Book Co.

Underwood, Barbara & Betty *Hostage to Heaven: Four Years in the Unification Church*, 1979, Clarkson N. Potter

Wood, Allen Tate with Vitek, Jack *Moonstruck: A Memoir of My Life in a Cult*, 1979, Morrow

Wooden, Kenneth *The Children of Jonestown*, 1981, MaGraw-Hill

Yamamoto, J. *The Puppet Master*, 1977, Intervarsity Press, IL

Yanoff, Morris *Where's Joey? Lost Among the Hare Krishnas* , Swallow/ Ohio University Press.

ARTICLES

Anderson, Susan M. & Zimbardo, Phillip G. "Resisting Mind Control" *USA Today*, November 1980

Arnin, "Cults, Deprogramming & Guardianship; a Model Legislative Proposal"   17 Columbia J. Law & Soc. Prob lems 163 (1982).

Behar, Richard "The Prophet and Profits of Scientology" *Forbes 400*, October 27, 1986

Collins, Glenn "The Psychology of the Cult Experience" *New York Times*, March 15, 1982

Conway, Flo & Seigelman, Jim "Information Disease: Have Cults Created a New Mental Illness?", *Science Digest*, January, 1982

Cornell, G.W. "Those Guru Cults: Religion or Exploitation?" *Reader's Digest*, February 18, 1977

Curran, Ron "Inside Scientology", *LA Weekly*, April 4-10, 1988

Delgado, Richard "Religious Totalism: Gentle & Ungentle Persuasion Under the First Amendment" *Southern California Law Review*, Vol. 51, No. 1, Nov. 1977

Farber, I.E. & Harlow, Harry F. & West, Louis Jolyon "Brainwashing, Conditioning, and DDD (Debility, Dependency, and Dread)" *Sociometry*, December, 1957

Fraser, Donald "Investigation of Korean-American Relations" *Report of the Subcommittee on International Organizations, U.S. Government Printing Office,* October 31, 1978

Glass, Leonard L. & Kirsch, Michael A. & Parris, Frederick N. *"Psychiatric Disturbances Associated with Erhard Seminars Training; Additional Cases and Theoretical Considerations" American Journal of Psychiatry* March, 1977 & November, 1977

Goldberg, William & Lorna "Group Work With Former Cultists" *Social Work,* March,1982

Hochman, John "The Jews of Jonestown" *Midstream,* April, 1985

Hochman, John "Pathology as Personal Growth: A 'Participant Observation' Study of Lifespring Training" *Psychiatry,* Vol. 46, August, 1983

Langone, M.D. *Counseling Individuals and Families Troubled by Cult Involvement* 1983, AFF

Langone, M.D. *Resource Handbook, Young People and Cults: A Preventive Approach* 1982, AFF

Langone, M.D. *Destructive Cultism: Questions and Answers,* 1982, AFF

Levine, Edward M. "The Case for Deprogramming Religious Cult Members" *Society,* March/April, 1980

Levine, Edward M. "Rural Communes and Religious Cults: Refuges for Middle Class Youth", *Adolescent Psychiatry*

Salvatore, Diane "The New Victims of Cults" *Ladies Home Journal,* August, 1987

Senders, Cherri & Maloney, Kathleen "Busting Rama" *LA Weekly,* January 22-28, 1988

Woodward, Kenneth L. and Woodward, Elizabeth "Why Are Teens Turning to Religion?" *Seventeen,* July, 1975

CONTRIBUTING AUTHORS

Rachel Andres Editor, *Cults & Consequences* -
> Director of the Commission on Cults and Missionaries, Community Relations Committee, Jewish Federation Council of Greater Los Angeles; Advisory Board Member of the International Cult Education Program and the American Family Foundation.

James R. Lane Editor, *Cults & Consequences* -
> Documentation Specialist and Writer, living in Los Angeles.

* * *

Marsha Emmer Addis - Chair, Commission on Cults & Missionaries; a Founder of the Cult Clinic of Jewish Family Service. Chair, Resource Committee, American Family Foundation.

Dr. Sandy Andron - The Director of High School Education, Central Agency for Jewish Education in Miami, Florida; National Board Member CAN; Board of Advisors, American Family Foundation.

Ellen Berlfein - Former Member of the Unification Church. She has a Psychology degree from the University of Colorado at Boulder and is currently a graduate student in Education Technology.

Chris Carlson - Former Member of the Unification Church.

Norman Cousins - Prominent social thinker and former Editor of the *Saturday Review.*

Henrietta Crampton - A Founder of the Cult Awareness Network and mother of a Former Cult Member.

Rabbi Maurice Davis - Exit Counselor; A Director of American Family Foundation; Board of Directors, Cult Awareness Network.

Esther Deitz - Founder and Former Director of B'nai B'rith Cult Education Project in Washington, D.C.

Richard Delgado - Professor of Law at the University of California, Davis.

Robert W. Dellinger - Former science writer at the Boys Town Center; former Assistant Editor of *Human Behavior* Magazine.

Arthur Dole - Professor of Educational Psychology, University of Pennsylvania; Consulting Editor of *Journal of Cultic Studies*; Consultant to American Family Foundation.

George B. Driesen - Attorney in Washington, D.C.; Advisory Board Member, American Family Foundation.

Paul Engel - First Vice President of the Cult Awareness Network; National Board of Directors, FOCUS; Former Member Unification Church.

Ron Enroth - Professor of Sociology Department at Westmont College in Santa Barbara; Author of *Youth, Brainwashing, and the Extremist Cults, The Lure of Cults* and *New Religions*, and other publications.

Rabbi Yehuda Fine - Founder and Director of the Jewish Institute; Member of the New York Task Force on Missionaries and Cults; Interfaith Counsel of Concern on Cults.

Dr. Martin Galper - Clinical Psychologist; non-coercive Exit-Counselor.

Don Haigler - Former Member of the Church of Scientology.

Steve Hassan, M.Ed. - Psychotherapist; Exit Counselor; Author of Combating Cult Mind Control; Former Member of the Unification Church.

Dr. John Hochman - Assistant Clinical Professor Psychology at U.C.L.A.; Former Vice Chair, Commission On Cults & Missionaries; Editorial Board, *Journal of Cultic Studies*; Advisory Board, American Family Foundation.

Judy Israel - Bureau of Jewish Education, Boston.

Randy Frances Kandel - Anthropologist; Attorney involved with cult custody litigation.

Galen Kelly - Exit Counselor, Dale System, Inc.

Barbara Bruno Lancaster - Former Cult Member; National Board Member FOCUS; Design and Production *Cults & Consequences*.

Dr. Michael Langone - Director of Research and Education, American Family Foundation; Editor, Journal of Cultic Studies; Co-Author, Cults: *What Parent's Should Know*.

Doug Lenz - Former Member of the Unification Church.

Edward Levine - Professor Emeritus of Sociology, Loyola University; Board of Directors, Mental health Association of Evanston.

Sydelle Levine - Former Director, Cult Awareness Network New York/New Jersey.

Meyer Lightman - District Director, Jewish Family Service, Los Angeles; a Founder of the Cult Clinic, Jewish Family Services, Los Angeles.

Marilyn Malek - Mother of a member of the Church Universal and Triumphant.

Carla Pfeiffer - Former Director, Kansas Enrichment Center and Norfolk Center.

Rabbi Stephen Robbins - Vice Chair, National Cult Task Force of the Union of American Hebrew Congregations; Chair, Committee on Cults, Central Conference of American Rabbis; Former Chair, Commission on Cults & Missionaries; Rabbi, Temple Emanuel Beverly Hills, California.

Mark Roggeman - Police Officer, Colorado; National Chair, Security for Cult Awareness Network; Exit Counselor.

Dr. Harold Scales - Private Physician, Teaneck, New Jersey.

Gary M. Scharff - Former Member of the Unification Church; Formerly with Options for Personal Transition.

Judith Schulman-Miller - Former Coordinator, Cult Clinic, Jewish Family Services, Los Angeles.

Jim Siegelman & Flo Conway - Cult Researchers; Authors, *Snapping: America's Epidemic of Sudden Personality Change* and *Holy Terror*.

Dr. Margaret Thaler Singer - Professor of Psychology, University of California, Berkeley; Recipient of the National Institute of Mental Health Research Scientist Award.

Dr. Louis J. West - Director, U.C.L.A. Neuropsychiatric Institute; Advisory Board, American Family Foundation.

Hillel Zeitlin - Psychotherapist; Exit Counselor, Baltimore, MD; Former Director, Project Yedid, and Options for Personal Transition.

Dr. Marjory Zerin - Co-Director, Westlake Center for Marital and Family Counseling; Member, Union of American Hebrew Congregation Task Force on Cults.

* * *

INDEX

Schmitt (replacement)

ORDER FORM

Friends • library • parents • clergy • students • teachers • synagogue or church
children • school • doctor • lawyer • therapist • Chamber of Commerce • PTA

CULTS
&
CONSEQUENCES

Please send book(s) to: **$14.95**

Name: _____

Address: _____   _____
                 Street   Apt. or Suite #

_____   _____   _____
City   State   Zip

☐   *Please send an announcement that this is a gift from:*

_____
Donor's Name

_____   _____
Street Address   Apt. or Suite #

_____   _____   _____
City   State   Zip

Enclosed is my check for: $_____

Please make check payable to: "CULTS & CONSEQUENCES"
(Postage Paid) Please allow 3-4 weeks for delivery.

St. Louis Community College
    at Meramec
    Library

Commission on Cults & Missionaries
Community Relations Committee

Jewish Federation Council of Greater Los Angeles
6505 Wilshire Boulevard, Los Angeles, CA 90048 (213) 852-1234